Wallpaper
a history

Françoise Teynac · Pierre Nolot · Jean-Denis Vivien

Wallpaper
a history

Foreword by David Hicks

For Monsieur Adolphe Halard

Translated from the French
Le monde du papier peint
by Conway Lloyd Morgan

Published in the United States of America in 1982
by Rizzoli International Publications, Inc.
712 Fifth Avenue, New York

ISBN 0 8478 0434 8 LC 81 86461

©1981 Berger-Levrault, 229 boulevard Saint-Germain, 75007 Paris.

All rights reserved. No part of this publication may be reproduced or
transmitted in any form or by any means, electronic or mechanical,
including photocopy, recording, or any information storage and
retrieval system, without permission in writing from the publisher.

Text filmset in Great Britain by Elephant Productions, London SE19
Printed and bound in France

Contents

Foreword 6

Preface 7

Introduction 9

Part I: From the origins of wallpaper to the age of machine printing 13

CHAPTER 1   The ancestors of wallpaper   15
- Incunabula   15
- The dominotiers   21
- Comparisons and contrasts in Europe   44

CHAPTER 2   Influences and discoveries   57
- From the Mogul empire to Cathay   57
- Flock wallpaper   66

CHAPTER 3   The golden age   77
- John Baptist Jackson (1701-77)   77
- Georgian and Regency papers   79
- German wallpaper makers   84
- Jean-Baptiste Réveillon (1725-1811)   86
- After the Revolution   95
- Panoramic or landscape wallpapers   102
- American wallpapers   120

CHAPTER 4	Grandeur and decadence	127
	Technical and artistic refinements in France (1815-30)	127
	The industrial age and the great exhibitions	128
	The union of art and industry	132
	The floral motif	141

Part II: The industrial age   143

CHAPTER 1	The last great styles	145
	William Morris, a new spirit in wallpaper	145
	Art Nouveau	146
	Young America	152
	Artistic influences in France	154
	From Jugendstil to Bauhaus	156

CHAPTER 2	Contemporary wallpapers	165
	The new German school	165
	New work in America	167
	England: old and new themes	170
	France between the wars	175
	France today	180
	Publishers of wallpaper	184
	Important wallpaper exhibitions	193

Part III: Wallpaper and the arts   195

| CHAPTER I | Wallpaper and literature | 197 |

| CHAPTER 2 | Wallpaper and painting | 201 |

| CHAPTER 3 | The flower as a recurrent motif in wallpaper | 205 |

Part IV: Manufacturing techniques		**213**
CHAPTER 1	Early techniques	**215**
	The raw material	215
	Marbled paper (sixteenth century)	216
	Mosaic paper (seventeenth century)	218
	Papier de tapisserie (seventeenth century)	218
	Block printing (eighteenth century onwards)	218
	Flock wallpaper (early nineteenth century)	223
CHAPTER 2	Industrial techniques	**227**
	Cylinder or drum printing	227
	Mechanical sizing, surfacing and gilding	227
	Machine printing (nineteenth century)	228
	Sanitary printing (late nineteenth century)	230
	Photogravure	230
	Flexography	230
	Screen printing	230
	New materials	231

Bibliography	235
Acknowledgments	239
Sources of illustrations	240
Index of names	241

Foreword

This splendidly illustrated history of wallpaper fills a gap on the shelves of libraries in institutions devoted to the history of decorative arts and will be welcomed by interior designers and product designers, such as myself, who can at a glance see the fascinating development of decorative wall-coverings from 1509 till 1980.

The sophistication, imagination and quality of these historic papers is overwhelmingly exciting and provides an immense challenge to present-day designers and manufacturers.

Perhaps the zenith of wallpaper designers' and printers' art are the amazing scenic papers by Dufour and Zuber and the more elaborate of William Morris's papers.

The text is erudite, and the colour reproduction excellent. This book makes an important contribution to the documentation of the history of decorative art.

David Hicks

Preface

Our approach to the history of wallpaper is to put the subject back into the framework of social, economic and artistic activity in each period, and differs therefore from the great pioneering works of Nancy McClelland, Henri Clouzot, Charles Follot and A.V. Sugden and J.L. Edmondson. We hope to contribute to the recognition of wallpaper as an accurate gauge of changes in society, of economic and technical developments as well as of the ups and downs of fashion and artistic taste. For all its links with the textile industry, wallpaper manufacture has its own place, but by being too often used as a mere replacement for more expensive materials wallpaper has been considered a sham substitute. Of course, the craft of wallpaper is one of illusion and *trompe l'oeil*, its scope ranging from precious silks to Flemish tapestries, Spanish leather to ceramic tiles. Wallpaper can offer the heavy drapery of velvet or brocade, the finish of wooden panels, or the solidity of marble. Being ideally suited to a decor of simulation and illusion, wallpaper developed a genre of its own in the nineteenth century – the panoramic paper. At the other extreme, there is the simple beauty of the *domino* paper, and the magic of the early prismatic papers, which foreshadow op art. The mean little wallpaper in the student's digs and the rich and grandiose *Armida's Garden* are both facets of the same art form, whose aim is to enrich the everyday.

The major problem that confronts the present-day researcher into the history of wallpaper is simply that so little of it remains *in situ*. If one looks at wallpapers preserved in public and private collections, one is seeing them literally displaced, removed from their context, so that only the style, important though it is, can be studied. Furthermore, any attempt to link documentary and archival sources, giving names and addresses or containing announcements or advertisements, with the papers themselves, which are for the most part anonymous, is an arbitrary and chancy activity, though a tempting one.

This book is the fruit of considerable research, but our aim has not been to offer a series of definitive proposals, rather to open new questions on both the past and the future. Our starting point in this quest has been the hope of reviving affection for this ephemeral and fragile material, and affection also for the people who by their effort and craft created such beauty, be it rich or simple. We aim to give recognition to all the forgotten craftsmen, whose names are lost to us, and to the pioneers whose achievements have been overlooked by other writers on the decorative arts. Our hope is that this book will inspire those who until now have not suspected the richness of the subject, and encourage those who already hold it dear, so that all who read this book will understand the urgency of supporting the difficult but essential work of researchers, curators and specialists. Wallpaper is first and foremost a popular art form, and needs a wide base of support if our interest, and the work of experts, are to bear fruit in the future.

This book also discusses the different techniques of manufacture, past and present, in the hope that the reader may better understand the state of the art today, with its successes and failures, and envisages what may come. But if our book serves only to make wallpaper better liked, its aim will have been attained.

Introduction

There is a clear magical or ritual significance in the wall decoration found on the buildings of the ancient civilizations of the world. When later the arts lost their overt sacred role, the magic became hidden: but although unrecognized and unexpressed, it did not disappear. So it is with wallpaper: its present purely secular use masks its original religious purpose. The origins of wallpaper are to be found in the Middle Ages, when popular icons, called *dominos*, representing the Almighty and the saints, were stuck onto the walls of lower-class dwellings in western Europe. There they performed a double function, being both a talisman against bad luck and a covering for the cracks and crevices in the wall itself.

The French guild of *dominotiers*, or makers of these images, was influential and well organized, and while it soon lost any connection with religious activity, in making decorative papers it kept on a tradition of high workmanship and a concern for craftsmanship. A peculiarly European art form, as much in technology as in style, wallpaper has maintained this splendid tradition, despite the passage of time and the consequent changes and influences. Over the years it has taken advantage of new substances and techniques in creative new ventures, but still using that most fragile of materials: paper.

All the European languages use terms for paper – *Papier, papel, papier* – that come from the Latin *papyrus*, itself derived from the Greek. The earliest scribes used either earthenware tablets (sometimes coated with wax), palm leaves, the bark of trees or thin sheets of lead. Later the Egyptians found a much lighter and thinner medium, the unrolled stem of the papyrus reed, which grows abundantly by the Nile. With the Roman conquest of Egypt, papyrus (the word now meaning the product not the plant) came into use over almost all the Greco-Roman world. Just before the Christian era parchment was discovered. The name comes from the city of Pergamum, where it appears to have been invented, according to the evidence preserved in the famous library there. Parchment was made from animal skins, and its greater strength and durability made it a serious rival to papyrus, which it eventually superseded.

The first real paper was made from linen fibres. In AD 105 the Chinese priest Tsai-Lun used it for writing out Sanskrit prayers that had been translated for him by Hindu savants. When in AD 751 the Chinese tried to recapture Samarkand from the Arabs, they were repulsed and some were captured. The prisoners gave the secret of manufacturing paper to the Arab world, where grammarians and poets, historians and geographers, astronomers and mathematicians preserved ancient texts and developed new sciences while western Europe was laid low by repeated barbarian invasions. The long caravans that crossed the Middle East and North Africa carried with them the culture of the ancient world, which was brought to Europe as much by the Moors in Spain as by the Crusaders. The recipe for making paper was taken to France by three men who had escaped from Arab prisons. Their names were Falguerolles, Malmerand and Montgolfier: names which are preserved only in the oral tradition of the Montgolfier family. (We owe our information to Mr Bernard de Montgolfier, keeper of the Musée Carnavalet in Paris.)

It was during the eleventh century that rag paper was first produced. A process of gradual improvement led to rag paper finally replacing both papyrus and parchment as a writing medium. By the seventeenth century paper was available in various qualities, suitable for a range of uses.

The European decorative arts drew their inspiration from the classicism of the Greco-Roman world, from the exoticism of Chinese painting and from the elegant formalism of Islamic patterns; and it is our hope that this book may show wallpaper to be one of the most delicate and subtle achievements of the union of these three civilizations.

Abbreviations used in the captions. BN: Bibliothèque Nationale, Cabinet d'Estampes, Paris. DTM: Deutsches Tapetenmuseum, Kassel. MISE: Musée de l'Impression sur Etoffes, Mulhouse. V&A: Victoria and Albert Museum, London.

The French in Egypt.
30 sheets in brilliant colours, designed by Deltil for Jacquemart and Bénard. French, 1816. Carlhian coll.

PART ONE
From the origins of wallpaper to the age of machine printing

Domino *paper lining a chest. French, 14th century.
Musée de Cluny, Paris.*

CHAPTER ONE
The ancestors of wallpaper

Incunabula

The early history of wallpaper can be traced by studying, in the first place, the French printers who, from the late medieval period, made simple religious illustrations from wooden blocks, and then the *dominotiers*, who from the same time were practising a similar art – the creation of small utility papers bearing a printed decoration. The examination of rare fragments of sixteenth- and early seventeenth-century decorative papers printed in England is of equal importance in shedding light on the evolution of wallpaper.

The first reference to '*dominotiers*, illuminators, sculptors and crucifix makers' (to whom Etienne Boileau, *Prévôt des Marchands* for Paris in 1260, granted the right to a coat of arms) is found in the important *Livre des Metiers* which lists the rules of the workers' guilds at the time of Louis IX. The twelfth century, religious to a fanatical extent, had only recovered with difficulty from the horrors of the Albigensian crusade. This murderous affair was started by Pope Innocent III in 1208, continued under the regency of Blanche de Castille and only ended with her son Louis IX's conquest of southern France in 1229, an event which was to assure for centuries to come the dominant position in Christendom of the Church of Rome.

During this time popular icons served two purposes. The clergy used them to preach the faith, while for the layman possession of a *domino*, as the crudely painted images were called, was proof that one was no heretic.

The dictionary defines *domino* as either the cape worn by bishops and other senior clergy (and thus a symbol of temporal and spiritual authority) or the enveloping cloak and mask worn as a disguise at a ball, and which concealed utterly the identity of the wearer – in itself a magical achievement. The etymology of *domino* is equally complex and symbolic. In Latin *dominus* means God the Father, or Christ, with the emphasis on the sovereignty of God. In colloquial Latin *mamino* meant the Virgin Mary, and a mother. It seems possible that *domino* is a contraction of *dominus-mamino*, expressing both the doctrine of the Trinity and the duty of the layman to the Church.

The *domino* was printed in rough black outline, with colour applied by blocks to enliven the drab design, the material often being too flimsy to allow much creative scope. All the same, once on the walls these pictures must have had some decorative effect and in them we can see the first stirrings of the idea of paper as a mural decoration.

Not until the fourteenth century were wood engravings, first used for printing on textiles, used to create a printed image on paper. Although initially the technique produced a fairly crude result, it was nonetheless a considerable step forward in producing a repeated image, which both reduced costs and made a larger market more accessible. *Dominos* became even more popular, as the introduction of printing helped the development of the *dominotiers*' art, even though they were always forbidden to own presses.

Other rules, newly introduced, increased both the wealth and the position of the guilds. Louis XI, in 1467, gave the guild members the right to a banner and exempted them from taxation and the feudal duty of *guet* or watchkeeping. He also carried in his train large rolls of paper painted for him by the illuminator Jehan Bourdichon, who had created the Book of Hours of Anne of Britanny.[1] These rolls would be hung, unfurled, on the walls at each stop on the royal procession. The *dominotiers* now shared a guild with stationers, paper makers and card makers. So they lost their connections with producing religious images, although of course playing-cards retain a special symbolism, derived

15

The Legend of Actaeon.
*Copperplate-printed paper for bookbinding.
Early 17th century. V&A.*

from magic, which unites kings and gods with figures from folklore, and are used both for games of chance and for divination.

Another change was occurring at this time, in the way paper of various kinds was distributed. The main means whereby *dominos* had been sold was through pedlars and packmen who carried them throughout France. In the fifteenth century in Paris paper merchants began to set themselves up in business. They could only trade outside the university quarter, where they set up shops in arcades, low and dark places stuffed with their merchandise. Business was done in the street, and awnings protected the shelves of fragile paper. As the profession became established, so the clientele, hitherto exclusively rural, became an urban one, thus creating further changes in demand. The guilds distinguished between paper merchants and makers of paper, the members of only three guilds being allowed to sell paper: the *marchands-merciers* or haberdashers, the richest group, who had shops that sold all kinds of merchandise both wholesale and retail, and who would stock any novelty; masters of the *dominotiers'* own guild, be they *cartiers*, *cartonniers* or *feuilletiers*, who were artisans and dealers, and finally the *colleurs* or cardboard makers, and with them the *regratiers* who would deal in small quantities, sold by weight or even sheet by sheet. These merchants, despite their guild titles, were forbidden by royal decree from manufacturing paper and from possessing any printing equipment, especially hand-presses.

The sixteenth century was to see in Europe a profound transformation of society through which the modern nation states were to come into being. Royal authority became absolute and centralized, thereby over-riding the power of the feudal lords. Their strongholds no longer held such strategic importance. Castles began to lose their military function and were soon to be transformed into residences and gracious mansions whose luxury favoured the development of the decorative arts. Wealthy Italian heiresses who married Renaissance princes of France were to bring with them artists from across the Alps, all encouraging a new informed taste and style of living amongst the nobility.

In Italy a taste for the Antique had been precipitated by the discovery in Rome of Nero's palace, the Domus Aurea, in which walls were decorated with grotesque masks, delicate garlands and painted landscapes which demonstrated an understanding of perspective. In sixteenth-century Italy commerce flourished and produced a new social class – the bourgeoisie. With access to great riches these people were able to construct their own homes. Cities and towns everywhere rapidly grew in size, and Europe became a vast workshop/building-yard where the arts blossomed. The

The Five Senses. *Lining paper with border.*
Woodblock-printed. English, early 17th century. V&A.

Tudor Rose. *Lining paper.*
English, 17th century. V&A.

Ceiling paper discovered in the Master's Lodge of Christ's College, Cambridge. Block-printed in black by Hugo Goes. English c. 1509. Reconstruction from fragments in V&A.

bourgeoisie kept its taste for popular images, at the same time following the example of the nobility and court life. In spite of their new-found wealth, members of this class could not always afford such luxurious items as Flemish tapestries, elaborate stucco or marble decoration, Cordoban or Venetian leather panels, Genoese velvets or painted ceilings. As a result the *cartiers-dominotiers* were called upon to supply papers as furnishings. These ceased to bear the simple religious images and now strove to imitate the appearance of the costly materials which were beyond the means of the *dominotiers'* new clientele.

The origins of wallpaper in Europe are difficult to establish because of the very small number of early examples, which have generally survived only in fragments. In Stuttgart, playing-cards dating from 1430 and a miniature print on a gilt ground from a wooden block, some paper originating from the south of France in 1490, printed with a fabric design (in the Olga Hirsch collection), and other extant remains from England, were all witness to the use of paper for a printed decoration or as a substitute for textiles, or, more important, as a wall-covering in its own right, from the beginning of the sixteenth century.

It is therefore clear that by this date the manufacture of paper was considerably advanced and that it was economically feasible to use paper for utilitarian purposes other than publishing books, woodcuts and engravings. Sheets of paper could by means of engraved wooden blocks be given a simple decorative appearance and could be used to line cupboards and chests or be affixed to the walls of lesser rooms.

In England at this time a guild comparable to that of the *cartiers-dominotiers* did not exist. The earliest datable evidence of wallpaper *in situ* was discovered in Cambridge, in the Master's Lodge of Christ's College during the course of restoration work there in 1911. The patterned fragments, now held by the Victoria and Albert Museum, were printed from a block measuring approximately 16 x 10 inches (40 x 27 centimetres) on paper already bearing letterpress on the reverse. A date of about 1509 is established by these traces of printing, as they include a poem lamenting the death of Henry VII in April 1509 and a Proclamation of Pardon dating from the first year of Henry VIII's reign. The latest alterations to the Lodge are thought to have taken place in 1509.

The paper is ascribed to Hugo Goes, a printer of Beverley, then in Yorkshire, and of Stonegate in York, who was working in Cambridge at this date. His rebus was known to be a goose, a play on his surname. A goose does appear on the right of the design in the paper, and on the opposite side is a Lombardic 'H'. The conventional split pomegranate design is of a type introduced into England through the medium of Italian silk brocades imported during the fifteenth century. The sheets of paper covered the beams and joists of the Lodge's hall and the dining-room and must, in repeating the same motif, have presented a continuous arabesque design similar to the ornamental decoration on painted Italian ceilings of that period. The notion of modern continuous wallpaper is present in these precious fragments, but our knowledge of the circumstances in which they were printed and used is, for this early date, quite exceptional.

The first known fact in the history of wallpaper is that printing by means of an inked wooden block was introduced at the same time for paper and for textiles. The patterns for the designs, for decoration in embroidery or lacework, were printed, or even drawn, onto paper. Some rare decorative papers have been associated with one of the earliest types of English domestic embroidery, 'black work'. This was linen embroidered with black silk, and dated from the beginning of the sixteenth century. A few monochrome papers display the same floral designs (scrolling stems and tendrils and formalized blooms decorated with lines, cross-hatchings and dots) as appear in the embroideries. These are now considered to have served as patterns for needlework and as lining- and wallpapers. A fine early seventeenth-century example is in the Ashmolean Museum, Oxford. It was used as a lining to the Court of Wards deeds from a charter box in Corpus Christi College, Oxford.

Blocks used for printing cloth were also used for paper: if the ornamental border was also transferred, no matter, as often the intention was to imitate the textile anyway. All this leads to the conclusion that the *domino*, at first a form of wall decoration used only by the lower classes, began to find a market among the petty bourgeoisie from the end of the fifteenth century. There is, alas, no hard evidence for this, and it is not likely that we will ever find anything but fragments of a complete wall decoration from the sixteenth or early seventeenth century. The wall-coverings that have survived are in leather, cloth or wood, and include frescoes and painted panelling. Paper is a fragile material, and its chances of survival are lessened by the attitude, common in the nineteenth century and the early part of this century, that wallpaper was a vulgar and imitative form. Paper as decoration was never seen as having a place in a noble household, so that someone designing a well-appointed modern apartment or recreating a historical ensemble would rarely consider using wallpaper. Only in contemporary Japan is paper considered the equal of more costly materials, and there the height of elegance is to own a notecase in fine leather that imitates the finish of paper.

Although few printed papers have survived the passage of time it can be assumed that in the six-

Paper with royal coat of arms from Nacton Hall, Suffolk. Woodblock-printed in black. English, early 17th century. V&A.

Fragment of paper with crown and motto 'Dieu et mon droit'. Woodblock-printed in black. English, first half of 16th century. V&A.

Paper with the motto of the Order of the Garter, from Besford Court, Worcestershire. English, 1550-75. V&A.

Paper with the arms of the Company of Mercers, London. English, early 17th century. V&A.

teenth century in Britain and in France they were increasingly used as decoration in modest middle-class homes. Indeed the rare Tudor and early Stuart printed papers are often sophisticated in design and were suited to cultivated tastes. Such papers have generally been discovered lining deed and charter boxes and other furniture, giving a clean, appropriate setting for their valuable and fragile contents. In just a few instances they have been found on walls.

Close in date to Hugo Goes's pomegranate paper is a fragment which is supposed to have originated from Broke Hall, Nacton, in Suffolk, built in the early sixteenth century. The fragment shows the Royal Device used by both Henry VII and Henry VIII, printed in monochrome. An outstanding series of armorial papers is now, like the previously mentioned examples, preserved by the Victoria and Albert Museum. These date from between 1550 and 1575 and were removed from Besford Court, Worcestershire, which was begun in 1550. The papers covered a wall surface and displayed an elegant, symmetrical design revealing an Italian influence similar to that of contemporary silverwork. The motifs, reversed out of black, include the arms of Elizabeth I, the Order of the Garter, grotesque masks, Tudor roses and urns filled with fruit and flowers. At the corner of each sheet is a quarter of the Tudor rose, four sheets being required to demonstrate the continuity of the design. The disposition of the lettering and such ornament as the urns meant that this formal paper decoration was designed for display on a large, flat, vertical surface, unlike the abundant floral patterns of many decorative papers of the Tudor period which could be viewed from any angle. (The same design has, however, been found on paper lining a deed box now in the Public Record Office.) Black and white decorative and armorial papers of this type were common up to the mid seventeenth century.

Little is known about coloured papers of this time. In 1896 two isolated examples were discovered at Borden Hall, Sittingbourne, Kent, a building which dated from the end of the fifteenth century. These fragments were then described by Lindsay Butterfield and Edwin Foley and dated to about 1600, but they were subsequently lost. The paper had been nailed to the plaster of the walls and ceilings with large flat-headed nails. On one fragment, a floral design, said to reveal the influence of Indian printed textiles, was printed in (or painted with) green, blue and black on a red ground. The other showed flowers printed in black and vermilion on a white ground.

Block-printed papers with stencilled patches of colour must certainly have existed from the early seventeenth century. Seven sheets of paper of this type, dating from about 1680 to 1700, were removed from Aldford House (now demolished) in

Park Lane, London, where they were used as wallpaper. Each is about 18 inches (about 46 centimetres) wide and shows a little scene of stag hunting, a house and garden or a lady fishing, filled out with birds, ducks, butterflies and stylized plant designs. The pictures are surrounded by stylized floral borders and were probably printed as models for embroidery. Three specimens from Aldford House are in the Whitworth Art Gallery, University of Manchester, and others from the same sources are at the Colonial Williamsburg Foundation, Virginia, USA. Another example in the same series was used as a lining paper for furniture and is in the Victoria and Albert Museum.

Waste paper was commonly used in producing decorative papers. The pattern of the Cambridge fragments was printed on the reverse of unwanted documents, and there were later instances of patterns for dual-purpose papers being printed over the texts of banned or waste literature. This process of overprinting a popular textile design was referred to as 'damasking', as is borne out by a letter in the records of the Stationers' Company written by the Bishop of London to the Masters in 1673, which ordered them to damask or obliterate copies of Hobbes's *Leviathan*.

In the sixteenth and seventeenth centuries two of the more important associations of London merchants were those in the wool and cloth trades. Such associations would either be limited partnerships or share corporations, an efficient system that returned sizeable and rapid profits. This was the cornerstone of British economic power. The printers of decorative papers and wallpaper and card makers did business in the area round St Paul's cathedral, near the leatherworkers and silk mercers of the East End, and they were often in touch with their French counterparts, the *dominotiers*, especially those in Normandy. Wallpaper makers did not use the old guild structure but a flexible modern system, strictly capitalist, with companies funded by the investments of the nobility and the prosperous middle classes of London. In this respect there was no distinction between craftsman, merchant and nobleman, and this in turn encouraged all ranks of society to use paper for decorative purposes.

The dominotiers
Jean-Michel Papillon

The French *dominotiers* began to make what they termed *papiers de tapisserie* in the seventeenth century, and the technique of manufacture remained the same throughout the century, although

Lining paper in the black-work style.
English, 17th century. Ashmolean Museum, Oxford.

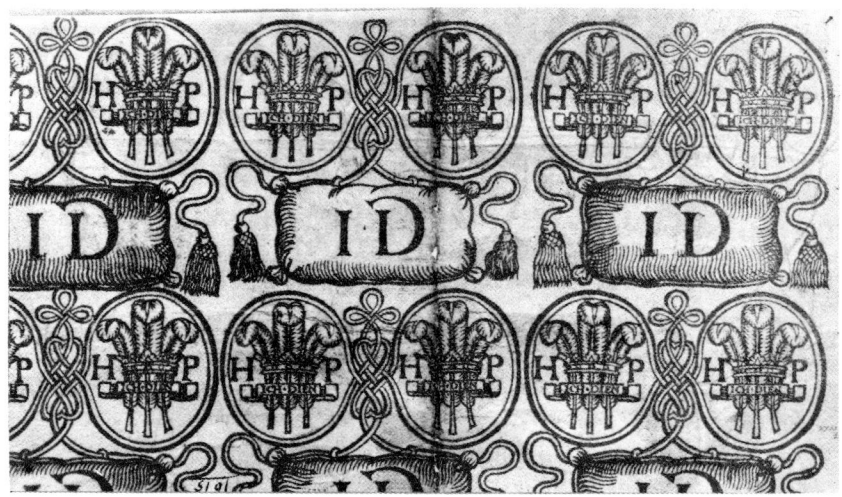

Paper with the arms, initials and motto of Henry Frederick, Prince of Wales.
English, early 17th century. V&A.

Domino *paper by J.-M. Papillon,
with design of boughs and bunches of grapes.
French. BN.*

*Paper by J.-M. Papillon from the
Château de Bercy, Paris. French,
c. 1725. Follot coll.*

the rest of Europe at that time was using utility papers printed with coats-of-arms and other motifs. As the name suggests, *papiers de tapisserie* were inexpensive imitations in paper of materials such as brocade, Indian chintzes, Spanish leather as well as tapestry, but they also imitated architectural elements such as cornices, wood panelling, mouldings and false ceilings. Such wall-coverings had the same purpose as more costly decors, for the substitution only gave a new direction to a way of life that was determined on comfort without losing a scrap of elegance. At first, suites of tapestry were used by the Crown and the nobility to cover the bleak walls of medieval castles, to create a little warmth in their immense and sombre rooms and to brighten them with a pattern of colours enriched by gold and silver thread; but above all sumptuous tapestries were clear proof of the wealth and taste of their owners. Similarly, the bourgeoisie used *papiers de tapisserie* to cover their walls and create the illusion of beautiful but inaccessible materials, such as the Spanish leather that keeps its warmth in winter but is refreshingly cool in summer.

By the end of the seventeenth century wallpaper was as widely used in France as in England. It is hard to provide tangible proof of this, because so few of the many *papiers de tapisserie* or figured papers produced in the sixteenth and seventeenth centuries have survived *in situ*. We do not know, either, of any paintings of the period that show wallpapers used in an interior. The only fragments that have come down to us are from bookbindings, or the linings of chests, boxes and other pieces of furniture.

In Richelet's 1680 *Dictionnaire*, the entry on *dominotier* reads 'a maker of marbled paper and other papers printed in different colours, and various figurative designs, which *used to be called dominos*'. Ten years later Savary des Bruslons wrote in his *Dictionnaire universel du commerce*: 'a dominotier makes a sort of tapestry on paper, which for a long time was used by the peasants and the poorer classes in Paris to cover the walls of their huts or their rooms and shops.' In 1713 he added: 'By the end of the seventeenth century, the technique had reached a high point of perfection and elegance. Quite apart from the larger quantities of paper that are sold for export abroad and in the principal cities of France, there is not a house in Paris, however grand, that does not contain some example of this charming decoration, even if only in a wardrobe or other private room.'

There are two main reasons why we do not have physical evidence of seventeenth-century papers. Firstly, very few bourgeois houses, let alone poorer people's dwellings, have survived. Secondly, those buildings that *have* survived the perils of war or destruction by fire, or just the process of urban development, have been regularly redecorated according to changes in ownership or fashion, thus

Lining paper glazed with gelatine, showing the influence of 'cabbage leaf' tapestries. German, early 18th century. P. des Ligneris coll.

Ballet Champêtre. Design engraved by Martin Engelbrecht. German, 18th century. P. Nollot coll.

burying for ever any traces of the fragile original decoration under layers of later paint and paper. In addition, the nineteenth century had a passion for the modern, unlike our own era which, cut off from its roots by the machine age, needs to get back into contact with the past. When the nineteenth century did pay any attention to the creations of earlier ages, it was the high points that were noticed, such as Réveillon's wallpapers, and the less flamboyant work of the *dominotiers* and their colleagues was overlooked or treated with mistrust. Historians of wallpaper did little to change this attitude: Henri Clouzot, for example, in his *Histoire du papier peint en France*, 1935, gives three times as much space to Réveillon as to the whole period before him. Not until June 1967, when the Musée des Arts Décoratifs in Paris staged an exhibition of 'Three Centuries of Wallpaper', was it possible to look once more at the splendid fragments of the *dominotier's* art that had remained hidden throughout the nineteenth century.

Even though the early wallpapers were all printed by the same method, they do have a wide variety of designs and colours. There are two main groups: the simplest papers repeat the same motif from a single wood block; the more attractive papers, which are made to join up into a whole, are printed from several blocks. The former use a range of geometrical symbols, such as cubes, lozenges and circles, as well as checkered and dot and line motifs. These were printed in black onto the sheet, which was then heightened with coloured size applied through cut-out stencils. These elements provide the background for wavy bands of images, mainly showing flowers, but sometimes birds and, rarely, people. The papers printed off several blocks unfolded into several widths or depths. This group includes *chinoiseries*, which will be discussed in more detail later. All these papers were glued down, their edges overlapping, and were surrounded with printed borders which were sometimes used to divide the paper into strips. Often the topmost edge would have a frieze with an architectural motif or an arabesque. So some paper makers specialized in flowers, others in imitating architectural details, marble, or panelling.

During the whole of the seventeenth century and the first half of the eighteenth there was no one who manufactured wallpapers exclusively. Rather there were groups of artisan shopkeepers, being card makers, *dominotiers*, paper merchants and wood engravers of all kinds. The paper they printed was used also for decorating books and boxes, firescreens and furniture. They also produced hand-painted sheets, printed from blocks, which could be cut up to make decorations for sticking onto tables and desks, or chairs and varnished chests. Some of them engraved alphabets, vignettes and tailpieces for printers; others engraved designs for embroi-

Paper for a harpsichord, by Jean Papillon II. BN.

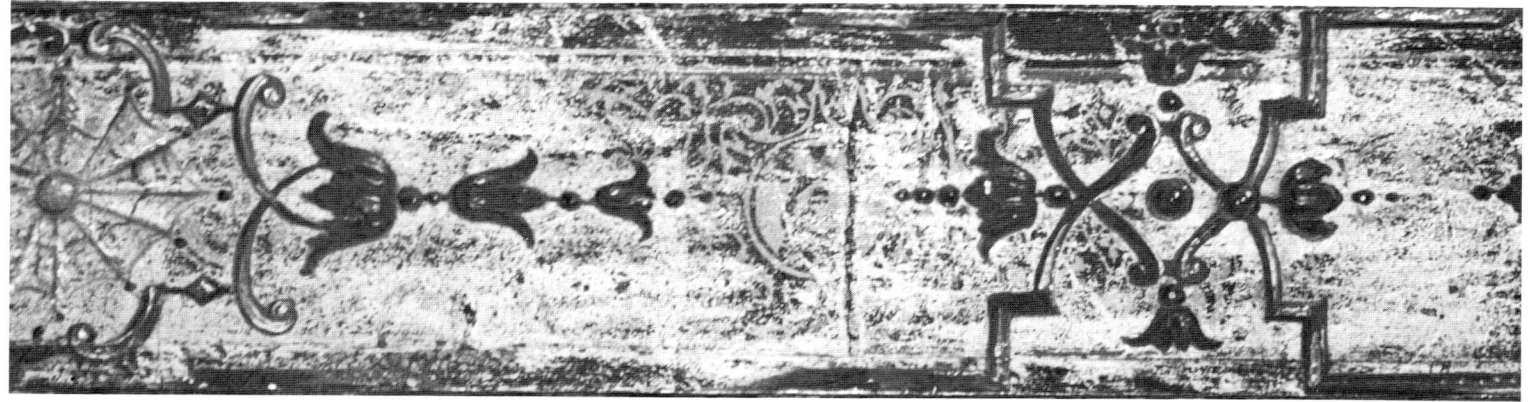

Paper from a Rückers harpsichord from the Château de Versailles.

Seahorse paper from the frame of a Rückers harpsichord. 1620. Mercier-Ythier coll. (The same paper but with the design in negative occurs on another Rückers harpsichord in Antwerp.)

Coloured paper for a harpsichord by Georg Christoph Stoy, Augsburg. Mercier-Ythier coll.

dery or for lacework for skirts or sleeves. The shops that most of the craftsmen also kept sold paper of all sorts – corrugated paper, wallpaper, manuscript paper – and ink, wax and glue.

The information we do possess on these early merchant-craftsmen is due to Jean-Michel Papillon (1698-1776), who was the last descendant of two generations of wood engravers. Apart from his *Traité historique et pratique de la gravure sur bois*, he also prepared a collection of engravings, of both his own and his forebears' work, and a manuscript, written a year before his death, which was intended as an addition to the *Traité* should a second edition be published.

According to this manuscript, the first member of the family, Jean Papillon I (1639-1710) was born in Rouen but set up his business in Paris, in the rue St Jacques, where 'he produced playing-cards and obituary announcements, but these found no market, and he was ruined .... He never engraved anything of real quality'. Jean had two sons, Jean-Nicolas, a second rate engraver who became a corn-chandler, and the father of Jean-Michel, Jean Papillon II. Jean-Michel described his father as 'one of the most accomplished engravers of his time. He was born in St Quentin in 1661 and brought up in Rouen and later in Paris, where he was taught by Noel Cochin, a skilful etcher and engraver.' It was from Cochin that he learnt to draw horses and horsemen, motifs that were to appear decorating his signature when he was apprenticed to Barberot, a haberdasher 'who dealt in stencils for lacework, drawings inked onto cloth for embroidery work, or for the stitched skirts called Marseilles work. Though his father had given him but two or three lessons in wood engraving, Jean nonetheless started to make engravings himself. But as he was only expected to design one skirt each day, the rest of his time being free, he was able to develop this skill on his own account. He worked out a method of engraving his skirt designs on wood, and of transferring them onto the material, so he could make two designs in two hours. This also increased his master's business, and as Barberot thought well of him, he made sure Papillon improved his mastery of both drawing and engraving... By 1684, Papillon had already engraved a number of worthwhile pieces and begun to make a name for himself with booksellers, as well as with the embroiderers, *gaziers*, upholsterers, ribbon makers and other workers for whom he provided designs.'

As we have seen, haberdashers also sold all sorts of paper, including wallpapers, so that Jean Papillon II would have become familiar with such work. His contacts with fashion and textile workers developed his ornamental vocabulary. The cutting and cross-cutting of his designs became more and more exact, and he was the first person to use a marking gauge to draw parallel lines. In 1686 he married Marie-Madeleine Chevillon. She was the daughter of a well-known bookseller who traded 'at the sign of the Colombe Royale' in the rue St Jacques. The marriage gave him the chance to engrave many vignettes, coats-of-arms, scrolls, fleurons and portraits to illustrate books. His taste ran to elegant arabesques and the repeated motifs of embroidery, which gave him the idea of printing from more than one block for his largest designs. Jean-Michel writes: 'To him we owe the invention of *papiers de tapisserie*, for which he started a fashion in 1688. His designs were well made and artistic, showing much skill in their arrangement. He developed the art of such papers to a level that has not been matched by his contemporaries or later designers, all of whom have imitated his designs because of their high reputation and taste.'

Poppies. *Paper printed from the first block engraved by J.-M. Papillon, in black with stencil colours. French, 1707. BN.*

At last wallpapers, previously confined to the size of a single woodblock, could be made in large decorative panels to form a continuous and coherent mural decoration in the same way that paintings did. Such papers were soon to be found in every middle-class house. Jean Papillon II himself did not therefore stop engraving vignettes, scrolls, obituary announcements and so forth, but also set himself up as a haberdasher in order to increase the scope of his business.

His son, Jean-Michel Papillon, was brought up in the engraving workshop, and at an early age showed an interest in the technique: when only eight years old, in 1706, he tried to engrave a block of boxwood, without his father knowing, but only managed to break the tools. A year later he tried again, with the help of his father who suggested a design of poppies, and provided a piece of pear wood, a softer material. Although a number of notches made by the inexpert cutting needed to be repaired, the end result was, to the father's surprise, not at all bad. This engraving had an honoured place in Jean-Michel's collection, though he regretted that the stencilling of the colours had been very badly done.

Jean-Michel Papillon had only one purpose in life: to make 'delicate wood engravings'. His preface to the Traité... de la gravure confirms this amply: 'Let me state here that my love for the Art has overcome the innumerable obstacles that seem to have been in my way and that I was drawn to becoming an engraver at all events by my own wish and, if I can put it in such a way, of my free will, even before I could have been fully aware of having such a quality. One of the first obstacles was the contrary attitude of my own father, whose firm opinion it was that I should not make my career that of a fine engraver, but as an engraver exclusively of wallpapers: which were of course his line of business... so I was made to work all day printing wallpapers, as likely colouring them in when I was not cutting out the blocks, as going to houses of quality to attend to the hanging of papers.'

But on the quiet he was perfecting his technique as an engraver by copying the work of such masters as Le Clerc, Pérelle and Callot. The finish of the son's work was much better than the father's, but he often had to leave his chisels aside for the gluebrush: 'While working for my father, I had almost every day to go and place or hang wallpapers: in 1719 or 1720 I went to the village of Bagneux, near Mont-Rouge, where a Swiss officer, Captain de Greder, had a very pretty house. After I had decorated a small room for him, he asked me to put mosaic paper on his library shelves.'

A few years after his father's death in 1723 Jean-Michel handed over the stock of the business and the blocks to Madame Langlois, a widow. What made him do so? Perhaps the way his father made him work at papers and not at the 'fine wood engraving' he wished for. We do not know. What *is* certain is that on 22 September 1723, Jean-Michel Papillon, described as a *graveur et bourgeois de Paris* married Charlotte-Madeleine-Thérèse Chauveau, daughter of the late René Chauveau, a sculptor and member of the Académie. His witnesses were his uncle Jean-Nicolas Papillon, the corn-chandler, and his cousin on his mother's side, Nicolas Thoyer, a master merchant who dealt in card and paper. From his wife's side there were René-Bonaventure Chauveau, her brother, an expert adviser to the courts, and her brothers-in-law, the Parisian merchant Charles-Francois Guérard and Jacques Chardon, a printer and bookseller. So he joined that section of the prosperous middle class who worked in the book and paper trades, which encompassed a number of different guilds. Jean-Michel Papillon was the first professional *tapissier* and, more importantly, the first historian of wallpaper: his writing recalls his métier with affection and vigour.

The anatomy of a workshop

In 1746 when Denis Diderot began to amass the material on the fine and decorative arts for inclusion in his *Encyclopédie* he visited the workshops of different professions, and consulted practical manuals and dictionaries, both French and foreign. He also asked the most famous manufacturers to supply him with illustrations for reproduction as engravings. The first articles were ready in about 1750, and the first volume of the work was published in July 1751. In a letter about wallpapers, Diderot recalled 'one craftsman, to whom I thought I had explained quite clearly what I required – I supposed a few hundred words and a modest illustration would be sufficient – but who brought me ten or twelve full sheets covered with illustrative diagrams, and three thick, large notebooks written in a fine hand. Whereas another wallpaper maker, to whom I made exactly the same request, only brought me a brief list of words, without definitions, explanations or diagrams, assuring me that there was nothing more to his trade worth knowing or writing down – this for a trade that produces such a variety of finished products, in so many different materials, using a whole range of techniques and machines.'

In July 1759, Diderot went to visit his sister at Langres, where his father had just died. It was there, at the beginning of this century, that Monsieur Violle, a government official, found seven sheets of wash drawings, all signed Papillon. P. Gusman published these drawings for the first time in the magazine *Byblis* in 1925, whereupon Henri Clouzot, keeper of the Musée Galliera in Paris, wrote to ask Violle if he might have the drawings, which he had seen by chance in *Byblis*, in order to write about them in the *Revue de l'art*. Since then the drawings have frequently been published, discussed and exhibited: they are crucial documents for the history of wallpaper.

The sheets of drawings are of different sizes, but are all about 12½ x 7½ inches (32 x 19 centimetres). When we came to photograph them for this book we were surprised to find under the frames and in the margins a very large number of annotations. These do not, unfortunately, enable us to give the drawings a firm date. Clouzot suggested 1738, which has been widely accepted but is in our view not feasible, for why would Diderot have been asking Papillon for diagrams six years before the first meeting of the *philosophes* which launched the

Pen, ink and wash drawings intended as engravings for Diderot and d'Alembert's Encyclopédie, *by J.-M. Papillon. French, c. 1759. Violle coll.*

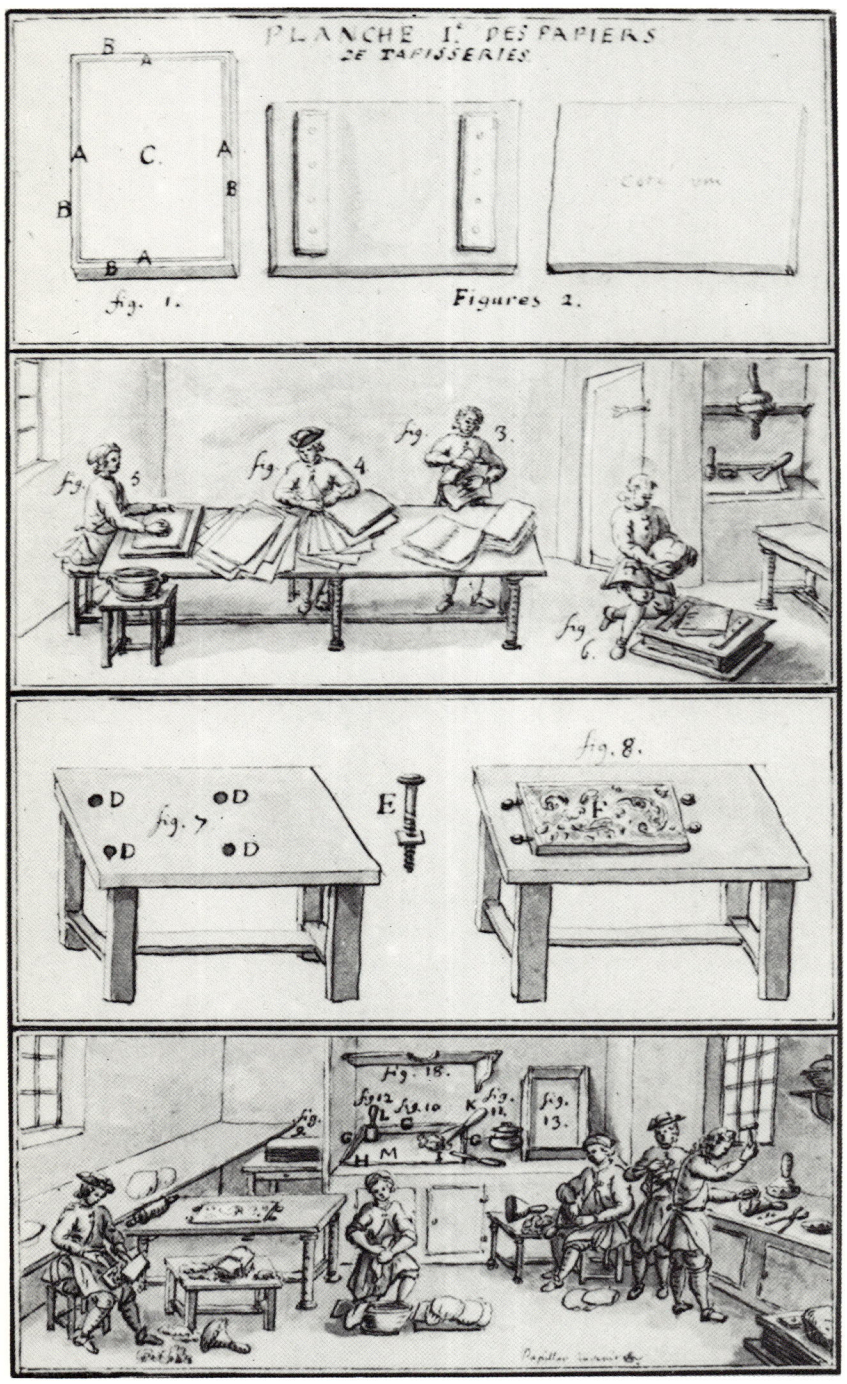

Sheet 1
Figs 1-22: the equipment needed for printing.

Strip 1
Fig. 1: the stock of paper for printing.
Fig. 2: planks to hold the paper during printing.

Strip 2
Figs 3-6: the paper is prepared, dampened and held ready for press between two planks, by means of heavy weights.

Strip 3
Fig. 7: the printing table, a solid structure with four holes and a vice for fixing down the printing block (D,E).
Fig. 8: the block fixed on the table.

Strip 4
At the back of the workshop, tools for inking the block.
Fig. 10 (H,G,M): a three-sided tub for mixing the colour.
Fig. 11: a small pan, probably for ox-gall.
Fig. 12: a pestle and mortar for lampblack (L), and palette knives (I,K).
Fig. 13: a trough.
Fig. 18: a shelf with fittings to hold the inking-pads.
In the foreground five workmen are making inking-pads: one is preparing the stuffing, another the leather by dampening it, the third places the stuffing round the stick, while the fourth positions the leather which is nailed down by the last man.

Sheet 2
Printing up the blocks.

Strip 1
Figs 14(N)-17: the inking-pad, the handle, the frame and the die.
Figs 19-22: the roller used to exert an even pressure on the planks (see fig.28).
Fig. 19(P): the part of the roller that holds the cushioning blanket, with a square hole at each end.
Fig. 20: the two spindles, the square end (Q) fitting exactly into the roller, the other end (R) taking the handles.
Fig. 21: the handles, which turn freely on the spindles.
Fig. 22: the roller with the blanket attached.

Strip 2
Left: a workman mixes the colour, while a second rubs two inking-pads together to ensure even inking. A third man inks a block with two pads.
Fig. 24: a man prepares a sheet from the stock of paper.
Fig. 25: another gets ready to place a sheet on the block.
Fig. 26: the sheet is placed on the block, starting at the top. (Papillon takes care to show how the workmen hold each sheet with both hands and their teeth, to ensure it does not get inked before it is in place.)
Right: a workman sews a blanket onto a roller. In the foreground, sheets being pressed.

Strip 3
Fig. 27: a sheet is placed on the block.
Fig. 28: a sheet is printed.
Fig. 29: the printed sheet is lifted off.
Fig. 30: apprentices hand the sheets on lines to dry.

Strip 4
Figs 31(A), 32(B,C): the newly printed sheets are piled up and separated from the waste sheets.
Fig. 33: a workman takes them to dry.
In another part of the shop two copperplate presses are being used to make proofs:
Fig. 34: a proof is taken off.
Fig. 35: a workman turns a lever to operate the press.

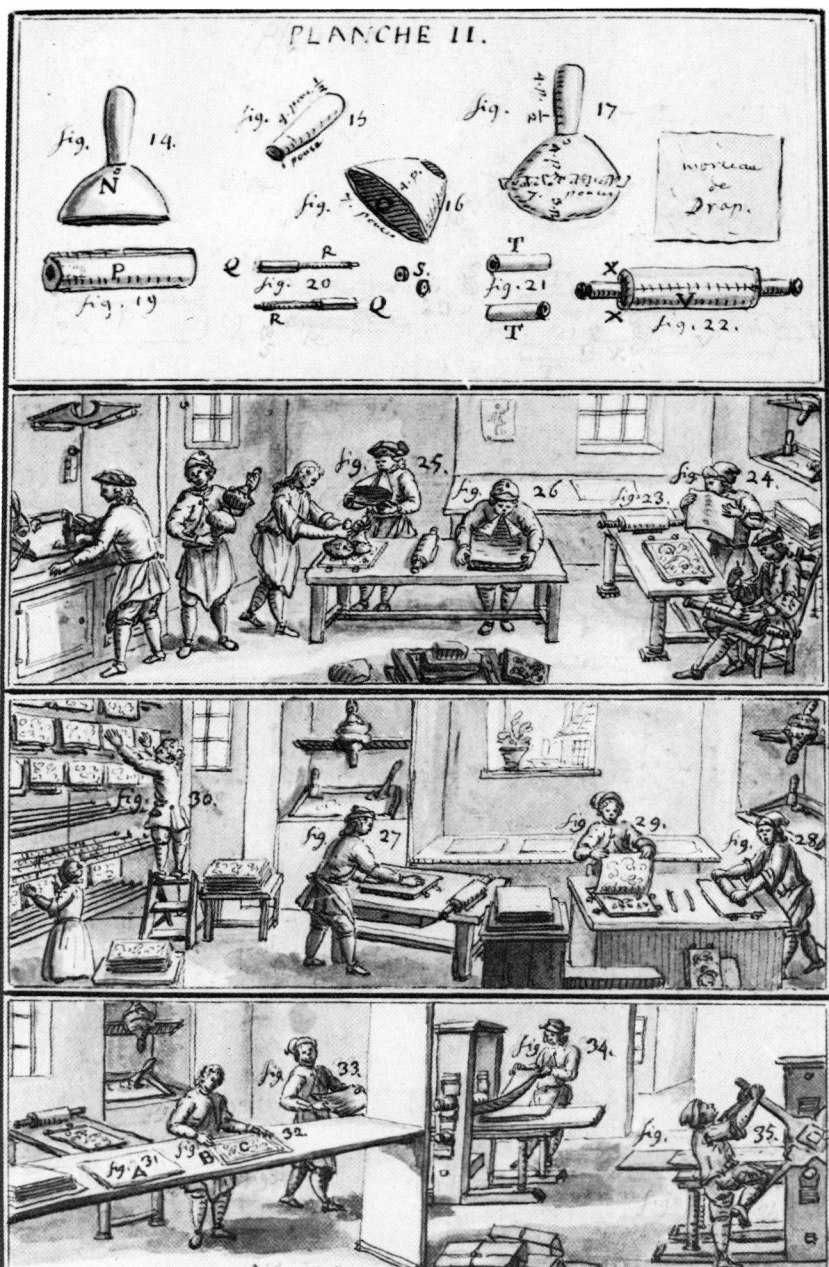

MARGINAL INSCRIPTION (instructions to the original printer)
'The engraver will give more depth to the third strip by reducing the space given to the tools, so that the whole is divided into four equal strips, as are the other sheets.'

Sheet 3
The first two strips deal with drying, checking and colouring the sheets, the third shows the outside of the workshop, in the rue St Jacques, and the fourth a house where wallpaper is to be hung.

Strip 1
Fig. 36: on a stool, a pile of reject sheets.
Fig. 37: an apprentice carrying sheets.
Fig. 38: a girl and her mother remove the reject sheets.
Fig. 39: a workman separates printed and waste sheets.
Fig. 40: a workman on a ladder hangs sheets to dry.
Fig. 41: a workman cleans marks off the paper.
Figs 42, 43: two workmen check the printed sheets.
Fig. 44: in the courtyard, two workmen wash down the materials in a large bath of hot water.

Strip 2
The brushwork room, where on a large trestle-table women are stencilling colour onto the sheets; the glue for this is being heated in the fireplace. The finished sheets hang from the ceiling to dry, and on the left the shopmen are shown packing them up.

Strip 3
The rue St Jacques and the St Séverin fountain. The inscription reads: 'View of the old shop, where Papillon first put up his sign, in the rue St Jacques by the fountain'. This sketch gives much detailed information about a contemporary row of shops: each one is close to the next and opens straight onto the pavement, the inside is shielded by blinds, and the owner's name and nature of his business are displayed prominently on signs and along the shop-front.

Strip 4
Inside a house where paper is to be hung.
Fig. 45: the walls are carefully scraped down.
Fig. 46: holes and cracks are filled.
Fig. 47: strips of paper are pasted over cracks.
On a table in the foreground there are strips of paper, a brush and a bowl of glue. Glue is being heated in the fireplace, and in the background three workmen are using a broom, sponges and hot water to soak the old decoration off the walls.

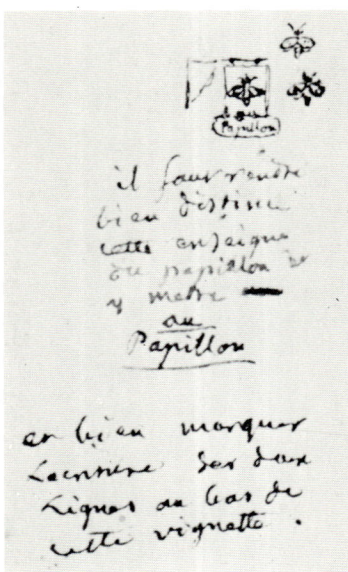

MARGINAL INSCRIPTION (instructions to the original printer): 'The butterfly sign [on strip 3] must be clearly drawn and the words 'au Papillon' included... and the two lines of writing at the bottom of this strip must be clearly rendered.'

Sheet 4
Workmen prepare to hang the paper, and trim the sheets.

Strip 1
Fig. 49: four workmen mark on the walls where the sheets will fall, and the lines of the borders and frames.
Fig. 50: three workmen trim the sheets with scissors.

Strip 2
Papillon shows the different ways of trimming sheets and borders according to how they will fall on the wall: they are joined at the top ('le chef', CBC), on the right or left ('côté à gauche', 'côté à droite', D), at right angles (à 'l'équerre',E), or at the bottom ('par embas', F). Papillon takes care not to repeat the same design in any of these sheets or borders, even while using purely floral motifs.

Strip 3
Workmen check the join marks on the walls.
Fig. 51: two men smear the plumbline with ochre, while two others, one on a table, the other on a set of steps, use a line to mark the upper border, and two others, one kneeling, one on a ladder, mark out the verticals.

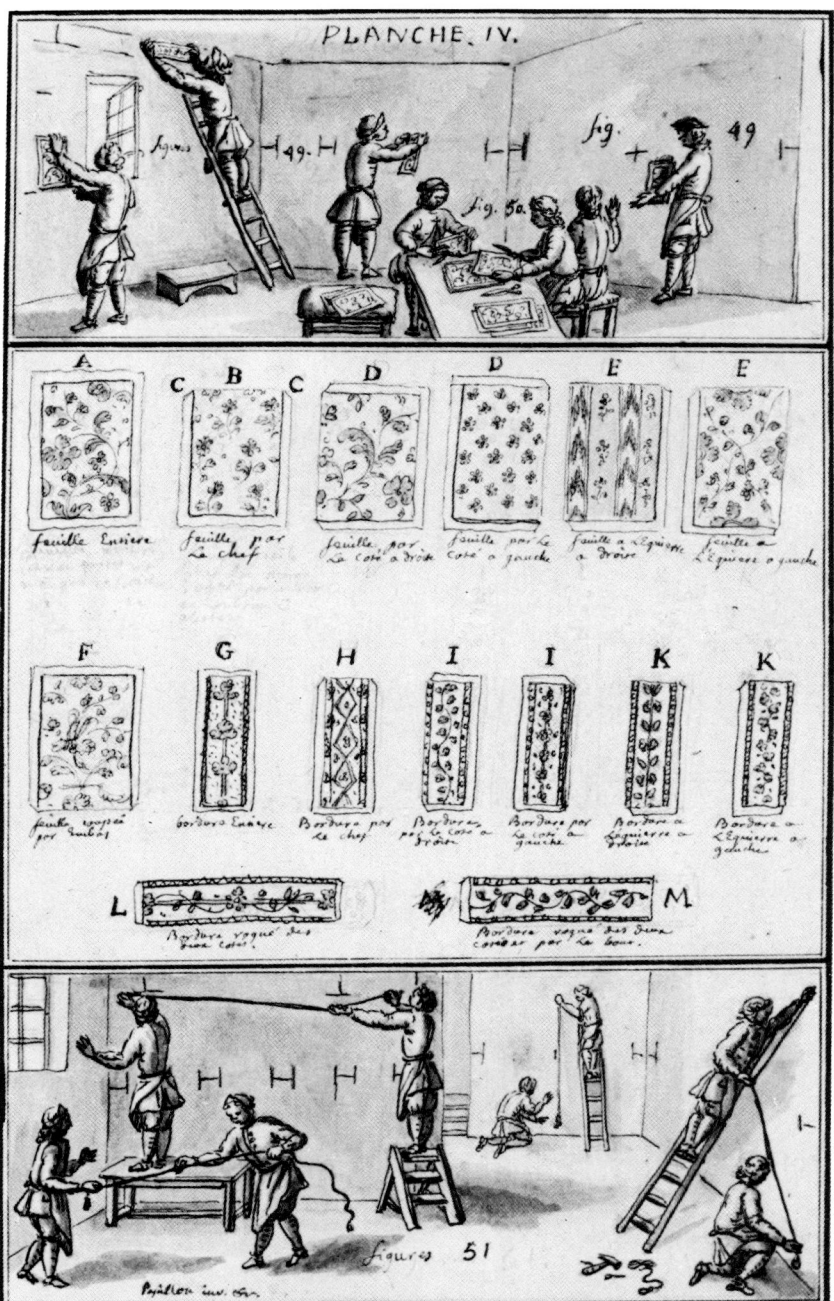

Sheet 5
This sheet shows how papers were hung.

Strip 1
Fig. 52: two men sitting at tables cover the sheets with glue.
Fig. 53: one man holds out a brush and glue to the man who is going to hang the paper (on the table the outline left after pasting the sheet can be seen).
Fig. 54: two workmen hand pasted sheets to the paper-hanger.
Fig. 55: two paper-hangers place the sheet, trimmed at the top, always starting at the top of the wall.
Fig. 56: a worker mixing glue.

Strip 2
Fig. 57: checking the verticals are straight.
Fig. 58: around the pasting-table, workmen cut out and glue the borders.
Fig. 59: the vertical borders are placed in the gaps between the sheets.
Fig. 60: borders are placed in the angle between two walls.

Strip 3
Fig. 61: placing borders at the top of panels.
Fig. 62, 63: three ways of gluing sheets.

Strip 4
Fig. 64: placing the bottom border on a panel.
Fig. 65: a panel decorated with alternating sheets and borders, the horizontal ones having been hung last. The right hand panel shows a landscape in the Chinese style, framed by a border with decorated corners.

Sheet 6

Strip 1
Fig. 66: two men placing a paper wainscot against a landscape paper.
Fig. 67: a complete panel, with borders, wainscot and frieze.
Fig. 68: panels divided by *trompe l'oeil* columns, wainscot and frieze.

Strip 2
Concealing joists and rafters with a false ceiling.
Fig. 69: two workmen placing a heavy paper across the rafters.
Fig. 70: others fill the gaps where the joins can be seen.
Figs 71 and 72: lines are marked out on the ceiling as a basis for decoration.

Strip 3
Fig. 73: workmen position a ceiling rose and friezes with floral motifs.
Fig. 74: the wallpapered rooms being presented to the master and mistress of the house.
Fig. 75: even the staircase, walls and ceiling have been wallpapered.

Strip 4
Fig. 76: an alcove with cupola ceiling is papered in the same way as a cupboard, but with a different paper.
Figs 77, 78: a workman papers a niche, marking out how the sheets (A,B,F) and borders (G,H,I) should be trimmed.

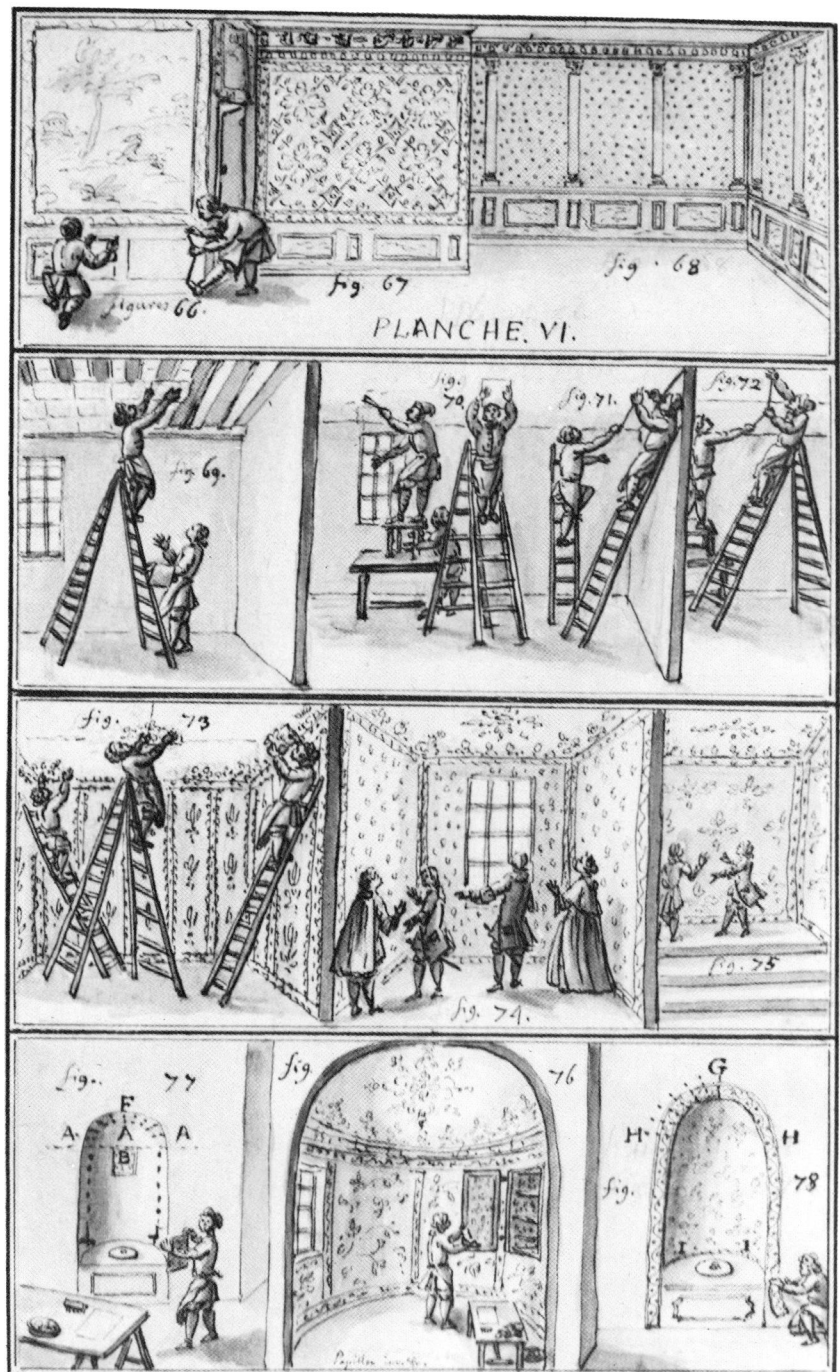

Sheet 7
The last sheet deals with the most difficult and unusual problems of hanging.

Strip 1
This shows the system for hanging flock papers which, like distemper papers, were quite fragile and could not be applied by brush.
Fig. 79: a workman fixes the supporting canvas to the wall with tacks, while in the background two workmen and an apprentice (holding the ladder) paste the sheets onto the canvas.
Fig. 80: workmen take down and roll up the sheets of canvas.

Strip 2
Fig. 81: workmen erect large canvas screens.
Fig. 82: workmen fix hinges onto the screens.

Strip 3
Figs. 83-85: workmen cover a chimney-breast with marbled paper.

Strip 4
Fig. 86: in the background, workmen nail a stretched panel onto the wall. On the right a workman brushes glue onto the back of a sheet, while opposite a woman positions a large sheet. On the left, two workmen cover a panel of flock paper with a cloth to protect its fragile surface.

idea of the *Encyclopédie*? As we shall see in due course, a large number of details suggest a date of after 1750. Our own proposal is the year 1759, when Diderot went to Langres to mourn his father and perhaps in his grief left behind the drawings he had just received; he himself declared that he did not intend to publish them.

Papillon's sketches are drawn in black pencil, heightened with black or sometimes sepia ink and with wash backgrounds. They were drawn from the life, and provide a realistic account, in a series of images like a cartoon, of working life in a wallpaper workshop in the first half of the eighteenth century. Each sheet is divided into four strips, which, if run together, provide a complete panorama of all the stages in making and hanging paper.

These drawings are of real value, both for the light they shed on the profession of the *tapissier*, or wallpaper maker, and for the information they give on interior decoration in the middle of the eighteenth century. The various techniques of the *dominotiers* were taken over by the *tapissiers*, though Jean-Michel Papillon's contribution to the *Encyclopédie* is hardly flattering to the former: 'Domino – a kind of paper, on which the outline, figures and designs are printed from crudely cut woodblocks, then colour printed by stencil, as for playing-cards. These papers are made in Rouen in particular, and other provincial towns. Their only market is the peasantry, who decorate their hearths with them. All *domino* papers lack taste: the designs are poor, the stencilling worse and the colours harsh.'

But why should Papillon deal so roughly with an art he had practised himself? Doubtless he was referring to the sort of wallpapers sold by pedlars at rural fairs, dull things printed off old blocks with no effort at fine production or modern decoration. Papillon, who was a member of the Société des Arts, saw himself as a real artist, determined on perfection, purity of line and elegant design. He treated the simpler work of his contemporaries without pity, but was just as critical of his own efforts. The creative ability of real artists such as Jean-Michel Papillon and his father transformed the *domino* into *papier de tapisserie*, which would now be welcome in the homes of the leisured bourgeoisie.

Papillon is as strict and precise in his account of how to hang paper as he is on its manufacture. Four of his seven sheets of drawings deal with hanging paper, and describe each stage in considerable detail. From the number of workmen shown – and the drawings depict with care the task of each one – hanging paper was the most delicate and difficult part of the profession. The drawings also show all the possible ways in which Papillon could use different papers. There were marbled papers for fireplaces and chimneys, papers with continuous designs for large wall panels, papers with landscapes in the Chinese style, edging papers to frame the whole, friezes, papers imitating wooden panelling, and floral designs and rosettes for ceilings (this was a real innovation, for all the other evidence of such papers dates from the early nineteenth century).

Papillon also takes care to show how to put up a false ceiling – in paper – and cover it with wallpaper, how to wallpaper a staircase and a circular room, tests of his workmen's real skill. He shows how to hang flock paper and distempered paper, and how to cover a screen or the round panels of a staircase. Fig. 81 is particularly important, as it foreshadows the print rooms found in Britain in the second half of the eighteenth century. Two examples are known, Castletown House in Co. Kildare and Hickstead Place at Bolney in Sussex, where the staircase walls have the same arrangement of engravings in

Ornamental paper designed by Roumier. Woodblock-printed by J.-M. Papillon. French, 1727. BN.

trompe l'oeil. Fig. 81 shows small framed pieces, but the drawing is not sufficiently detailed to show whether they are frames fixed to the stair panels or engravings pasted inside a paper border. In either case, we can assume that Papillon would not have gone to the trouble of showing this particular way of hanging paper if it was not a system he regularly used, so that even if he was not the inventor of the print room he can be considered its inspiration. We can be sure that his depiction is absolutely authentic, as much when it shows the specific task of each apprentice or craftsman as when it shows a workman perched on a stool placed on a table because all the ladders are already in use (fig. 70).

Large brocade paper printed in black (probably the underlying design for a flock paper). J.-M. Papillon, French, 18th century. BN.

Trade card of Ramponneau, an inn-keeper. J.-M. Papillon, French, 1761.

Papillon himself, our eyewitness to all this activity, is not identifiable among the team who work under his name.

Although his workshop produced a considerable quantity of papers, very few of his wallpapers have survived. The collection of the Cabinet d'Estampes in Paris contains only seven examples. Apart from the design of poppies already mentioned, there are two large blocks (illustrated on p. 76 of Papillon's *Traité*) that join to form a continuous pattern imitating cut velvet, engraved in 1746 for Monsieur Martin the elder, the Royal Varnisher, and (on p. 80) a large block for mosaic paper with flowers and butterflies in a scroll.

Martin, together with his son, created a famous series of varnish finishes that imitated Chinese and Japanese lacquers. According to an announcement in the *Mercure* of March 1770, Martin the younger offered at his shop at the sign of the Malle Royale in the rue St Antoine 'flock papers an ell across [about one yard] in one piece without joins, each piece with a border in a range of colours, sold by the square ell'. As Papillon had engraved the two blocks for paper imitating cut velvet in 1746, perhaps Martin was already selling flock papers then, although the first blue flock papers were not imported into Paris until 1753. We will come back to this question in the chapter on flock papers.

Another design (illustrated by Papillon on p. 77) has motifs of flowers, mosaic patterns and stippling was cut in pear-wood in 1727 for the sculptor Roumier, who had designed it. Figs 5 and 6 on p. 81 show two oddments of wallpaper designs. As the same designs could be used for wallpapers or textiles, we can add two blocks which Papillon calls 'blocks for painted cloth' (fig. 2, p. 80) and a 'small block for painted cloth' (fig. 4, p. 81). Finally, we can add to the material in this collection the design reproduced by Clouzot for a very fine arabesque paper with the mark of Papillon and the rue St Jacques opposed. Félix Follot discovered this paper when the Château de Bercy was demolished in 1860, and there may well be other papers that have disappeared that would add to Papillon's *oeuvre*.

Just as Papillon's wash drawings explain the different techniques for making wallpaper, so his *Traité* on wood engraving gives us a detailed, affectionate and sometimes naive picture of the busy world of the *dominotiers*, whose first historian he was, as well as being one of the most famous manufacturers of wallpaper. His account lists the names of his colleagues, their relationship with the law and the other guilds, and outlines clearly the web of connections between the printers, engravers, illuminators and booksellers both Parisian and provincial, which makes it so difficult for us to give an exact provenance to any creation of this group of craftsmen.

Papillon's rivals

During the seventeenth century and the first half of the eighteenth the *dominotiers* adopted new techniques of printing and manufacture, began to use papers of a better quality, and developed colours that used ink, oil or water as a base; their craft thereby reached a considerable height of perfection. These changes are proof both of the gradual development of wallpaper technology and of the real creative achievement of these craftsmen, an achievement too long underestimated. Almost all the names of these craftsmen that have survived have been found in archive sources, in newspapers or in Papillon's *Traité*. Only a handful have been found on the borders of surviving wallpapers. We have perhaps a hundred names in all, and must ask how many more have been lost with the passage of time, or how many craftsmen are represented by surviving, unidentified papers. As each maker would have had a range of papers, the total extent of manufacture must have been extremely wide. Indeed, some *domino* papers carry, in addition to the name of a maker, a design number, and some have engraved stamps such as 'A Paris chez les associés – no 97' or 'sold by Aubert rue St Jacques, Paris, at the sign Au Papillon, under royal patronage –no II'.

It is very difficult to estimate the level of production of wallpapers. Even though we know the size of the urban population, and can estimate from the different phases of urban development how many buildings might need redecorating, we still cannot guess at what proportion of the population would have used wallpaper for redecoration.

One factor that led to a more general need for wallpaper was the development of printing, as a great deal of such paper was used in bookbinding. During the sixteenth century about 200,000 books were published, each edition being about 1000 copies, that is about 2 million books in all, each requiring two sets of endpapers in marbled or *domino* paper. Paper makers also printed large numbers of sheets coloured by stencil, not only for book covers, but as linings for boxes and chests. This type of paper was at first produced like any other, but gradually became more specialized and diversified as demand developed. In the course of the eighteenth century, wallpaper began to establish an identity of its own and so become a separate manufacture. Wallpaper makers and wood engravers created a whole range of papers suitable both for bindings and for wall-coverings, such as marbled paper, with its infinite range of effects, and paper with floral designs, or with scrolls, garlands or groups of people. It is often difficult to establish how certain papers were meant to be used. Among the papers produced by Remondini at

A card seller. Engraving.

A card maker. Engraving by Martin Engelbrecht. German, 17th century.

Faiseuse de Cartes. Eine Kartenmacherin.

Bassano, for example, we find the same designs used for both endpapers and wall-friezes. The fact that the *dominotiers'* paper was used in the book trade explains why they set up shop near the printers, booksellers and stationers, who in turn would need to be near the universities. Thus in Paris the trade was first established in the rue St Jacques, near the Sorbonne. This street was a vigorous centre of commerce, with its rows of shops for craftsmen, booksellers, printers, haberdashers, *dominotiers*, papermen and stationers. After the fourteenth century the guild structure became more rigid and controlled. It became necessary to

Lining paper. Italian, early 18th century. V&A.

be admitted to a guild as master in order to follow a profession, and an unqualified trader could lose his stock and his rights. There were frequent squabbles between the *dominotiers*, paper makers and wallpaper makers and the other guilds, as the goods they produced could equally well have been made by engravers as by printers and artists. A series of royal edicts protected and defined their rights.

In 1586, a royal charter gave the guild of *dominotiers* and makers of wallpaper and hand-coloured images the right to print pictures and portraits from mythology, from the Old and New Testaments, and to make papers to hang on walls. Other edicts followed in 1597, 1608, 1649 and 1660. In 1597, Henri IV's edict mentions 'makers of papers and other materials as wallpapers and suchlike'. The later edicts increased the rights and position of the *dominotiers*. In 1708, the painters' guild, with the help of a Commissioner, tried to impound Jean Papillon's stock of papers, on the grounds that they were printed and coloured by brushwork. Papillon blocked this move by reference to a 1660 decision in favour of engravers. In 1732 the wood engravers won an action brought against them by the copperplate engravers, on the grounds that they only used copperplate presses to produce counter-proofs for wallpapers, and owned no copperplate engraving tools. This decision was confirmed by a decree on 6 March 1739. But in 1768, a law was passed allowing a *dominotier* to use his press only when a master printer (or his deputy) was present. Once the work was finished, the press had to be chained and padlocked. In 1776 the wallpaper makers joined the guilds of papermen, binders and joiners, and in 1785 the paper, card and wallpaper merchants obtained a royal decree granting them the right to practise the 'craft of painting and printing paper for use on furniture.'

The shops in arcades down the rue St Jacques were often continuations of workshops that opened onto an inner courtyard. Quite dark inside, the shops had large bays, containing a display of wares under an awning, and later a glazed window as shopfront. We have the names of only nine *dominotiers* in the rue St Jacques. First and foremost is the Papillon family, who set up shop near the St Séverin fountain in 1663. Shortly after his father's death in 1723 Jean-Michel Papillon moved to the rue du Pont St Michel, as we know from one of his trade cards. (He returned to the rue St Jacques in 1766.) Then the widow Langlois bought from him his workroom, shop and sign. (Her son, a printseller, adopted the sign A la Renommée.)

Hoping to gain trade from the confusion, Didier Aubert set up shop under the sign Au Papillon near the Hôtel de Saumur. The experiment led to a court case brought by Madame Langlois, which she lost. Papillon writes: 'Aubert was my pupil in wood engraving, but his business was selling wallpapers, and this brought him into dispute in 1740 with Madame Langlois, who also sold my wallpapers. The best way to explain the matter is to say that the case was over my sign Au Papillon, which her father-in-law had taken over, before the marriage, for his shop, still in the rue St Jacques. When after a few years the widow Langlois (to whom I had sold my stock of woodblocks) wanted to leave her father-in-law to set up her own business, she put up the same sign too. The court case resulted: she lost, and the sign Au Papillon remained with Aubert.'

*Address card of Petit,
a paper and print merchant. French. BN.*

A L'IMAGE NOTRE-DAME.
Rue du Petit-Pont proche le petit Châtelet du côté de la rue Galande, vis-a-vis un Marchand de Draps.

PETIT, successeur de feu M. GUERARD, Marchand Mercier à Paris, Tient Magasin de toutes sortes de Papiers pour l'Ecriture et l'Impression; Papier d'Hollande de toutes grandeurs pour l'Ecriture et le Dessein; à Lettres, satiné, doré sur tranche. Papier de toute grandeur, battu, lavé et verni pour écrire. Papier battu, lavé pour les Mathematiques; Papier bleu d'Hollande; Papier gris à dessiner: Portes Feuilles d'Accademie de toutes grandeurs et autres; veritable Encre de la Chine pour dessiner; Crayons, Porte Crayons. Colle à bouche; Compas et Regles: Papier reglé pour la Musique et le Plainchant; Livres de Musique. veritable Encre double et luisante; bouteilles de cuir bouilli et autres; Ecritoires de Bureaux et fermantes à clef, de poche et de valise; Cornets de plomb. Vernis blanc pour Découpures et pour Meubles: Registres de toutes grandeurs; Regles pour les Comptes Etrangers, Partie double et Journeaux: Boites pour les Bureaux; veritables Plumes d'Hollande, de Cignes et de Corbeaux: Canifs. Poinçons, Grattoirs des Meilleurs; Pain à cacheter. Sandarac pour l'Ecriture; Cure-dents, Tablettes, Porte Feuilles garnis d'argent, et autres. Papier marbré, doré, argenté et façon d'Indienne de toutes sortes, venant d'Allemagne; Papier marbré à fleurs pour Tapisserie, et imitant le Marbre pour les cheminées: toutes sortes de Papiers de couleur, Découpures fines et d'Allemagne, Cartons dorés pour faire des Reliquaires. Tient Magasin d'Ecrans à main, peints et en decoupures; il vend seul les Ecrans Historiques, et les fastes du Roi en 6 Ecrans tres interessants; quarante sortes de Canons d'Autel pour dire la Messe, à choisir, entr'autres le beau Drevet, tant en Cartes qu'en Cuir dans des Cadres dorés, peints très-proprement: le Jeu de la Récréation spirituelle pour les Communautés; le Jeu d'Oie, Damiers. Corail du Sieur Dupré, ci devant Associé du Sieur Dufresne, pour blanchir les dents sur le champ, les affermir et les entretenir; il fabrique aussi la Cire d'Espagne. Assortiment de Papiers à l'aune d'Angleterre, les plus nouveaux, pour tapisser les Cabinets. Papiers façon de tontisse de toutes sortes de desseins et couleurs, les fait poser à la Ville et à la Campagne. Estampes de bons Auteurs, dont il est actuellement possesseur des Planches; et diverses belles Estampes de Balechou et autres assorties. Fait envois et commissions pour la Province, et le Pays Etranger. Le tout à très juste prix.

AVIS
Pour ne se pas tromper sur les demandes des Papiers Marbrés.

Papiers Marbrés à fleuron Rouge et fond Bleu, pour Relieurs. Sur Caré.
Papiers Marbrés à grand Placard Rouge pour Relieurs plus cher que celui ci dessus. Sur Caré.
Papiers Marbrés façon de Marbre pour les Cheminées de toutes couleurs et Desseins. Sur Caré.
Papiers Marbrés à fleurs de toutes couleurs et Desseins pour tapisser les Cabinets.

Marbled papers. 18th century. J.-D. Vivien coll.

Jacques Chauveau, who traded at the sign of the Two Columns, perfected the method of printing wallpaper from several blocks *à rentrure*, that is, by printing each colour from a separately engraved block. This involved using register marks *(rentrées)* on each block. This development spelt the end of the brush and stencil method for adding colour. The oil-based colours he used, thinned with turpentine, gave a varnished finish to the paper, which meant that papers were, for the first time, washable to some extent.

The Chauveaus were a family of paper makers, founded by François Chauveau (1613-77), a well-known Parisian engraver. The family also included René Chauveau, who died before 1723 and was sculptor by appointment to the Crown. It was his sister's daughter – Jacques' sister – Charlotte who married Jean-Michel Papillon. Jacques Chauveau

Address card engraved by J.-M. Papillon. French, 1758.

had studied under Jean-Michel's father, Jean Papillon II. The last member of the family was Pierre-Joseph Chauveau, Jacques' son, who was a pupil of Jean-Michel. He too set up in the paper business in the rue St Jacques.

Another name in the list of *dominotiers* is that of Masson, 'peintre et graveur sur papiers', whose business was taken over by one Miyer. Panseron, too, was an engraver, a pupil of Vincent Lesueur, and his shop was at the sign of La Vérité, where he made papers 'of a special quality'. Also recorded are Basset, who in 1770 began business at the junction of the rue des Mathurins and the rue St Jacques; Crépy the elder, who could be found at the sign of St Louis, just below the St Séverin fountain; and Jean-Gabriel Huquier and his son Daniel, who opened a shop in 1766 in the rue des Mathurins. We should not omit Desventes who from about 1773 to 1774 was near the Hôtel de Lyon in the rue St Jacques, opposite St Yves, nor Le Fort, who was at 62 rue St Jacques in 1789. These last three important names prove that although by the end of the eighteenth century wallpaper making was becoming an independent trade, its business centre was still the rue St Jacques, which must have been a busy area, frequented not only by students and *literati* but by merchants and craftsmen and their apprentices. It is also worth noting that family links joined *dominotiers*, stationers and printers: Jean Papillon II married the daughter of a well-known printer, Chevillon, whose cousin was Nicolas Thoyer, a master stationer. As we have seen, Jean-Michel Papillon married a Chauveau: his wife's brother-in-law was Chardon, a bookseller and printer in the rue du Petit Pont.

The Parisian *dominotiers* who worked outside the rue St Jacques include Fournier, at the sign of the Good Workman, rue Carré St Martin, who was the first person to join sheets end to end to make rolls; Lavoisières, who specialized in paper that copied natural woods; the father-and-son partnership of Lebreton, who had a reputation for marbled papers, and lastly Boulard, on the Quai des Gesvres, who made the earliest distempered papers. The first papers to imitate silk were made by Lecomte, whose shop was in the rue des Prouvaires. A technique for copying muslin and linen, which was to be widely used in the nineteenth century, was first perfected by Chenevard in 1797.

In spite of the fact that each guild was independent, the paper trade, if we may call it that, brought together not only creative artists (engravers) but skilled craftsmen (printers, binders, paper makers and paper hangers) as well as merchants (booksellers, haberdashers and stationers). When, after the middle of the eighteenth century, the manufacture of wallpaper became independent of the work of the *dominotiers*, the trade also moved away from its connection with books. It became part of the furnishing business and consequently moved away from the university district to the area round the faubourg St Antoine.

The provincial scene

The provincial *dominotiers* became established at the same time as those in Paris, and their papers remained popular until the middle of the nineteenth century. By the end of the seventeenth century provincial people were using both the *domino* paper and decorated papers made specifically as wall-coverings. They preferred simpler tastes, though, more in the popular tradition, economical and straightforward. People did not change their values so rapidly, or fall victim to the latest fashion or technical innovation. For a long

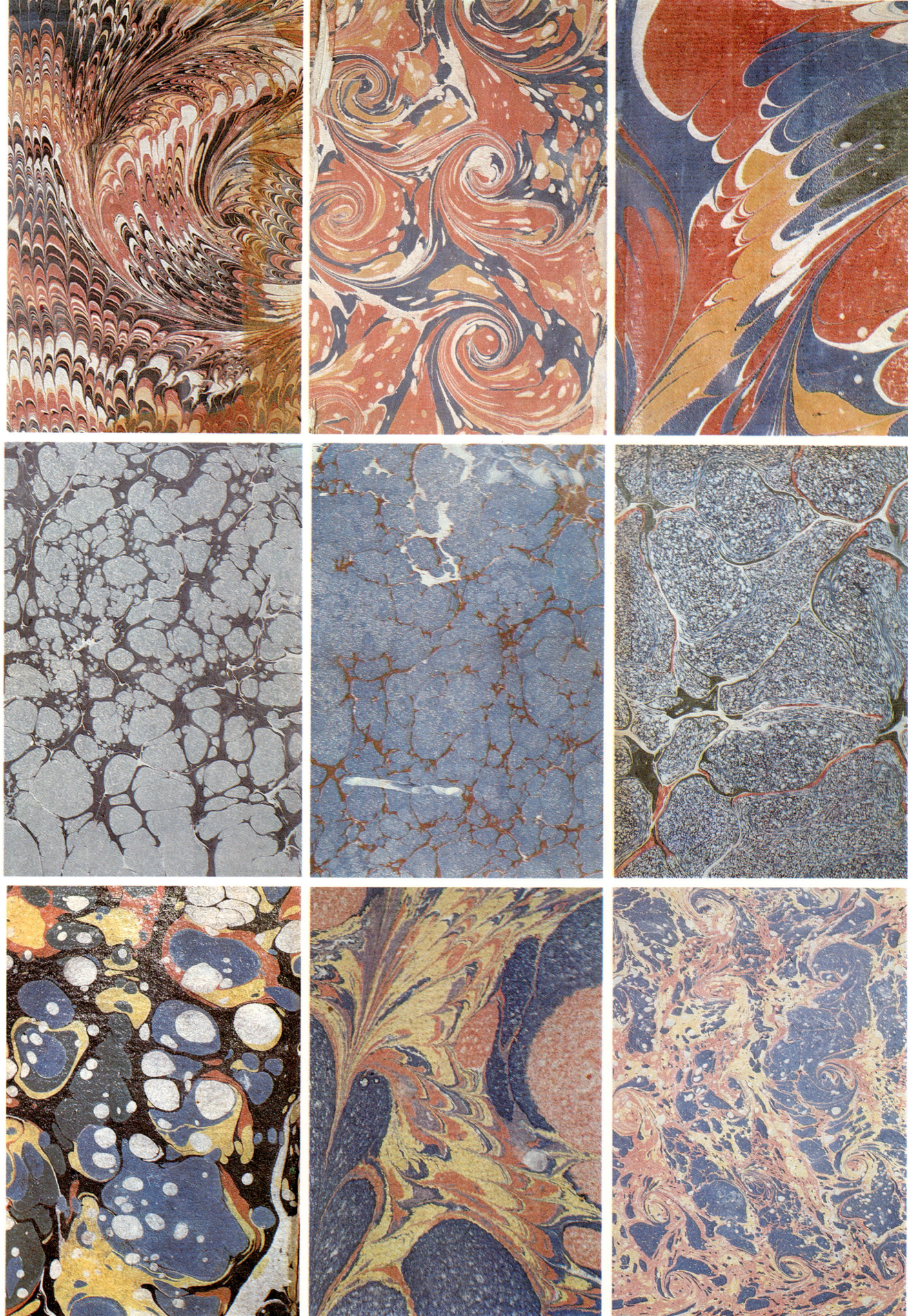

Lining paper. Early 18th century. H. Cuny coll.

Lining paper. French, 18th century. P. des Ligneris coll.

Domino paper. 18th century. Nobilis coll.

time they adhered to their preference for the simple charm of paper in small sheets bearing the same design.

It was in the traditional centres for making linen and cloth that the paper makers first became established. From the early seventeenth century Rouen was the major provincial centre for wallpapers: from there the names of the makers Le François and Tierce have survived, together with Amy, Chevallier, Guillaume Benoît, Soury and Morand. The silk and textile business in Lyons made this city the other financial and commercial capital of France; a number of wallpaper makers and *dominotiers* were in business there in the late seventeenth century.

As to the trade in Besançon, we are indebted to the work of Monsieur Petit-Jean of the Institut d'Archéologie who records the names of France, the widow Tissot, St Agathe and Labourey. Also in Besançon in 1780, Dominique Obermann, a native of Alsace, set up a manufacture of paper that was taken over after his death by Jean-Pierre Bourier. The city of Orléans, too, was well known for its *dominotiers* such as Rabier-Boulard, Huquier and Pelle. Jean-Baptiste Letourny was among the best known, and his son continued the business – 'where one could always find a selection of flock papers and all sorts of *dominoterie*' – until 1843. Also in Orléans, Jean Leblond (1688-1771) went into partnership with his son-in-law Jean-Baptiste Sevestre (1728-1805) who signed his products Sevestre-Leblond after Leblond's death. The business then passed to Pierre-Fiacre Perdoux.

At Le Mans there was also a fair amount of wallpaper, produced mainly by hand: we know of Jacques Gaugain, or Sillé (1723-72), and his widow, as well as Joseph-Jean Portier (1751-1831), one of Sillé's workers, who set up on his own in 1785, and Pierre Leloup (1769-1844). There is an account of Gaugain's workshop in Cordonnier-Detrie's *Trois papiers dominos de Jacques Gaugain et de sa veuve*, published in 1930. At his death Sillé left 139 blocks engraved with floral designs, and his widow, Elisabeth Bourmaux, took over the business. She lived in a house not far from the shop and workroom, in the parish of the Crucifix, with her daughters, her son-in-law, her grandchildren and their nurses, as well as her mother and her aunt, and the workmen. She sold the business in 1779, and seems to have let out rooms for a living thereafter. The same source tells us that Portier made his name with floral papers, in fresh colours, often printed by stencil.

As to Bordeaux, papers discovered at the episcopal palace at Saint-Pandelon in the Landes tell us about the Duras business in the place Dauphine. Their products used the normal *domino* repertoire, such as flowers, Chinese landscapes, scrolls and fluted backgrounds, but heightened these with

Domino *paper, printed in black with stencilled colours.
18th century. J.-D. Vivien coll.*

Domino *paper. 18th century. Nobilis coll.*

*Paper with branches, flowers and fruit
on a striped background, printed in black with red,
yellow and blue stencilling. Pierre-Fiacre Perdoux,
Orléans. French, 18th century. J.-D. Vivien coll.*

Domino *paper. 18th century. P. Nolot coll.*

designs overprinted in black. They had a limited stock of images, but by using the same blocks with different colours achieved an almost infinite range of variations. On one unmarked paper, the crisscross foliage and the central bouquet are first printed in black on a blue ground, then a second time, slightly out of register, in yellow, to give a truly vibrant effect.

As was common at the time, these craft workshops would be family businesses. The father would perhaps engrave the wooden blocks, the son would be responsible for printing the sheets, helped by apprentices who would also look after the cleaning and maintenance of the equipment. The lightest and easiest tasks would be left to the children, for example drying and sorting the sheets, while the women would often add the colour, either

Stag hunting scene. Fragment of wallpaper from Aldford House, Park Lane, London. Block-printed in black with hand-stencilled colours. English, late 17th century. Whitworth Art Gallery, Manchester.

by stencil or by brush for more delicate work: hence their charming name *pinceauteuses*. It would often happen that the chief worker or journeyman would marry the daughter of the house, or the son marry into another family in the same trade. Perhaps for this reason, the head of the family might die without an heir, and often his widow would take over the business, as we have seen with Langlois, Gaugain and so forth.

Although part of the bourgeoisie, these craftsmen were never very rich, and their work was hard. The material they produced was delicate and not long-lasting, though it delighted their contemporaries and deserves a central place in the decorative arts for its variety and beauty.

Comparisons and contrasts in Europe

Progress in England

In England by the late seventeenth century wallpaper was assured a place in interior decoration. The manufacture of wallpaper was encouraged by urban expansion, especially after the Great Fire of London of 1666, and by the rapid and general diffusion of material wealth amongst the middle classes as well as landowners. Three parallel developments occurred in the history of wallpaper during the late Stuart and Hanoverian period. In the first place the production of flocked paper hangings was perfected, providing acceptable wall-coverings which were cheaper than fine textiles or embossed and gilded leather panels. In the second place the importation of Chinese wallpapers with their graceful designs and accurate colour stimulated the paper stainers to offer stylish alternatives. Finally the production and marketing of block-printed wallpapers was gradually developed to meet an increasing popular demand – as the patents, commercial directories and advertisements of the period show. It is these last circumstances which are outlined here; flock hangings and Chinese wallpapers are the subjects of the next chapter.

In the late seventeenth century France held the lead in paper manufacture; in 1687 she exported to England, and to the Low Countries, paper to the value of two million *livres*. But the English paper industry was making progress. In 1685 John Briscoe patented machinery for 'the true art and proper for making English paper . . . both as good and as serviceable and especially white as any French or Dutch paper. The following year saw the foundation of the White Paper Makers' Company on the patent of Dupin, Hampshire, French and Co. After 1690 Acts of Parliament encouraging paper making speeded up improvements.

Paper hangings were the product of what was then described as 'paper staining', which compares with the German term *Buntpapier*, meaning paper with coloured decoration. Early paper stainers' advertisements indicate the variety of styles offered for sale in London. In 1680 George Minnikin, stationer of St Martin's le Grand, was selling 'all sorts of colourd paperhangings'. In 1690 Edward Butling of Southwark advertised 'hangings for rooms in lengths or in sheets, frosted or plain. Also a sort of paper in imitation of Irish Stitch, of the newest fashion and several other sorts viz., flockwork, wainscott, marble, damask, Turkey work etc'. Wallpaper designs of this period tended to echo the current fashions in embroideries and woven textiles such as damask or brocade silks. In his diary for 8 January 1665/66, Samuel Pepys mentioned the 'counterfeit damasks' which lined the walls of a closet in his home. The formality of the stylized floral decoration of the early Stuart utility papers was relaxed. Now formalized blooms and fruit and wide scrolling foliage were either disposed around vertical serpentine stems, or freely set against simple diaper patterned grounds or treated symmetrically as flat patterns in the manner of Italian brocades. As the eighteenth century progressed, so the characteristic vine, oak, tulip and rose motifs showed greater naturalism. The influence of Indian cottons and Chinese art further encouraged a new range of imagery and the use of brighter colours.

Competition within this field was doubtless heightened when Huguenot craftsmen from France settled and established workshops in England shortly after the revocation of the Edict of Nantes in 1685. The London Patent Office received its first application for a patent for printing wallpapers in 1692. William Bayley had invented a new art 'for printing all sorts of paper of all kinds of figurs and colours whatsoever, with several engines made of brass and other such metals with fire, which will be useful for hanging on walls or rooms.' In 1699 John Houghton explained in his *Collection for Improvement of Husbandry and Trade* that paper tapestry was widely available and fairly priced. The base paper was strong and thick, and the rolls in which it was sold measured room heights – proving that manufacturers assembled sheets into rolls before printing them. Throughout the eighteenth century sheets of paper measured either 32 x 22½ inches (approx 81 x 57 centimetres) ('Elephant') or 35 x 22½ inches (approx. 89 x 57 centimetres) ('Double Demy'). A 'piece', later meaning a roll, was generally 11½ yards (approx. 10.5 metres) long and was made up of 12 or 13 sheets.

The growth of the wallpaper industry did not escape the notice of Queen Anne's government, which was burdened by a national debt and the need to raise supplies for Marlborough's campaigns in the Low Countries. In 1712 it began to levy duty on paper 'printed painted or stained to serve for hangings' of 1d per square yard, raised to 1½d in 1714. Duty on plain paper had been charged since 1694, and a paper stainer's licence cost £4 a year. Duties were raised in 1787 and again in 1809; wallpaper tax was eventually repealed in 1836. From 1773 import duty on wallpaper was levied at a rate of 1½d per square yard, papers carried by the East India Company being exempt. (From 1792, during the Napoleonic Wars and up to 1825 heavy import duties were imposed. A shilling rate continued up to 1846 when it was reduced to 2d and was finally abolished in 1861.)

For all the restrictions this tax imposed, the manufacture of wallpaper increased rapidly, as did the number of businesses. A glance at the surviving literature shows the originality, stylishness and quality of English papers. They became a sign of novelty, a reaction against traditional decoration. So the Palladian William Kent used wallpaper in preference to the old-style velvet hangings when around 1720 he decorated the Saloon at Kensington Palace, designed by Sir Christopher Wren. This was the first time that wallpaper had been used in a royal building anywhere in Europe. Matthias Darly, a printer and wallpaper maker in the Strand, London, provided 164 engravings for Chippendale's *Gentleman's and Cabinet Maker's Director* of 1754, a number which was considerably increased for the third edition in 1762. In this book, Chippendale writes that his furniture is perfectly suitable for a lady of quality's dressing-room 'especially if the walls are covered with Indian paper'.

Robert Dossie's *Handmaid to the Arts* (1758) gives us a careful account of the different methods for printing wallpapers, and making marbled paper, papier mâché or stucco paper. He describes how 'spangled' paper is made, using powdered isinglass to give a convincing effect of velvet embroidered with silver. 'It can be used most effectively, as the richest and most elegant paper I have ever seen was printed in this way, on a yellow spangled ground, with a design of flowers and herds of deer. The effect was so much that of embroidered velvet that even at a few feet in good light the illusion was not apparent.' In 1763 Thomas Mortimer published his *Universal Director*, which tells us that wallpaper had become an important element in British trade. But the most valuable work we have on English papers is that of John Baptist Jackson, published in 1754, as Jackson was both a professional and an artist. We will discuss Jackson's work in detail in Chapter 3, as he is one of the great names in English wallpaper.

German decorated papers

The Germans perfected a number of techniques for making decorated papers, and they exported their products all over Europe, where they were used for different purposes. Not surprisingly, the country that created both the wood engraving and the printing press was also involved in the early development of wallpaper.

Wood engraving was invented in Germany towards the end of the fourteenth century, and made possible for the first time the exact repetition of a decorative motif. With the perfection of printing from moveable type, achieved in Mainz in the fifteenth century, the way was opened, indirectly, for the decorative printing of paper. The Germans were also the first to use marbled paper for endpapers in books. The technique of marbling was learnt from the Turks, who had themselves

Paper found in a house in Hyde Street, Brentford, Middlesex. Block-printed with gilded effect on the border. V&A.

Domino paper glazed with gelatine. South German. DTM.

Paper printed in black with blue stencilling. French, 18th century. P. Nolot coll.

Frieze with chiaroscuro medallion, from Douglas Ford House. English, late 18th century. V&A.

*Brocade paper. Gold on a white ground, Augsburg. German, 1710. DTM.
(A similar example is in the Olga Hirsch Collection,
and another, dated 1700, in the Kunstgewerbe Museum, Basel.)*

*Varnished 'bronze' paper. Woodblock-printed on a green ground.
South German, 1720. DTM.*

obtained this special craft from the Persians in the sixteenth century. Travellers in Persia have left us many descriptions: 'this beautiful paper comes from lower Tartary, from Balk, Bokhara or Samarkand. They make it in all colours, apart from black, and it is either mottled or sometimes speckled with silver: sometimes the paper is decorated with painted flowers, sometimes with Moorish designs in the lightest silver, but never so as to interfere with the calligraphy or distract the reader.' (The Turks not only made splendid marbled papers but also learnt at an early date the use of the stencil, to make silhouette pictures. These decorate a large number of contemporary manuscripts.) During the course of the seventeenth century, marbled paper came to be made all over Europe.

The first wood engravings served a dual purpose: one was the making of images, in the form of prints, the other the making of decorations. This technique was perfected in Germany, and gave rise to a considerable variety of papers, such as *Brokartpapier* or brocaded paper, which is also called Augsburg paper, from the town where it was first manufactured. The designs were borrowed from brocade work, and the delicate decorations were heightened with gold, giving these ornated papers the splendour of goldwork. These elegant and fragile papers are also signed, by such craftsmen as Jacob Euderlin (*c.* 1700), Johann Michael Schwibecher (1695-1748), Joseph Friedrich Leopold (1670-1750), Johann Michael Munck (1710-1762), Johann Carl Munck (1730-1794), Simone Haichele (*c.* 1750), Johann Georg Eder (1762-1796) and Georg Christoph Stoy (1670-1750).

The most important of these was Stoy, a merchant and maker of decorated paper who was born in Nuremberg. He later moved to Augsburg, where in 1703 he married Anna Maria Euderlin, daughter of Jacob Euderlin and widow of the paper marbler Mathias Fröhlich. The papers he made are considered to be among the most beautiful in Germany and had a reputation throughout Europe.

Nuremberg was also an active centre of paper making. One name that has come down to us is that of Georg Nikolaus Renner (1803-55), but most renowned must be the Reymund family, Johann Michael (d. 1765), Andreas (1754-82), Georg Daniel (1770-1815) and Paul (1764-1815). (The name Reymund suggests a connection with the great Remondini family from Bassano.) Another important centre was Fürth, where Johann Köchel (1682-1726), Georg Meisch, Johann Meisch (d. 1849) and Johann Lechner (1766-1838) practised.

German manufacturers, like the *dominotiers* in France, made papers that copied varnished wood (*Fladerpapier*) and copperplate printed papers. But one of their special native products was the *Herrn-*

Adam and Eve in Paradise.
*Brocade paper, gold
on a violet ground. Nuremberg,
South German, 1780. DTM.*

*Brocade paper. Gold on
an orange ground.
Augsburg. German, 1730.
DTM.
Note the influence of Persian
designs. (A similar paper in
the Olga Hirsch Collection is
signed by Johann Michael
Schwibecher.)*

Herrnhuter Kleister Papier. German, 1780. DTM.

Vases of flowers. Domino *paper made by Rizzi in Varese. Italian, 1770. An identical version in the V&A is inscribed 'Giuseppe Rizzi Varese Lombardo, via San Mardula 10' in the margin. DTM.*

huter Kleisterpapier which combined a block-printed image with decorations made by either a wooden comb, rollers, or painted by hand. The technique was developed in the small village of Herrnhut in Saxony. The evidence suggests these papers were intended for bookbindings or as lining papers for furniture: there is no evidence for their use as wall decoration. No real wallpaper manufacture was established in Germany before the end of the eighteenth century.

Italy: new discoveries

Italy's rich artistic heritage has created a burden of prejudices it is difficult to avoid. It is conventional to think that for reasons of taste, tradition and climate the Italians have never been interested in wallpaper. Taste has dictated a preference for marble, brocades or gilded stucco, tradition has demanded that antiquity's choice of fresco as a mural decoration be respected, and lastly the Italian climate is not reputed to be generally suited to wallpaper. So modern specialists, a number of them quite important, have not hesitated to affirm that Italy has no wallpaper. Who indeed could believe that a country that has given the world a culture in marble could have recourse to a material as ignoble and fragile as paper?

But given that the French *dominotiers* and their German and English contemporaries made wallpapers as well as playing-cards, engravings and marbled paper, it is ridiculous to suppose that the Italians did not do the same. In fact, there were plenty of wallpaper makers all over Italy: in Milan, for example, Alberto Ronco (born c. 1610), Giulio Cesare Bianchi (1735-80), Geronimo Cattaneo (born c. 1780), Giovanni Angiolini (born c. 1730); in Palermo, Mario Labo, Giovanni Benedetto Castiglione (1610-65); in Bologna, Carlo Bertinazzi, del Bettuzzi; in Florence, Guaniesi Baleni (born c. 1596), Antonio Benucci; in Rome, Egidio Petit, Angelo Topai, Luigi Valadier (1726-85); in Varese, Antonio Baratti, Giulio Giampicoli, Giuseppe Rizzi; and above all from Bassano the Tizzi and Menegazzi families and the famous Remondinis.

The first member of the Remondini family was Giovanni Antonio (1634-1711) who set up his business in Bassano in 1650 and was the greatest printer of his day in Europe. The dynasty continued with his son Giuseppe (1677-1750), his grandson Giambattista (1713-76) and his great-grandchildren Giuseppe and Giovanni. Count Giovanni Batista Remondini, who was the last to bear the name, bequeathed to the Museo Civico in Bassano in 1849 a collection of these wallpapers which had been produced with the same delicate craftsmanship for five generations.

*Landscapes in octagonal lozenges, and butterflies
framed with beribboned garlands. Remondini, Bassano. Italian, 18th century. DTM.*

*Ducal Palace, Venice.
Remondini, Bassano. Italian,
18th century. DTM.*

*Venetian landscapes in medallions
with floral garlands on a blue ground.
Remondini, Bassano. Italian, 18th century. DTM.*

*Paper from a room in the Palazzo Carminati,
San Stae, Venice, now rehung in the Ca' Rezzonico.
After Sebastiano Ricci, Italian, 18th century.
Museo Correr, Venice.*

The family produced papers for bookbindings and for lining furniture, as well as wallpapers called 'flowered papers', both polychrome and gilded, marbled papers and others with an oyster-shell decoration. Some of their papers are called *zigrinate*, meaning they imitate the effect of flames, others *radicate*, from their patterns of fine lines. In his book *Altes Buntpapier*, Dr Mick discusses ten Italian papers. His fig. 15 is a perfect example of the papers that were produced in Bassano in the last quarter of the eighteenth century. (There are two specimens of this paper, one in the British Museum, Olga Hirsch Collection, and one in the Victoria and Albert Museum.) The paper shows a circular view of Venice (the Riva degli Schiavone, Ducal Palace and Piazzetta) in a yellow octagonal frame, surrounded by a large garland of green foliage and red and ochre flowers on a quartered blue and white ground. There are other versions of this paper, for example with the view in oval form, linked with butterflies framed by flowers, the whole frieze showing a striking creativity within a remarkably simple form. There are a number of admirable other papers, all with floral motifs: bunches and bouquets, garlands and wreaths. One splendid example has its design surmounted by an eagle. It dates from the early nineteenth century and must have been made for the American market.

The Remondinis also made splendid series of papers, often using the same blocks but varying the colours, showing large bouquets of flowers on a background, or flowers laid out in a regular, circular or convoluted pattern. These papers, which carry the signature 'cum privilegio fratri Remondini de Joseph', show the immense variety and inventive scope of those working in Bassano. In 1957 the Museo Civico in Bassano acquired 800 woodblocks from Varese, which complement the wallpapers from Count Remondini's 1849 bequest, and make this an excellent collection. The blocks are mainly in pear- and apple-wood, sometimes in walnut. In the second half of the nineteenth century, the Menegazzi factory continued the manufacture of similar papers, while in Varese the Remondini's woodblocks were successfully reused.

From the same factory over the centuries came religious images, calendars, games, pictures of animals, and numerous sheets to cut up and use for decorating furniture, some showing people, some flowers and fruit. These papers were used all over Europe and in America. (In Milan, the Bertarelli Collection, at the Castello Sforzesco, contains 6000 wallpapers, the majority originating from Bassano or Varese.)

During the preparation of this book we found, in the library of the Union des Arts Décoratifs in Paris, two cloth-bound albums containing samples of some 350 papers. The annotations on these papers, in sepia ink, leave no doubt that they came from

arland of flowers surmounted by an eagle.
merican market. Italian, late 18th century.
vico di Bassano del Grappa.

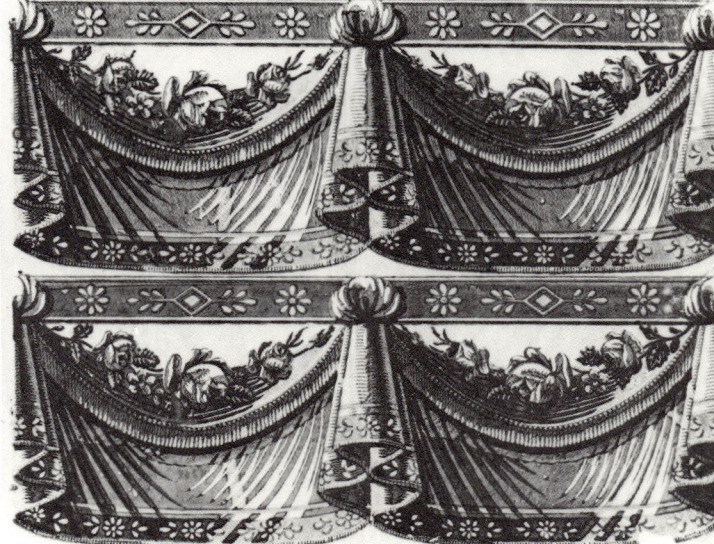

Frieze of drapery and flowers.
Remondini, Bassano. Italian, c. 1800.
Museo Civico di Bassano del Grappa.

The piazzetta in Venice framed by a garland of multicoloured flowers.
Remondini, Bassano. Italian, late 18th century. Museo Civico di Bassano del Grappa.

Chinoiserie *engraved and coloured designs on paper. Remondini, Bassano. Italian, 18th century. P.Nolot coll.*

Italy and were almost certainly prepared for salesmen. In one of the two, the papers are printed in oils, a technique that was not much used in the eighteenth century. The designs include motifs of flowers, stripes, diamonds and squares, and imitating picot. One of the latter is identical to a blue printed paper pasted onto the back of a pair of pastels dated 1770. The pastels come from Avignon, a town that retained its papal connections until the end of the eighteenth century, which would suggest that the papers came from Rome, from the workshops of Egidio Petit, Angelo Topaï or Luigi Valadier.

But it is to Venice that the wallpaper enthusiast must turn for something special. On the second floor of the Ca' Rezzonico, a museum concerned with eighteenth-century Venice, a room and alcove from the Carminati Palace at San Stae have been reconstructed. The walls are covered with a mid eighteenth-century wallpaper, printed in chiaroscuro and showing antique ruins, columns and arches, enlivened with figures, much in the manner of Sebastiano Ricci (1695-1734). The English wallpaper maker John Baptist Jackson spent a great deal of time in Venice, and it is likely that they met. Certainly Jackson drew his inspiration, both in subject-matter and in technique, from Venice. It is also likely he visited Bassano, as his collection includes a number of splendid chiaroscuro pieces. The wallpapers from the Carminati Palace show that the Venetians did not despise wallpaper, despite the problems of a humid climate, but did not know how to preserve it.

In addition, we must not forget the Chinese papers that Italians had sent from London, such as those at Stupinigi or the Trenzanesio Palace near Milan.

Italy still has many more surprises in store for us: the few examples we have shown merely point the way. A full account of the palaces and villas where wall decorations are still intact, together with an analysis of municipal archives, would produce a rich harvest of valuable and interesting facts which would act as a corrective to current generalizations.

Domino *paper probably made in Rome. Italian, c. 1770 P.Nolot coll.*

Wallpaper in the domino *style. Remondini, Bassano. Italian, 18th century. Museo Civico di Bassano del Grappa.*

Floral paper. Remondini, Bassano. Italian, 18th century. Museo Civico di Bassano del Grappa.

Paper from a shop in Kingston-upon-Thames, Surrey. English, 18th century. V&A.

Lining paper for a chest. English, late 17th century. V&A.

'Chintz' paper with a floral design from Salisbury. Early 18th century. Whitworth Art Gallery, Manchester.

CHAPTER TWO
Influences and discoveries

From the Mogul empire to Cathay

Indian and Chinese work

There was a considerable level of commercial contact between West and East during the Middle Ages. The silk and spice route, with its aura of mystery and adventure, linked Byzantium to China by caravans which traversed the Turkish empire. The other route was by sea: Arab coasters plied between Shiraz in the Persian Gulf and Canton, and the goods were sold into Europe through Venetian merchants. But the Turkish capture of Constantinople in 1453 closed the door on the Orient and its distant splendours; the Mediterranean ceased to be the centre of Western trade which moved northwards, and Italy lost her leading commercial position, even though artistically she shone as never before.

Not until the sixteenth century was Europe again to trade with India and China. Portuguese ships, following the route around the Cape of Good Hope discovered by Vasco da Gama, reached Calcutta, and Eastern markets were again open to Western entrepreneurs. Lisbon became the port of entry for silks and spices and the first porcelain to reach Europe. During the Netherlands' war of liberation against Philip II of Spain, the Dutch took Spanish and Portuguese ships captive, and sold their precious cargoes to the kings of France and England. The foundation of the British East India Company in 1599, and of the Dutch East Indies Company in 1602, marked the beginning of British supremacy in the India trade. The British and the Dutch were well organized, with a multinational monopoly on trade with the East. The Dutch based their operations on Batavia, whence they spread to China, Korea and Japan: they alone had the right to trade in Japan. But Paris remained the most important market in Europe during the seventeenth century. On the Ile de la Cité, at the sign of Noah's Ark, one shop, according to John Evelyn in 1644, sold curiosities of all kinds, natural and man-made, Indian and European, useful and decorative, such as boxes, ivories, porcelain, dried fish, pictures and other fantastic and exotic objects. The word 'Indian', as used by Evelyn, for a long time meant anything from the Far East, work from China or Japan as much as from India itself. Similarly, Coromandel screens, those masterpieces of Chinese art with panels of incised lacquer decoration, take their name from the western coast of India, on the Bay of Bengal, where they were bought by European merchants. But there were two products from the East in particular that changed European styles of decoration completely: Indian cotton and Chinese

Calico takes its name from Calicut, near Madras where it was first made. Originally it was a cotton material painted by hand with designs of flowers and bouquets, whereas today calico usually means an unprinted material. In the seventeenth century India was still under the Mogul yoke, and while influenced by Chinese art the Indians produced work to the taste of their masters, the Mohammedan princes. Calico would be printed and painted in series, and sold in packets of five to twenty-five rolls of differing sizes. These were known as *diwar giri* and were used to protect walls, or, rather, the backs of people seated against a wall. When they were introduced into Europe in the seventeenth century, these cottons took the world of fashion by storm. The nobility and the bourgeoisie would pay any price to get calicos with which to clothe themselves and decorate their homes. In France new manufacturers tried to set up in competition with the imported cloth, which was a real source of concern to the French economy, in that the English and the Dutch made all the profit on the trade. But the new European makers of painted

The Arrival of the Portuguese Traders in Japan *(16th century)*.
*Screen painted by Nanbar Byobu, Kano School. Japanese.
Musée Guimet, Paris.*

The Indian. *Silkscreen reproduction of a 1790 woodblock-printed paper.
Cole and Sons. English, 1973. (William Morris
designed a similar paper in the late 19th century, now reproduced by Sanderson.)*

*Indian design on embossed paper by Paul Balin.
French, 1870-80. Nobilis coll.*

*Frieze in an Indian style.
18th century. Follot coll.*

cottons also threatened the traditional manufactures of wool and silk. The problem was not only economic but social: it has been estimated that half a million people moved in an exodus of workers from France, taking not only their money with them but, more importantly, their skill. As we have noted, the revocation of the Edict of Nantes in 1685 sent Protestant craftsmen in a flood from France into Holland, Switzerland, England and Germany. The majority of the new cloth manufactories that were set up in Europe in the last part of the seventeenth century were headed by refugees.

The first native manufactory of calico was set up in Marseilles in 1648, and others followed in the southern Languedoc, Saintonge and Vivarais regions. When Louis XIV had rid France of the Protestants (who had almost complete control of the market and manufacture of Indian cloth) he could not stop them importing their goods any more than he had been able to control their counterfeit manufacture. But in the fight against France's economic plight and to protect the silk and wool industries, Claude le Peletier, Colbert's successor as Comptrolleur Général des Finances, forbade the importation of cloth from India and the manufacture in France of the popular Indiennes made to similar designs; this embargo covered the years 1686 to 1759. He also ordered that the woodblocks used to print on cloth be destroyed. As a result, the craftsmen working in cloth turned their hands to making paper, taking over to the new material their techniques and their decorative vocabulary.

Their technique consisted in engraving each part of the design onto a separate block, so that the whole design would reappear once all were printed, and also in printing each colour separately. This meant that wallpapers could be used to make up a continuous decor. Jean Papillon, in 1688, made the technique his own, and created a market for it. The new product was an immediate success, and was soon widely used. It changed people's concept of wall-covering radically, opening the way to the representation of landscape in wallpaper.

The new technique was also suitable for floral designs in the Indian or Persian style, which soon became popular decorative motifs. (In France, Réveillon was a great exponent of this style.) It is possible to see in wallpaper one of the main origins of the asymmetry of the rococo style – the other being the designs on porcelain from Japan, which was imported from the early eighteenth century.

In 1759, through Madame de Pompadour's intervention, the ban on importing calico was lifted. This gave a further impetus to the wallpaper industry, which had been growing in strength and scope throughout the second half of the eighteenth century. The importation of Indian textiles developed at the same pace: 115,000 hundred-

Design for an India paper. Watercolour. German, 1810. DTM.

India paper in Mme de Warrens' bedroom at the Château des Charmettes. French, 18th century.

Sherkan *Reproduction of an old paper by Nobilis. French, 1976. Nobilis coll.*

Chinese paper from the Château de Maintenon, Eure-et-Loir. 18th century.

Chinese paper. 18th century. MISE.

weight of cloth was landed in Marseilles in 1788, six times the quantity for 1700. The market for Indian cloth – whether in excellent or execrable taste – continued throughout the nineteenth century and has lasted until today.

Chinese papers

The East India companies also introduced Chinese papers into Europe. Originally, they were not sold, but given as gifts to foreigners at the conclusion of a sale. The delicate hand-painted designs on rice paper soon, however, attracted interest in their own right. Because the paintings did not follow the conventions of western perspective, nor used effects of light and shadow – thus distributing space in a quite novel way – they could be comfortably looked at from a variety of angles. The same qualities meant that their motifs could be used in repetitive patterns.

Jean-Michel Papillon tells us that his father had bought for 180 *livres* five sheets of paper from the captain of the Compagnie des Indes, who had himself bought them in Surat. The design of one sheet, of Japanese origin, was identical to those that covered the dais in the governor's palace in Japan. There was one large sheet, measuring 1 *pied* by 20 *pouces* (about 13 x 21 inches, or 32.5 x 54 centimetres) which Papillon describes as being gilded and encrusted with pearls. This sheet was sold to a Monsieur de Villayer for 120 *livres* in 1721. The four other sheets, rather smaller in size, he sold to the wife of a Fermier Général who used them to line the inside of a chest and a box. Despite the exorbitant prices charged for Chinese papers, the demand for them rapidly exceeded the supply, because delivery times were so long: eighteen months' delay was not unusual. Not surprisingly, attempts were soon being made in England and in Holland, Flanders and Germany to copy the papers, but as the copiers did not understand the purpose or the methods of Chinese iconography, errors and mistakes in interpretation were bound to occur.

Chinese paper was of course imported into London, where it was rapidly imitated by English manufacturers, who exported their work all over Europe. It seems that even the Chinese wallpaper found in the Levantine suite of rooms in the hunting lodge of Stupinigi near Turin was an import from London.[1] In England itself Chinese paper and its imitators had a considerable following: the paper could be used to show off the Chinese porcelain and lacquer furniture that the East India Company had brought in. Such articles were sold in the coffee houses of Mincing Lane, in London. In 1695 an auction of sixty-six pieces or lengths of Japan paper for hangings was held at the Marine Coffee House in Birchin Lane in the City of London. It was in such

Chinese paper with pheasants, flowers and fruit. Gouache and distemper, second half of the 18th century. V&A.

Chinoiserie panel with design of birds within a border, from a house in Wotton-under-Edge, Gloucestershire. English, c. 1740, V&A.

Chinese paper in two panels with scenes of everyday life. Woodblock-printed and distemper-painted. First half of the 18th century. V&A.

places that fashionable and courtly society congregated, and these oriental goods found immediate success. An entry for 1693 in John Evelyn's diary refers to Queen Mary's China and Indian cabinets, screens and hangings. John Macky's *Journey through England* of 1722 describes a room in the Palace of Wanstead as being 'finely adorned with Chinese paper, the figures of men, women, birds and flowers, the liveliest [the author] ever saw come from that country.' The Duke of Bedford is known to have purchased a set of these paper hangings for Woburn Abbey in 1573.

The Chinese had been making paper for over a thousand years and had used large decorated paper hangings for ritual and architectural purposes.[2] There were two principal types of Chinese wallpaper. In the first place were the studies of birds, insects, flowers and foliage. These decorations were generally composed of twenty-five sheets, each about 12 feet (3.5 metres) in height and were non-repeating in design. Ink outlines and a paint similar to tempera or body colour were applied to pale coloured grounds. Articles of luxury, the papers were pasted onto stout cartridge and fixed to canvas. Some exquisite and accurate studies of plants and birds are as fine as any painting produced in the style of the Ch'ing dynasty. These were popular up to the middle of the eighteenth century, although attractive examples were highly prized long after. The Prince Regent purchased sets from the firm of Crace and Sons in 1802. One was installed in the Pavilion at Brighton (now replaced by a similar Chinese wallpaper given by Queen Victoria in 1856) and the other is presumed to have been the one presented by the Prince in 1806 to Temple Newsam House, Leeds, where it can be seen today.

The second type of Chinese wallpaper depicted landscapes and scenes of daily life and became fashionable after 1750. Sometimes referred to as a panoramic paper, the wallpaper in the hunting lodge of Stupinigi is one of this type. Individual panels designed to fit together form a coherent whole guiding the eye around in a circular sweep. The idea of depth and unlimited space results from the absence of any perspective, or rather from the presence of numerous focal points. A fine example was presented to Lord Macartney, Ambassador to Peking around 1792, and later used to decorate the board room of Coutts Bank in the Strand, London. Within a naturalistically coloured landscape of hills and pine trees are represented over 300 figures, occupied in village activities such as rice and tea cultivation, gardening and pottery. A specimen of a comparable paper in the Victoria and Albert Museum shows in intricate detail an outdoor theatrical performance.

In his journal of 1770 the explorer Sir Joseph Banks declared that 'a man need go no further to

study the Chinese than the China paper, the better sorts of which represent the persons and such of their customs etc. as I have seen'. Banks's remarks foreshadow those of the French wallpaper manufacturer Joseph Dufour, one of the creators of panoramic papers. For his wallpaper *Les Voyages du Capitaine Cook* of 1806 he published a descriptive account of each scene, stressing its edifying and informative aspects: 'an immense curriculum of things to teach children'. The exoticism of the Orient in both the Chinese papers and the late European panoramas of distant lands was an irresistible attraction.

During the latter part of the eighteenth century, Chinese papers were printed from woodblocks and coloured by hand, a change brought about by the wishes of the importers. These painted engravings portrayed gentle landscapes suited to European tastes. Papillon deplored the fact that the Chinese had allowed the market to influence them into producing such facile work. The results were mediocre, and did not command a good price. Writing in 1766, he said 'the Chinese papers that are made today cannot compare at all in beauty with what was available twenty or forty years ago'. The drop in quality changed the market, and in any event European influence changed the traditional uses for such papers. At first it was the Chinese who conformed to European practice, for example by following Western conventions for representing space. Then manufacturers in London, Paris and elsewhere were at pains to meet the popular demand for these sought-after hangings and produced effective *chinoiserie* wallpapers and panels. An elaborate domestic reproduction bearing a Georgian excise stamp of about 1740 was removed from a house in Wotton-under-Edge, Gloucestershire, and is now in the Victoria and Albert Museum. The plant and bird motifs are not repeated and it is hand painted. Panels for overmantels and overdoors would sometimes show Chinese floral decoration curiously mixed with classical ornament printed from etched plates and hand coloured, as examples in the Museum of London illustrate.

This taste for the East found a place in all the decorative arts: in architecture, furniture, textiles, porcelain, as well as wallpaper. In architecture, buildings in the Chinese taste decorated eighteenth-century parks, such as the Chinese pavilion in the 'wilderness' at Retz, the pagoda at Chanteloup and Kent's pagoda at Kew. The pavilions at Sans Souci near Potsdam, at Drottingholm near Stockholm, and the Royal Pavilion at Brighton are among the finest examples. Also in England, Chippendale used Chinese forms and motifs in his furniture designs. Painted or lacquered panels, original Japanese or Chinese work, were inserted into pieces of furniture manufactured in Europe. (The Martin brothers made varnished imitations of the same panels.) Chinese and Japanese porcelain was to suffer the same treatment. Some items were copied and then 'interpreted' for the European market with superficial Oriental decoration, while the originality of others was corrupted by the addition of bronze decoration.

Papillon distinguished between Chinese and Japanese papers on artistic and practical grounds. In his *History of Japan* Engelbert Kaempfer (1651-1716), a Prussian naturalist and explorer, describes the large panels of paper on frames that could be used as screens or moveable walls to change the shape of rooms at will. The Japanese made considerable use of these *fusumas*, as they did of the screens of translucent paper called *sojii* which functioned as windows. These papers were manufactured at the ancient capital of the empire, Miaco, at Jedo and at Nagasaki, the only port that was open to the authorized traders of China and Holland. We wonder what has become of these papers, and of the embossed papers made (according to Papillon who himself tried out the technique) by using shaped blocks on dampened paper, then heightening the designs with colour.

The European taste for Chinese paper continued to develop during the nineteenth century, side by side with a deepening appreciation of Chinese and Japanese culture brought about by better acquaintance. Authentic Eastern forms – in architecture, flora or costume – are correctly portrayed, but manufacturing processes using a repeated pattern gave the overall designs a disturbingly European feel. Chinese paper created many possibilities for wallpaper in Europe, both in the way it was used, for example the display of several large panels together, and in its artistic style with its fine drawing and bright, fresh colours. This was in addition to the revolutionary effect that the exotic vocabulary of Chinese design had on Western applied art and decoration as a whole.

Chinoiserie *paper with garlands and bunches of flowers, masks and butterflies around Chinese scenes. From a house at Berwick upon Tweed, Northumberland. Block and stencil printed, then varnished. c. 1700. V&A.*

Hunting scene from the Old Brewery, Watford, Hertfordshire. Distemper paper. Chinese, c. 1800. V&A.

Album of chinoiserie designs by Jean Pillement. French, 1773. Bibliothèque des Arts Décoratifs, Paris.

Chinese panorama. Lithograph by Desfossé from the Maigret sales catalogue. Carlhian coll.

Flock wallpaper

Flock paper printed in black, green and orange on a cream-coloured ground. Attributed to Hermann Schinkel of Delft. Dutch, 17th century. V&A.

Flock papers can be defined as papers that imitate the finish of velvet or tapestry by means of powdered textiles glued onto the paper surface and following a printed design. Each European country has a particular name for such papers: for example *papier tontisse, papier velouté* or *papier soufflé* in France, *Velourspapier* or *Samtpapier* in Germany.

The first reference to flock paper comes from Nuremberg, where a technical description, dating from 1470, was found in a small handbook from the Monastery of St Catherine.[3] In the archives of the Alte Kapelle at Regensburg a sheet of flock paper, probably of Italian workmanship and dateable to 1450, has survived.[4] It shows a hunting scene, and is in red on a white background.

Between these precious fifteenth-century fragments and the splendid English hangings that were to delight Paris there were three centuries of trial, experiment and development before the new wall-covering was perfected. Many European countries developed a technique that prepared the ground for flock paper, which would have been produced in Germany, Italy, Holland or France had it not first appeared in England at the beginning of the eighteenth century. It was first introduced in France in 1753. There it had an immediate success, being called *papier d'Angleterre*. French manufacturers tried to resist the fashion, then imitated it and finally claimed it as a native product. Throughout the century it was developed to a level of quality that neither the technical developments of the nineteenth nor the further achievements of the twentieth century could surpass.

The taste for materials with applied or flock designs originated in Venice in the early sixteenth century. As conventional wall-coverings were extremely expensive, the Venetians set about finding a substitute that would appear similar and cost less, and hit upon the use of wool clippings applied to leather, a method that also rendered the leather more resistant. It is worth noting that the technique, which was soon to be found all over Europe, could also be used on fabric and paper, and frequently adopted a design vocabulary borrowed from Turkish stuffs. Flock material can be divided into two main groups: those imitating the designs of brocades and velvets from Utrecht, and those copying tapestry designs, particularly landscapes and historical scenes.

In Germany and the Low Countries both leather and cloth were used, and a number of examples of flocked cloth have survived. During the seventeenth century, for example, Hermann Schinkel in Delft worked as an engraver, printed wallpapers and made flocked textiles. In Nuremberg

Flock paper with flowers on a quatrefoil ground, showing influence of calico designs. The joins between each sheet are clearly visible. 18th century. V&A.

Boar hunt. Flocked canvas wall hanging. German, c. 1660. Whitworth Art Gallery, Manchester.

Flock paper from Ivy House, Worcester. English, 1679. V&A.

Johann Hauntsch (1595-1670) created a paper on which the design was heightened by means of metallic powders applied with a brush into the varnish and mixed with powdered colours. The resulting spangled effect was gained by the strong contrast between matte and gloss, with highlights reflected from the metal. Johann Hauntsch's descendants carried on the business until the beginning of the nineteenth century, and flocked textiles imitating tapestries were also made in Kassel and Vienna.

Apart from imitating tapestries, flocked textiles could also be used effectively to copy embossed and painted leathers. Using similar floral designs, the same contrast between background material and relief could be achieved, the weave of the cloth creating a rugged effect and the powdered wool a contrasting softness. Other materials, with lyre-shaped designs, are rich but austere and robust, and must have appealed to the practical tastes of the Germans and the Flemish. Towards the end of the seventeenth century, the influence of Daniel Marot becomes more apparent. His designs, which in particular create the effect of curtains or draperies and can be compared to those of Jean Berain, have an air of elegance and lightness that heralds the refinement of the eighteenth century. A Huguenot decorative sculptor, Marot (1650-1700) moved to Holland after the revocation of the Edict of Nantes in 1685 and became architect to William of Orange, later William III of England.

Savary des Bruslons tells us that flocked textiles were also produced in Rouen and Paris: his *Dictionnaire universel de commerce* of 1723 deals extensively with their manufacture. In particular, he confirms that the first flocked textiles imitating brocade were made in Rouen, where later the first effects of foliage as in tapestries were achieved. In Paris, he says, a manufacturer in the faubourg St Antoine 'tried his hand at groups of figures, bouquets and grotesques, and was reasonably successful'. But Savary des Bruslons adds a note of caution: 'Pro-

Flock paper in brown on a beige ground. From the Château de Bosmelet, Auffay, Normandy. Early 18th century.

Fragment of flock paper in brown on a turquoise ground. From the Château de Bosmelet, Auffay, Normandy. Early 18th century.

vided they are made by skilled men, these kinds of tapestry can be taken, at first glance, for the real thing, but they have two basic faults about which nothing can be done. Firstly, they are very susceptible to damp, which can do them great harm. Secondly, they cannot be folded up and put in a wardrobe or taken from place to place like a proper tapestry, but they have to be rolled up on large wooden cylinders which takes up a lot of space: this is a nuisance.'

As to the first use of paper rather than cloth as a base, one very close contender is François, or Le François, a successful paper maker in Rouen who 'created in his workshop papers imitating tapestries and figured velvet'. This claim was published in an article in the *Journal économique* for March 1755, by a Monsieur Tierce, who was Le François' successor in business and who was claiming that France was the first to invent flock papers. As evidence he produced the engraved blocks that Le François had used between 1620 and 1630. Tierce printed these blocks onto paper, not using ink but a thick varnish to which he applied powdered wools of various colours, thereby making a perfect imitation of figured velvets or tapestries in the manner of Chinese papers, which he also possessed. These papers were called *papiers soufflés* (blown papers) because of the way the powdered wool was literally blown onto the glue-covered paper. How was it, though, that if Le François had made flocked papers in the seventeenth century no trace of them existed when Tierce wrote about it a century later, either in Paris or in the provinces? There are a number of possible reasons.

Firstly, there is no evidence that Le François used the blocks in question to print onto paper, though we do know he was able to imitate very fine tapestries in cloth. Tierce himself says that when he 'bought the stock from Le François' son, he improved the techniques used, and in particular developed the cloth side of the business, with less attention to the paper, as he felt the former to be much superior.' It is hardly in Le François' favour that Tierce was ready to let the wallpaper business slip at a time when the wallpaper industry was flourishing and expanding.

The second possibility is that Le François did in fact manufacture flocked papers, and that none have survived because they were so fragile. Savary des Bruslons makes it clear that even flocked cloths were difficult to protect. It could also be argued that the thinness of paper sheets would make it very difficult indeed to fix them onto walls; this was still a major problem a century later. In any case, the effort was not a success, and could not have caught the public imagination in the way *papier d'Angleterre* did in the early eighteenth century.

In 1634 in London Jerome Lanyer, who is presumed to have come to London as a Huguenot refugee, obtained an exclusive manufacturing

The Chinese Vase *French, 1860.*

Flock paper. English, c. 1700-25. V&A.

Chinese Decoration. *Designed by Poterlet for Zuber, 1861. Bohème coll.*

Fantail draperies. Partially flocked paper, designed by Mery for Zuber, 1826. MISE.

patent from Charles I for 'affixinge Wooll, Silke, and other Materialls of divers Collours uppon Lynnen, Cloath, Silke, Cotten, Leather and other substances with Oyle, Size and other Ciments to make them useful and serviceable for hangings and other Occassions, which he calleth Londrindiana.' Lanyer was not English, and his surname could be an anglicization of the French *lainier*, meaning a workman who puts powdered wool onto cloth. (There was also a Lainier family of musicians, from Rouen.)

In the 1630s Jerome Lanyer could not have made a commercial success of flocked papers, as England did not have a quality paper-manufacturing industry, France being Europe's main source of paper. Paper manufacturers in the Champagne area traditionally supplied Flanders, the Low Countries, Germany, Austria and Switzerland, while those of Angoumois and Guyenne exported to England and Spain by sea. This export market was much reduced by Louis XIV's wars, and the revocation of the Edict of Nantes led to an exodus of the best craftsmen to other European countries, which were thereby able to found their own industries. Moreover there were very few technical publications available from which to acquire the necessary knowledge.

In 1685 John Briscoe perfected a machine for making a paper that was claimed to be as white as French or Dutch paper and as good a quality in all other respects. With its own paper industry, England ceased to be dominated by France.

Shortly before 1700 Abraham Price founded the Blue Paper Warehouse at Aldermanbury, London. An early advertisement bearing the arms of William III (1694-1702) offered for sale, dyed through, blue 'sugar loaf' and royal purple papers sold by the ream and used in the Warehouse's wall hangings 'after the mode of real tapestry'. The public were warned against imitations made of a thin and common brown paper daubed over with paint. Pure blue paper was highly prized.[5] A proclamation of 1666 had forbidden the sale or import of foreign blue paper, as Charles Hildyard had received a patent for his manufacture of an English paper of this kind. Abraham Price diversified his production, offering designs of Irish work, floral damasks or marble and wainscot papers along with the flock tapestry papers in blue which were soon to enjoy a great vogue in France. The flock designs would be applied either by stencilling or printing from a woodblock, in some adhesive substance onto which the coloured powdered wool would be spread. By this means flock papers could be made to a very high standard, partly because of the fine quality of English paper, partly because of the delicacy of colouring and the quality of the designs.

Two technical developments were to help English manufacturers escape from the restrictions suffered by their French rivals. Firstly, sheets of paper could be stuck together end to end in rolls (each about 36 feet, or 11 metres, long) before they were printed, which freed the design from the limitations of a small format. Secondly, the papers could be printed with a base colour in distemper. (Jean-Michel Papillon had been against this technique and so did not recognise its value, from which his successor, Réveillon, was to benefit so much.) Above all, wallpapers were now accessible to every rank in society.

A rare late seventeenth-century paper showing a crimson flock pattern of a floriated gateway on a white ground was discovered at Saltfleet Manor, Lincolnshire. Flock papers of the early eighteenth century ranged in design from simple scrolling foliage to the most luxurious imitations of figured velvets from Genoa and Utrecht. These displayed vertical mirror-image patterns which gave wall surfaces a dignified rhythm. Outside the Victoria and Albert Museum, excellent examples are preserved at Temple Newsam House, Leeds, Clandon Park, Surrey, and Christ Church Mansion, Ipswich.

Flock wallpapers from the Blue Paper Warehouse and other factories in London had a remarkable success in France, which led to a 'paper war'. The situation was not eased by the Seven Years' War that broke out between France and England in 1756. If we are to believe Madame de Genlis, a passion for all things English ruled in France at the time: 'ladies would wear nothing but English dresses in poplin, muslin or English linen... They sell their diamonds to buy English steelwork and glassware. Our splendid Gobelins tapestries are put aside to make way for blue English wallpaper... The English could never have tried to imitate our fine tapestries, so they have put them out of fashion with their wallpapers.'

British flock wallpaper was soon adopted by the highest French society. In 1753 the Duc de Mirepoix, the French Ambassador in London, had sent some blue papers to Paris. Lord Albermarle, the British Ambassador in Paris, ordered some to decorate his house in Passy. In 1754 Madame de Pompadour, mistress of Louis XV and arbiter of fashion in the French court, put blue paper on the walls of her wardrobe at Versailles and in the corridor linking her apartment to the chapel. Four years later she wallpapered the bathroom at the Château des Champs. So wallpaper was received into the royal residences of France.

It is puzzling that a product, probably known about in France from the 1630s, had to wait until the 1750s to excite such interest. This may be explained by the fact that France was not a single economic entity, but was divided not only by internal customs frontiers but further split in two by the influence of the two largest cities, Paris and Lyons.[6] Any innovation could only spread slowly if it did not have the support of these two key centres. Moreover, wallpapers fell into the same category as the domino papers, which were despised by the upper classes as the property of the common people and the middle classes. In any case these papers were not strong enough to support flocking.[7] As to the rest of Europe, Italy never lost its conservative taste for fresco, and Germany and the Low Countries, with their traditional preference for leather, wood and textiles, were not to take up wallpaper until the nineteenth century, while the Spanish for a long time believed wallpaper was not right for their climate.

By subjecting France to a despotism of taste, Louis XIV rigidified society into an arbitrary and petty pattern that fettered the economy: the nobility and the court at Versailles lived in the King's shadow, and anything that did not receive the royal approval was doomed from the start.

In England, on the other hand, flock papers, along with other types of paper hangings, became increasingly popular during the first half of the eighteenth century. Both the aristocracy and the middle classes used them, and William Pyne notes that the Great Drawing Room of Kensington Palace was papered for George I around 1720.

Wallpaper in France did not receive royal approval until the Duc de Mirepoix and Madame de Pompadour used it in their private rooms: the fashion spread, and soon everyone had to have blue English wallpaper. We can get an idea of things from the journal carefully kept by Lazare Duvaux, who was a jeweller and merchant. He noted the following orders for paper, after 1748:

5 October 1748 – for the Countess de Maurepas
Four frames of cloth and India paper. [The term, 'India meaning either Chinese or Japanese]

Nov. 1748 for M. de Boulogne
A screen with six five-foot sheets of India paper on both sides

Dec. 1748 for M. Jacquet
One sheet of paper on a gold ground, 4 *livres*

Jan. 1749 for the Princesse d'Enrichemont
Mosaic paper to cover a wardrobe, 9 *livres*

Jan. 1749 for Me. de Sauvigny
Two sheets of paper on a gold ground, pasted into a cupboard, 12 *livres*

April 1749 for Mgr the Duc de Bouillon
Covering in cloth thirty-six frames and pasting with white paper covered with India paper, for making and stretching, 2 *soldi*

Flock decorative panel. Designed by Mader for Dufour, 1812. The same motif is used in the scenes from Molière (see p. 117). Bibliothèque Forney, Paris.

Flock frieze. French, c. 1800. Nobilis coll.

Flock paper. Reproduction of an Adam design by Follot. French, 1965. Follot coll.

Flock frieze. French, 19th century. Nobilis coll.

Frame-like border. French, c. 1800. Nobilis coll.

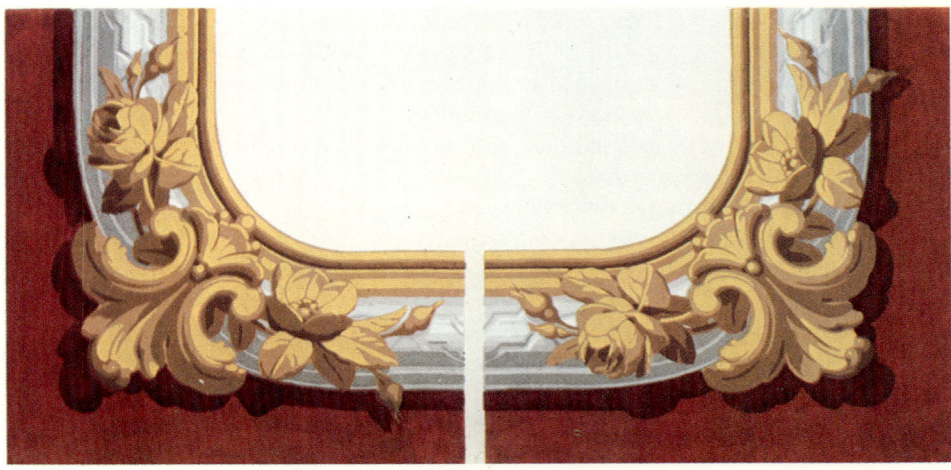

23 June 1749 for the Abbé Annison
  Restoring four panels of India paper, setting them back up and extending them top and bottom with two sheets in frames, 24 *livres*

23 July 1748 for Madame la Marquise de Pompadour
  Cloth, pasting and stretching ten small panels with India paper, 66 *livres*

8 May 1750 for the Dowager Princesse de Rohan
  Two sheets of floral paper

25 Jan 1751 for Madame la Marquise de Pompadour
  Cloth and making up six small panels in fine paper for the bath wardrobe, delivery, fixing etc. 32 *livres*

March 1751 for M. de Caze, Fermier Général
  Restretching a screen and recovering it entirely in white paper

August 1751
  Cloth, making up and restretching forty frames for the eight wardrobes (three frames in paper) and eight frames for the fireplace at Bellevue, 310 *livres*
  Supplying six missing sheets, 28 *livres*
  Carriage, 27 *livres*

Nov 1753
  For a large mahogany screen, sheets of fine paper and fitting, 60 *livres*.

So we see that the nobility at court did use wallpaper, but preferred Chinese paper for screens and tapestry papers for wardrobes or lining furniture.

The rise of flock wallpaper in France

In 1735, a Master Simon asked for permission, which was refused him, to manufacture tapestry papers depicting foliage and landscapes, and using wool clippings to achieve that result. Twelve years later, in 1747, Papillon engraved a series of blocks for Simon Etienne Martin,[8] which imitated figured velvet and were probably used to print a ground for powdered wool. Finally, in 1754, Roquis, trading in the rue du Cloître St Germain, announced in an advertisement that he possessed 'the secret of English paper, imitating figured velvets, and suitable for lining small rooms'. The following year Didier Aubert, whose shop Au Papillon was in the rue St Jacques, managed 'after difficult and costly experiments to make *papiers veloutés* as beautiful

Monochrome flock paper mounted on canvas. English, early 18th century. V&A.

Flock paper in green and beige on a pink ground. English, 1720. DTM.

Flock paper after Réveillon's The Two Pigeons, *1785, an example of which is at Clandon Park, Surrey. V&A.*

Decorative panel with frieze of drapery. Brown flocking and imitation bronze decoration on a wooden ground. Zuber. French, c. 1810. DTM.

and perfect as English papers, after the finest damask designs. The papers are nine *aunes* by twenty inches wide'. (An *aune* is about 44 inches, or 112 centimetres.)

Aubert added that he was able to supply suites of paper, designed to match the furniture, for large rooms. His success can be measured from the fact, mentioned in *La feuille nécessaire*, that in 1759 he opened a second factory in the rue de Charenton, near the faubourg St Antoine. Another craftsman, Jacques Chéreau, was making folding screens and firescreens in flock paper.

The outbreak of the Seven Years' War in 1756 stopped trade between France and England, and led to a remarkable expansion of wallpaper making in France. In another issue of *La feuille nécessaire* in 1759 it was reported that 'Monsieur Aubert has set up a factory for flocked materials which are much superior to those English papers which have to be pasted onto cloth and need the added expense of frames.'

Mlle d'Henery was a wallpaper merchant and also, it seems, a patriot: in the *Mercure de France* of July 1774, she announced that at her shop in the rue Comtesse d'Artois she 'makes and sells only French wallpaper'. The French government also took steps to protect the manufacturers. Decrees of 27 February 1765 and 1 December 1766, by increasing the customs duty, levied twenty *livres* on each hundredweight of flock or flock paper imported from abroad. The number of manufacturers increased, attesting to the vogue for flock papers: Jean-Gabriel Huquier set up shop in the rue des Mathurins in about 1765, and we know also of Crépy[9] in the rue St Jacques, Garnier in the rue Quincampoix, Poilly,[10] son of a famous engraver, and Lecomte, from Lyons, whose flock papers were made with silk clippings. Two English manufacturers also set themselves up in Paris: Lancake, or Lancoke, with a factory at Carrières and a shop in the rue St Antoine, and the firm of Windsor, which was established in the rue de Bagneux in 1779.

But flock papers gradually ceased to be so fashionable, and after 1780 newspapers carried many small advertisements from private individuals who wanted to get rid of their flock papers (demonstrating that it could actually be taken down). Taste now demanded the distempered papers in Pompeian style, of which Réveillon had made himself such a master.

Although flock papers lost some of their exclusivity and impetus, they were still manufactured in the nineteenth century. Technical developments such as the cylinder press and the paper roll meant that costs could be reduced, and there were several successful ventures, notably in borders. In the twentieth century powdered wool gave way to synthetic flocks.

So who won the 'war' over flocked wallpaper? Neither France nor England, though it is amusing to note that the most French of wallpaper designers, Réveillon, owed the beginning of his remarkable career to an Englishman. When Lord Albermarle imported wallpapers from England for his house in Passy, no one knew how to put it up correctly. Finally, Réveillon's opinion was asked, and it was he who worked out how it was done. In general, however, wallpaper itself benefitted most from the conflict by acquiring a wider role. In France in the eighteenth century wallpaper had been closeted in wardrobes and cupboards, but in the nineteenth it was to emerge from there and become accepted as a decorative medium in any social context.

Notes (pp. 56-75).

1. Stupinigi was built in 1730, according to a design by Juvara. 'The walls were entirely covered with wallpaper, distemper painted, which represented scenes from life in China in the mid eighteenth century. Highly fashionable all over Europe, these papers were commissioned from studios where many artists worked . . . Figures from various social classes were scattered throughout the landscape. The hands of two very different artists could be distinguished, one slender, graceful and fluid, and the other broader and more curved. The sheets were divided by borders.' (Catalogue of the Museo dell'Arredamento Stupinigi, ed. Noemi Gabrielli, Turin, 1966.)

2. Sir William Chambers described their use from his own studies in *Designs for Chinese Buildings*, 1751.

3. Haemmerle, *Die Buntpapiere*, Munich, 1961.

4. Pierre Gusman, in *Panneaux décoratifs et tenture murale*, mentions a St George design dating from 1425 in the Weigel Collection. We have been unable to trace it.

5. The colour blue was much used in England (and later in France) throughout the eighteenth century. It showed off the fashionable dark mahogany furniture and went well with collections of blue and white Chinese porcelain.

6. For a very long time Lyons was a much more important centre of commerce than Paris. In 1781 the 'industrial area' (comprising St Etienne, St Chamond, Virieux and Neuf-ville) had a turnover of 211 million francs, whereas Paris totalled only 25 million.

7. Canvas is a much stronger base, and can be made to the dimensions of the panel to be papered. It is easy to put up, with tacks on a frame, avoiding the disadvantages of glue (stains, drips, threads coming unstuck.) The first flock paper was mounted on canvas frames.

8. A decree of 18 February 1744 gave Simon Etienne Martin (younger brother of Guillaume Martin) the exclusive right to make all sorts of items in relief in Chinese and Japanese styles.

9. Crépy the elder, at the sign of St Louis, in the rue St Jacques, the third shop below the fountain of St Séverin in Paris, 'keeps a shop of English and flock paper for furnishing, the beauty of whose designs and the vividness and evenness of whose colours are of superior quality... he undertakes to match materials and to supply suitable cloth, and hangs wallpapers in the town.' (*Almanach du Dauphin*, 1770.)

10. 'Monsieur N.B. de Pilly, a skilful engraver, sometimes amuses himself by making black and white designs for flock wallpaper and transferring them onto blocks of copper or wood in relief, which will then be used for printing.' (Jean-Michel Papillon, *Traité... de la gravure sur bois*, Paris, 1776.)

Paper with border. The tulip leaves are flocked. Zuber. French, early 19th century. MISE.

*Paper by J.B. Jackson, showing influence of Sebastiano Ricci.
English, 18th century. V&A.*

*Trade card of James Wheeley. English c. 1758.
British Museum, London.*

CHAPTER THREE
The golden age

The eighteenth century and the early part of the nineteenth were to witness the expansion of block-printed wallpaper in Europe. In England John Baptist Jackson was the most remarkable and creative artist in the field. While Germany did not follow the general fashion for wallpaper, it was developed to perfection in France by Jean-Baptiste Réveillon. In the nineteenth century the Zuber and Dufour factories introduced landscape papers which were highly successful in America.

John Baptist Jackson (1701-77)

Of all the British makers of wallpaper in the eighteenth century, Jackson was one of the most remarkable and original. In his own forceful and rhetorical book *An Essay on the Invention of Printing in Chiaroscuro, etc* (London, 1754) he passed on the secret of his inventions and expressed to his contemporaries and posterity his love for the masterpieces of Italian and classical art, both in painting and sculpture. Born in 1701, Jackson was apprenticed to the engraver Edward Kirkall (1695-1750). Kirkall was a wood engraver and etcher, and was particularly noted for his suite of twelve engravings (published in 1732) using both techniques together, the wood engravings supplying the intermediate tones. Jackson went to Paris in 1726, to continue learning engraving under Papillon. Relations between the two men were not good: in his *Traité . . . de la gravure sur bois* Papillon listed the monograms of known contemporary and older engravers. For the monogram EK he wrote 'English painter called Ekwits, who trained Jackson in painting and etching. Of Jackson I have more to say – he was well known to Parisian printers in the 1730s for passing on to them a lot of mediocre engravings.'

Papillon goes on to claim that Jackson had stolen designs from him to sell as his own. The fraud being discovered, Jackson was thrown out of the workshop in the rue St Jacques. But it seems unlikely that Jackson could have lived for five years or more in Paris by selling 'mediocre engravings', nor that his dishonesty would not have made other printers and engravers close their doors to him.

Whatever the truth may be, Jackson left Paris for Rome. There he discovered the Rome of antiquity, and the work of Raphael and of Piranesi, which was to have such an influence on his own work. After Rome he moved to Venice, where he married, and was to live until 1746. This was the Venice that Canaletto and Tiepolo knew, still brilliant though the lustre was fading, a city of festival and masquerade, full of pictorial treasures. Titian and Tintoretto particularly drew his attention. Jackson soaked up the atmosphere of Venice, with its flamboyant intertwined and curving baroque forms, found in furniture, mirror frames and interior decorations, which were often designed by the artists who had provided the accompanying pictures.

When at last he returned to England, Jackson tried unsuccessfully to live by his engraving. He therefore decided to use his technical and artistic skills to produce wallpaper, and entered a workshop at Battersea, near London. There he produced large sheets of paper bearing engraved illustrations. These were designed to be set within a simple wallpaper decoration or contained within printed frames, and were certainly a novelty calculated to appeal to a cultivated taste. Printing in four oil colours was a new departure; by overprinting he claimed to produce 'ten positive tints'. A contemporary account gives us an idea of the effect that these papers created: 'those who have seen this new sort of paperhanging distended in a room have

Engraved dedication by J.B. Jackson. English, 1731. V&A.

*Italianate landscape with figures and ruins.
J.B. Jackson. V&A.*

*Paper from Doddington Hall, Lincolnshire. Attributed
to J.B. Jackson. V&A.*

allow'd that this method of printing comes nearest to the finishing of the pencil of anything that has hitherto been performed.' (*Enquiry into the Origin of Printing in Europe by a Lover of Art,* a booklet published in 1752 and discussed in Edna K. Donnell, Metropolitan Museum Studies, Vol 4, 1932, Part 1.) A connoisseur of the day, Horace Walpole, found a use for wallpaper reproductions after Old Master paintings. Writing to Horace Mann in 1753, Walpole explains that his parlour at Strawberry Hill was hung with 'Jackson's Venetian prints which I never could endure, infamous as they are, to be after Titian, but when I gave them the air of barbarous bas-reliefs they succeeded to a miracle.'

Drawing on his studies in Venice, Jackson reproduced such works as Titian's *Massacre of the Innocents,* Primaticcio's *Dream of Polyphemus* and Tintoretto's San Rocco *Crucifixion.* Also issued from the Battersea factory were papers which displayed small landscapes in roundels within baroque frames. Such papers served the fashion for print rooms, thought to have been started around 1750 by Lord Cadogan, where fine engravings were pasted directly onto walls and framed by paper borders. These formal arrangements were linked by paper swags and imitation ribbons. Jackson's wallpaper showed an Italian influence. The landscapes are in fact little *vedute* of houses, ruins and riversides or *fêtes galantes* framed by branches on an even background, which alternate with small roundels showing butterflies or flowering branches. The delicacy of this arrangement, which recalls the way engravings were placed on the walls of print rooms, links the rigidity of the Neoclassical symmetry to the baroque handling of the frames, where the sweep of the edge carries on into the subject itself. So there is a double effect of *trompe l'oeil* in that the flowering branches form the border of the picture and are also an element within it. This illusion of images seen in mirrors is accentuated by the chiaroscuro printing.

In his booklet published in 1754, Jackson talks of himself in the third person, intending his knowledge and his personal qualities to be of benefit to his contemporaries and to confound his 'lamentable predecessors'.

'When all has been said, it could be considered out of place to confer on Mr Jackson the merit of having invented this skill – for an invention is what it is... In truth, since the beginning of the sixteenth century, no-one, apart from Mr Jackson, has tried the Italian method.' With disarming frankness, Jackson quotes Pascal on the title-page of his book: 'Those who are capable of invention are few – those who can never invent are many, and in consequence the stronger'.

It is correct that Jackson was an innovator in his use of wallpaper to create large decorative panels.

To achieve this, he used several sheets of paper fixed together before printing. An even more important innovation was his use on wallpapers of the technique of chiaroscuro printing, which he had almost certainly learnt in Paris, from Jean Papillon I's pupil Vincent Lesueur or from Jacques Chauveau. Jackson claims his discoveries were made for his country, not for himself. 'Such was his love for his native land that, after giving all his time to comprehending these discoveries, he returned, strengthened by his experience, to contribute to the enrichment of the country to which he owed everything, in order to increase its trade and create work for his fellows, to whom he leaves his discoveries as an inheritance, although as a free man he could have kept all the profit for himself until the end of his days.'

Jackson's oil-printed papers were proof against dampness and darkening by smoke, as they could be washed. In design his large panels are closer to what Réveillon was to produce twenty years later in France than to the work of the *dominotiers*. Jackson railed against Chinese papers and *chinoiseries* generally, complaining that lions leapt from branch to branch like pussycats, houses floated in the air, clouds and sky were under the ground, that all the elements, men and women were in complete confusion, and that all the animals were monsters. His own works were surrounded by festoons and garlands of flowers or imitations of stucco framing, in the purest baroque Venetian taste. He produced grand landscapes in the manner of Piranesi, their grey cameos framed by rococo ornament. The wallpapers at Harrington House, Gloucestershire, depict large landscapes with ruins, trophies and scrolls in green, sepia and grey, with baroque frames. These stunning compositions are evidence of Jackson's inventive style, which responded well to contemporary English taste, already looking to Palladianism.

For his fellow countrymen without the means to buy the originals, Jackson also made large *trompe l'oeil* papers showing antique statues placed in stuccoed niches. 'The most elegant engravings, the statues of antiquity, are placed within niches, in chiaroscuro on paper panels . . . . Thereby, those who cannot acquire the statues themselves, may obtain them in reproduction . . . Among the works of sculpture that will be thereby made available to the everyday Englishman are the *Apollo Belvedere*, the *Dying Gladiator* and the *Medici Venus*.'

Clearly, Jackson made an original contribution to wallpaper in Britain: in using large decorative panels he made framed landscapes available, as Arthur and Robert were to do later. But although Jackson opened a shop in London's Regent Street, it may be that his work was not fully appreciated by his contemporaries. Thomas Bewick, in his memoirs, published in 1780, says that Jackson ended his days in an asylum on Tweedside. Less fortunate than his contemporary Thomas Bromwich, who obtained royal patronage, Jackson was nonetheless a tasteful innovator, and a true artist who achieved the *tour de force* of combining a number of influences, foreign, ancient and modern, into a truly original expression.

Georgian and Regency papers

By the end of the eighteenth century London had become the most important financial centre in the world. Industrual improvements were benefitting British products, and trade and mercantile life flourished. In the year 1798, 14,000 ships berthed in

Chiaroscuro ceiling paper.
Block-printed. English, 1769. V&A.

the Port of London. Witness to this activity were the City and the East End, with their numerous artisan workshops of craftsmen, tanners, dyers and paper makers, serving the needs of the fast-growing populace of the metropolis.

The enterprise of wallpaper manufacturers was as keen as it had been at the beginning of the century. Following the success of flocked paper and Chinese papers, printing in water-based pigments from as many blocks as there were colours in the design was developed to sophisticated heights. It was this method that gave the famous French manufacturer Jean-Baptiste Réveillon such success. The expanding market for luxury wallpapers was met by a number of talented and fashion-conscious designers. Writing in 1741, Lady Hartford praised the quality of English papers, and the *Covent Garden Journal* of 1752 did not hesitate to compare English paper with the best silk, claiming that they could

Floral wallpaper. Ink and watercolour. Attributed to the Eckhardt brothers, London. English, late 18th century. V&A.

Stencil-printed paper. English, 1780. V&A.

Block-printed paper in two colours on white. English, mid 18th century. V&A.

Stork and fountain. Paper from George Hill House, Sussex. Block-printed. Attributed to the Eckhardt brothers, London. English, c. 1790. Whitworth Art Gallery, Manchester.

only with difficulty be distinguished from each other.

In 1753 Edward Deighton obtained a patent to manufacture paper by a new system: the design, engraved on a metal plate, was printed by a cylinder press and the colours applied by hand with camel-hair brushes. Robert Dossie tells us this method was used exclusively for India papers, where the freedom and variety of design could not be conveyed by outline printing.

John Baptist Jackson's contemporaries were particularly concerned with producing *chinoiserie* papers and papers that imitated woven materials. For example, Thomas Bromwich, at the Golden Lion, Ludgate Hill, established a business that flourished between 1740 and 1850. He offered in his catalogue papers copying gilded leather, checkerwork, chintzes, calico and embroidery. Bromwich was appointed Master of the Worshipful Company of Painter-Stainers in 1761 and two years later he received royal patronage. Horace Walpole had recourse to Bromwich to provide papers for his decorative schemes, including a gothic frieze drawn by his friend Richard Bently. In her diary for 1771 Mrs Phillip Lybbe Powys praised Bromwich's work at Fawley Court, Buckinghamshire, arranging cut-out borders, festoons, and Indian baskets against pink and green Chinese papers.

One feature that distinguishes English wallpaper manufacturers from their French counterparts is that the English designer would often be responsible for the whole interior decoration, even the furniture – a role that the French *tapissier* was to have a century later. The Crace family were numbered among the most important of such decorators. The firm was established in 1750 and benefitted from the patronage of George III and the Prince Regent. John Crace, whose father Edward started the firm, decorated the Theatre Royal, Drury Lane, the Opera House in Covent Garden, and Carlton House, where there was a large Chinese drawing-room and a picture gallery in Strawberry Hill Gothick. Frederick Crace, who was responsible for the decoration of Windsor Castle, also worked at the Royal Pavilion, Brighton, between 1817 and 1823. Crace asked the painter Robert Jones for 'Chinese drawings' as models for the green and white paper for the library and royal bedchamber. The resulting strange, symmetrical designs of flowers and dragons bear little resemblance to real Chinese art. John Gregory Crace, one of the fist historians of wallpaper, worked on the decoration for the new Houses of Parliament and led the family firm into the machine age.

During the late Georgian period the brothers Francis, Frederick and Anthony George Eckhardt ran a successful business in London printing silks, cottons, calicos and wallpapers. They opened a factory on Sloane Street, Chelsea, in 1786 and a number of patents granted to them from this time up to the end of the century showed the range of their technical virtuosity. Scarcely any attributable examples of their work have survived, but we know that their designs imitated damasks, silks and lace. Papers were printed from woodblocks or copper plates, and large numbers of workers were employed in colouring and finishing by hand. Designs ornamented with gold and silver leaf simulated the sheen of woven silk; these can be compared with the productions of Anthony Eccard of the Hague who took out a patent in 1768 for printing flock papers with gold and silver. In 1791 the Eckhardts moved to larger premises at Whitelands in Chelsea, which were soon to be announced as the Royal Patent Manufactory under the patronage of the Princess Royal. The brothers subscribed to Thomas Sheraton's *Cabinet Makers' and Upholsterers' Drawing Book* of 1793, in which the use of wallpaper was specified and their own productions were praised for their grace and fine technique.

Another distinguished wallpaper manufacturer of this period was John Sherringham of Great Marlborough Street, London, whose business was established by 1786 and closed in 1802. He travelled in Europe and employed Continental designers to produce the elegant 'arabesque' papers which were the basis of his reputation. Sherringham's fine work was remembered in the mid nineteenth century by the decorator Mawer Cowtan, owner of a wallpaper firm, who described him as 'the Wedgwood of Paperstainers'.

Paper imitating figured silk. J.-B. Réveillon. French, 18th century. Follot coll.

Paper with medallions and imitation marble. English, 1789-99. From Segerhof, Blumenrain, Switzerland. Historisches Museum, Basel.

By the end of the eighteenth century manufacturers were catering for the luxury market, producing papers that imitated costly materials or stucco decoration. But such efforts were soon to be prejudicial to the progress of design. French manufacturers at this period were seeking originality of form and expression which suited the materials with which they were working. Trading restrictions imposed during the Seven Years' War from 1756 to 1763, and between 1779 and 1825, isolated British designers. The impressive French historical landscapes or scenic decorations were little known and never found as great a market in Britain as they did in the United States. The industry was heavily taxed: duties and licences were raised in 1787 and again in 1809.

The increasing demand for cheap wallpapers was apparent from the end of the eighteenth century, and mechanical devices to speed up production were being patented. In 1764 the engraved printing cylinders designed by Fryer, Greenough and Newbury of the City of London received a patent, as did the more successful cylinder printing machine using hand-engraved copper rollers invented by Thomas Bell in 1783. Even the block printers struggled to speed up their procedures by moving the blocks mechanically. But the calico printing machine, which was the forerunner of the first steam-powered wallpaper printing machine, was not in use until the 1780s. Moreover, the absence at this stage of continuous lengths of paper hampered the development of full mechanization. These difficulties, combined with increases in duties and licence costs, depressed the wallpaper industry. It seemed as though the brilliant productions of Sherringham and the Eckhardt brothers had temporarily exhausted the English initiative.

Chinoiserie *paper. Design attributed to the Eckhardt brothers, London. 18th century. V&A.*

Landscape with ruins. Early 19th century. V&A.

Gothic ceiling paper from a house in North Ockendon, Essex. Block-printed with stencil colours. English, c. 1775. V&A.

Embossed leather panels in several colours on gold. Avignon. Early 18th century. DTM.

German wallpaper makers

From the sixteenth century onwards, grained papers *(Fladerpapier)* and other fragile materials were used to cover doors and ceiling panels. But the makers of these ornamental papers turned to making a more durable wall-covering – embossed and painted leather hangings, which were in use up to the end of the eighteenth century. From the sixteenth century onwards there had been a considerable volume of trade between Venice and the merchant towns of northern Europe, particularly those of the Hanseatic League. Nuremberg became a marketplace for goods from Lübeck, Danzig, Breslau, Vienna, Venice, Genoa, Lisbon, Marseilles, Lyons and Strasbourg. In this economic heartland the influences of the Midi and the north met. From Venice came the splendid embossed and figured leathers called *guademeci*, gilded and painted, and with the added quality of warmth.

Although his fragile papers have not survived the wear and tear of time, Johann Hauntsch, in the mid seventeenth century, transferred onto paper the decorative motifs and techniques of leather, sometimes using powdered minerals such as mica. The method for applying the colours to the design was similar to that used for applying flock, and we should not forget that the earliest known formula for making flock paper is from a small book, dated 1470, from the St Catherine monastery in Nuremberg. In fact, the flock textiles made in Berlin, Kassel and Vienna were very widely used in Germany. They were often copies of Flemish tapestries depicting scenes from mythology; or else they imitated the panels of decorative leather hung on walls, using large patterns of boughs, framed by columns, borders and valances. These copied the arrangement of woodwork and wainscots in use at the time.

Another wall-covering only used in Germany, mid-way between wallpaper and printed textile, was *Wachstuchtapete*, which was first made in the eighteenth century and became very popular. The cloth base was soaked in oil and wax, then painted and varnished. It was as a result quite waterproof and was also used for rainwear. The material had the elegance of wallpaper and the durability of cloth, with the added advantage of being washable. It was made in various places, at Dresden, Kassel and Vienna, but the most famous manufacturer was undoubtedly Johann Andreas Benjamin Nothnagel in Frankfurt.

The son of a pastor, Nothnagel was apprenticed to Kiesewetter, in whose studio the animal and landscape painters J.N. Lentzner and J.G. Trautmann were working. In 1753 he took over sole control of the studios, which received in 1791 the honour of an Imperial appointment. His reputation was such that he received commissions not only from all the courts in Germany but also from the kingdom of Naples. Goethe, in *Dichtung und Wahrheit*, describes a visit to Nothnagel's workshops, and a sketch by the Frankfurt painter Christian Morgenstern shows a craftsman painting a flower on the unrolled sheet of cloth, which is hanging vertically. This technique appears very different from that described by Papillon, but woodblocks and copper plates were sometimes used to apply the basic design, with only the colours being added by hand. The makers of this waxed cloth were also wallpaper makers: it should not be forgotten that Chinese papers, which were copied to a high standard all over Germany, were also produced by this method, giving them the precious quality of lacquer panels.

These durable materials remained fashionable for a long time, which accounts for the limited use of wallpaper in Germany. In 1766, in her travel diary, Mrs Calderwood noted that the Germans did not yet have the taste for wallpapers in their homes. Leather and velvet were still widely used. However, in the mid eighteenth century, under the influence of French and English taste, wallpaper began to appear in Germany, and a number of factories opened in the various principalities. For 1760, we find the names of Riesewitz in Rheinburg, and Pontet in Hanover, a 'genuine English manufacturer'. C.W. Kolbe and Johann Pally advertised in 1767 that they made all sorts of papers for walls in the latest styles. In the same year Sonnin and Baldo were in business in Berlin and in 1770 they opened up in Potsdam. Two firms competed for the chief position: Isaac Joel in Potsdam and Wessely and Neumeister in Berlin, who both specialised in arabesque, Indian and 'Etruscan' papers in Réveillon's style. They offered panels, wainscots, overdoors, roundels, wreaths and borders. At Leipzig in 1755, Gottfried Philipp Wilhelm was making marbled and Turkish papers as well as other kinds of wallpaper. The first State Factory was opened in 1781, with B.G. Beck as director, employing as many as five hundred workers.

The most famous pioneer of German wallpaper was Johann Christian Arnold (1758-1842), the son of a pastor. He was educated in Latin, Hebrew and mathematics, and was first employed as a clerk in the Baumann bank in Frankfurt. He became a student of the landscapist C.G. Schutz (1718-91) who had a considerable influence on him. Leaving the bank, Arnold opened a wallpaper workshop that contained twenty-five presses. He worked in Kassel for Jerome, King of Westphalia (1806-13). As a result, he was made an adviser to the town's assembly of merchants in 1813, and later became a member himself. His considerable output covered the period from the closing years of the eighteenth to the late nineteenth century, and reflects the series

Paper imitating earthenware tiles in yellow on a blue ground. J.C. Arnold. German. c. 1820. DTM.

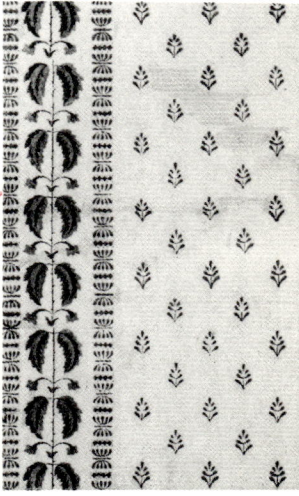

Paper with blue motifs and brown frieze on a yellow ground. J.C. Arnold. German. c. 1825. DTM.

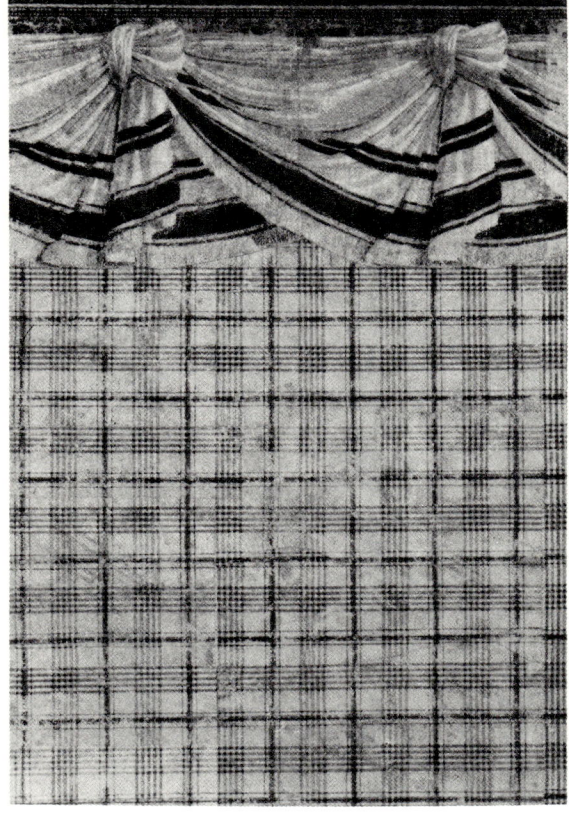

Drapery frieze and paper imitating a check fabric. Blue and sepia on white. J.C. Arnold. German, 1825. DTM.

of styles of the time, showing the same ornamental language as in France. Arnold's designs are Neoclassical, reflecting first the style of the late Louis XVI period; followed by that of the Directoire and the formal Empire style. After 1815 the bourgeois Biedermeier style dominated his work. Arnold also made a few early designs in a Renaissance and rococo style.

Finally, the Behagel brothers in Mannheim began a paper-making dynasty that spread all over Germany. Their nephew Jakob founded the firm out of which was to develop the famous Englehardt workshop – a name associated with the golden age of German wallpaper.

Jean-Baptiste Réveillon (1725-1811)

The artistic and political climate

It is well known that architects, painters and engravers in the eighteenth century were expected to make a voyage to Italy, to study at first hand the sources of European art, the archaeological discoveries of Pompeii and Herculaneum and the surviving Greek buildings at Paestum. At no other period did the past exert such influence on the arts and on political life. After the Revolution, French institutions were inspired by Ancient Rome – the Directoire, the Consulat, the Empire. In the arts, the new style, later to be called Neoclassical, was to embrace the decorative arts (wallpaper, textiles, furniture) as well as painting, from Panini to Hubert Robert and David, and, with Houdon, sculpture. Architecture and fashion were also affected: the style of clothes at the turn of the century was inspired by Greek, Etruscan and Roman models. Neoclassicism was a reaction against the baroque, which had ended in the lightweight rococo style, with its exaggerated asymmetry, curves and counter-curves, and scrolls. But the resulting return to an ancient purity, with its rigour and simplicity, did not exclude any elegance or grace of line. Rather, symmetry now confined the fluid arabesque, and the firm oval of a frame was bordered by a fine ribbon or a laurel wreath.

The Neoclassical movement began around 1750, when François de Marigny, the brother of Madame de Pompadour, was put in charge of royal buildings. He appointed Jacques-Germain Soufflot director of the Gobelins tapestry factory. After two tours in Italy Soufflot (1713-80) was to introduce the new style into architecture and the arts. The architect of the church of St Geneviève (now the Panthéon) in Paris, Soufflot formed a close friendship with Charles de Wailly, architect of the Odéon and friend of Hubert Robert. All these men developed their taste for the antique through a Rome revealed by the genius of Piranesi: 'Piranesi's giant vision took in all of Rome – Etruscan, Republican and Imperial . . . . In the succeeding decades, the number of sites portrayed in his engravings and the variety of his approach to the subject were to astonish Europe.' (Michel Gallet, 'Charles de Wailly, peintre architecte dans l'Europe des lumières', catalogue of an exhibition at the Hôtel de Sully, Paris, 1978.)

A number of talented craftsmen worked at the Gobelins factory, including Jean-Baptiste Huet (1761-1811), Joseph-Laurent Malaine (1745-1809), La Vallée-Poussin (1740-93), Cietti and Prieur. They and their contemporaries were to give the designs of wallpaper and textiles a basically antique flavour. The limits and ornamental vocabulary of this style were to be defined by numerous publications of 'Italian views'. In 1754, for example, Cochin and Bellicard published their views of Herculaneum. Huet specialised in panels decorated with vases, roundels, arabesques and rural scenes. La Vallée-Poussin published a suite of engravings of Roman scenes: *Nouvelles collections d'arabesques propres à la décoration des appartements*. Prieur published *Cahiers de sujets arabesques utiles aux artistes et aux élèves*, followed in 1783 by *Suites de frises et ornements*. We must add to the list Piranesi's own *Vasi, Cippi, Candelabri* of 1778 and Ponce's 1789 publication *Les arabesques des bains de Livie et de la villa Adrienne avec ses plafonds de la villa Madame*. Another direction was taken by Jean Pillement's (1727-1808) designs, published in England, which supplied the Lyons silk industry with endless Chinese subjects and designs of floral garlands and trelliswork. These were also widely used by the Gobelins factory.

Technical developments

In the second half of the eighteenth century a number of important technical developments made possible the production of wallpaper on an industrial scale. Most of these developments, which freed the paper maker from the constraints of the *dominotier*, came originally from England. Réveillon adopted them at once, whereas Papillon had not. One idea from England, that of pasting the sheets together into a roll before printing them, had an important effect. The 27-foot (8.2-metre) roll of paper freed the design from the format of the single sheet, and so designs with several repeated motifs began to be replaced with complete wall-high panels.

In about 1760 wallpaper makers began using the printing method developed for Indian textiles. The paper was printed from a block placed on top of it, and the design transferred by taps from a mallet. This method was necessitated by the length of the rolls, which were laid out on long tables; the numerous blocks for the colours had to be registered precisely.

Another major change in printing was the introduction of water-based or distemper colours, which changed the appearance of wallpapers completely. The base coats would be painted in by hand before printing. Distempers, which dry quickly because of their water base, created a rich and solid matte background. Greater variety and subtlety of colours, as in fresco painting, began to be possible.

Social and economic change

We find the first industrial systems of the eighteenth century in those manufacturing systems where the division of tasks allowed for the faster and better achievement of the finished product. Each worker became a specialist, and different phases of production were more strictly controlled, so that output increased. Réveillon, with characteristic acumen, made the most he could of this system, though he thereby hastened the destruction of the craft tradition. The family workshops of Papillon and the other *dominotiers*, where the engraving, printing and hanging were all done by the same workers, were to last for only a few more years.

By 1789 Jean-Baptiste Réveillon was in charge of an enterprise employing three hundred people (excluding children), who were divided into four groups: the engravers, designers and painters, the printers and tinters, the paper-hangers, and the porters, packers and colour grinders. Two chemists were in charge of preparing the colours and inks. The annual salary bill came to 200,000 *livres*. In addition to this Réveillon owned his own paper-making business.

He was well aware that his success depended on the skills of his designers, engravers and printers. We do not know whether he actually employed designers from the Gobelins factory, or if he only had their designs copied (copyright being unheard of at the time). He was certainly in touch with the best designers, and he did have his superb engravers make copies of designs for chintzes and decorative sculptures and reliefs. When they came to be printed, the designs prepared by his designers would be transferred onto woodblocks by the wood-engravers.

By organizing the manufacture of wallpaper into a unified process, where the work was divided into simple, repeated tasks, Réveillon created a modern system, an early example of a production line. His system anticipated nineteenth-century factories in which machine power was to increase output even further. Both the manufacturing process and the commercial aspects were kept within the business, so excluding middlemen. The fact that Réveillon's own firm manufactured the paper and the inks allowed closer control over quality and increased his returns. This control extended to the point of sale, as the showroom room was next door to the workshops. The whole enterprise was made possible by an extraordinary publicity campaign which was continuously being maintained. Thus Réveillon's own flamboyant character added to the reputation of his splendid wallpapers.

The rise and fall of Jean-Baptiste Réveillon

The life of Jean-Baptiste Réveillon was one long, slow but continual movement upwards, by means of patronage, intrigue and socializing. Forty years of courage and speculation (he writes ingenuously that he was always ready for effort and had a natural taste for taking risks) brought him to a pinnacle of glory from which the events of one single night were to topple him. This ordinary middle-class haberdasher became a person of historical importance by means of his innate business sense and flair for publicity. But he embodied a decaying system, and in the end preferred to withdraw completely rather than survive within it.

Réveillon was born in 1725 into a bourgeois family: the parish register describes his father as a *bourgeois de Paris* which suggests a reasonable standard of living. His handwriting and literary style further suggest that he was educated with some care. Despite what he said in his *Exposé justificatif* written in 1789, just after the riots, his childhood and early life were not unhappy (as nineteenth-century historians would have us believe). In 1741 he was apprenticed to a master haberdasher. Three years later he was working for M. Maroy, a haberdasher in the rue de la Harpe, where he and his mother lodged. Réveillon soon became indispensable to his employer, and in 1753 he bought the business, including the stock, the shop and the sign. This was financially a very worthwhile transaction. On 7 July 1754, he married Maroy's daughter, and her dowry of 8,000 *livres* cleared his debt. So he found himself a merchant, selling ink and pencils, irons and rackets and mirrors.

Réveillon did not, however, see a future as a shopkeeper giving him enough scope for his talent or ambitions. The fashion for English wallpaper gave him his chance: as we have seen, he was the first person to learn to hang it properly, and this ensured his immediate success. He became an importer and retailer of English wallpaper. Realis-

Landscape medallion set in a Pompeian-style panel. J.-B. Réveillon. French, late 18th century. DTM.

Neoclassical decoration. Design no. 191 of the Nicolas Dolfuss company. French, 1792. MISE.

ing that selling alone, though profitable, would not fulfil all his ambitions, he opened his own workshops. The first was at L'Aigle in the Orne district, a long way from Paris, so as to escape the attention of the card makers, *dominotiers* and copperplate engravers, who retained the exclusive right to make wallpapers. Even if he did not make a fortune, at least he would have a better reputation for quality than his contemporaries.

By the end of the 1750s the *dominotiers* began to lose their exclusive rights in the manufacture of wallpaper; as with all wall-coverings, manufacturing became freer and the specialists moved their shops to the faubourg St Antoine, near the furniture makers. In 1759, therefore, Réveillon set up his workshop in the rue de Charonne in Paris, with showrooms in the rue de l'Arbre Sec. Thanks to the patronage of the Lieutenant de Police Lenoir, Réveillon got the better of those *dominotiers* who were trying to retain their monopoly on wallpapers. To protect himself further, he bought himself into the guild of copperplate engravers and of the gilders and sculptors. Although to follow a profession, one was supposed to serve three years apprenticeship and then be elected a guild member, this system was often abused. Consequently money went into the State's coffers, but the crafts and trades fell into the hands of the wealthy.

The journey from his father-in-law's shop near the rue St Jacques to the showrooms in the rue de l'Arbre Sec was soon accomplished. The little bourgeois haberdasher had become an entrepreneur and merchant, whose wallpapers were very highly considered. As his workshops in the Marais were now too small, he leased in 1763 the outbuildings of the Folie Titon.

Titon du Tillet was an ostentatious financier, who had built a folly, a pavilion with outbuildings and charming gardens. For the interiors, Delafosse provided the paintings, Colignon the sculptures and Fontenay the ceilings. The five acres of gardens included a box-tree maze, an arbour, a quincunx with statuary, a kitchen garden, a garden in *parterres* with an orangery on one side, stables and offices. Near by were two other follies, the Folie Regnault and the Folie Méricourt.

Réveillon's business went well: he made India papers, papers with pastoral scenes and flowered papers of all kinds. In 1767 he became the proprietor of the Folie Titon – a master stroke of publicity, as it was a place that any person of quality in Paris would be expected to know, and its brilliant reputation could only add lustre to that of the notable wallpaper merchant. The huge and sumptuous workshops, where each day nearly four hundred people were employed, were open to the

Two panels with mythological figures, sphinx and garlands. J.-B. Réveillon. French, late 18th century. DTM.

Decorative panels with fountains, putti, flowers and garlands. J.-B. Réveillon. French, late 18th century. DTM.

Decorative panels. J.-B. Réveillon. French, late 18th century. DTM.

public and to visitors, and were recommended in guidebooks such as Thiéry's 1786 *Guide des amateurs et des étrangers voyageurs à Paris*.

To improve the supply of paper, both in quantity and quality, Réveillon bought a small paper mill at Courtalin. By a happy chance this brought him into contact with a talented young architect, the pupil and *protégé* of Soufflot, Etienne de Montgolfier, whom he employed in enlarging the mill. The business at Courtalin had been started by Etienne Delagarde in 1767, and when Réveillon bought it it was being run, somewhat shakily, by his widow. Réveillon made the younger of her two sons director, who after a visit to Holland became the best paper maker in Europe. Under his control, the mill produced the first wove paper, without wiremarks or irregularities.

The Folie Titon at the end of the 17th century. Engraving. Musée Carnavalet, Paris.

The business went from strength to strength. Réveillon gave up the shop in the rue de l'Arbre Sec in 1776 to move to showrooms in the rue du Carrousel, by the Tuileries. He became the most sought-after member of his profession, an arbiter of taste, although he sometimes suffered from legal problems. He was very anxious to get a royal warrant for his two products, the wallpaper he made in Paris and the white paper from Courtalin. His efforts were at last rewarded in 1783 and 1784. The *Mercure de France* carried this announcement in July 1784:

'His Majesty, in order to show his satisfaction at the progress achieved by Monsieur Réveillon in making plain papers and wallpapers, wishes to award him, in accordance with the *Arrêt du Conseil* of January 13th last, and under Letters Patent, the title of royal warrant holder. A stamp with the royal coat of arms and the words "Manufacture Royale" will in consequence be fixed to all the rolls of paper produced at the two factories. Monsieur Réveillon has royal permission to engrave, colour, print, paint, flock and sell wholesale or retail all sorts of paper, card, stuff, textile, leather or skin. Further, he may carry on his profession without let or hindrance from any guard, assignee, officer or member of any guild or corporation or artisans or tradesmen, whether or not he has been accepted as a member of such a guild or corporation.'

After this royal recognition, Réveillon was to bring himself to the attention of the highest in the kingdom, as well as to the intelligentsia and the masses, by literally putting up the largest wallpaper ever created. The Montgolfier brothers had been experimenting with balloons at Annonay, and on 12 September 1783 tried a first ascent in Paris, in the gardens of the Folie Titon but because of stormy weather the result was not a complete success. A second, and triumphant, attempt was made at Versailles a week later, in the presence of the King and the royal family and an audience of 100,000 people. This second balloon (which had been made in five days) was about seventy feet high, and carried the King's cypher and portrait, framed by a sun. But it was called *Le Réveillon*, and thus raised to the skies the name of the king of wallpaper. The sight of the balloon, with its gold and blue decoration, on twenty-four bands of painted paper fixed onto canvas, must have been splendid.

Montgolfier's enterprise would not have been possible without the technical achievement of Réveillon's workshops, which gained him an unparalleled reputation. He arranged a number of other ascents of his works at the Folie Titon. His name filled the newspapers and inspired popular art as well as fashionable songs. One would have thought that fame enough, but he also tried to get himself presented with the Necker gold medal. (This, together with a prize of 1,200 *livres*, was awarded annually to the inventor of a new process that enriched the art and industry of France.) Réveillon received the medal on 28 March 1786. He had applied for it in 1784 for his invention of wove paper, but Didot and Joseph de Montgolfier (Etienne's brother) paper makers at Vidalou-lès-Annonay, opposed him, claiming they had invented it earlier, and won. In 1785 the medal was not awarded, there being no invention of sufficient merit. So Réveillon got the medal he coveted, awarded perhaps for the sake of peace and quiet.

At the height of his fame, Réveillon could still surprise with his innate savoir-faire. So it was when the Hindustani ambassadors visited the famous factory and sumptuous house. They were surprised to read their names and titles, and the date of their visit, on a vignette Réveillon was printing. With a combination of style and delicacy, their gracious host had had the engraving done in Arabic characters.

His success caused much jealousy, and made him enemies. The social order he represented was beginning to collapse. Like many men who have risen to wealth and power from humble origins, Réveillon was hard on his subordinates (for example he dealt harshly with a strike at the Courtalin factory in 1775), though his severity was masked by a thin veneer of paternalism. In November 1789 he set up a fund for his workers who suffered loss through illness or redundancy. But this measure seems to have been dictated by the pressure of events rather than by any spontaneous sense of philanthropy.

The year 1789 was hard for the people of Paris. Cold weather and famine put 80,00 unemployed out onto the streets. Réveillon had been elected to the preliminary assembly for convoking the Etats Généraux on 27 April, but he seems to have had little concern for the claims and accusations expressed there. He was, however, unaware of the explosion that was to occur that very day. A group of demonstrators marched to his factory, shouting 'Death to Réveillon' and throwing mud and dirt all over the façade. Troops were protecting the factory, so the rioters looted the house of Henriot, a colleague and friend of Réveillon. The following day, workers from the district swelled the number of rioters to an angry three thousand. They marched on the Folie Titon and sacked it, burning the furniture, paintings and drawings, although the factory suffered little. The Revolution had begun. The rioters destroyed the main house, and broke doors and windows in the factory, though the plant remained intact. The gardens were ruined, the statues destroyed, the wine cellar looted, the works of art burnt. Even the famous gold medal was stolen. The French guards, helped by Swiss guards, tried to put a stop to the riot by firing running volleys to clear the streets, and ending with bayonet charges. Over three hundred rioters were killed.

An extract from the *Journal d'une femme de cinquante ans* kept by the Marquise de la Tour du Pin, describes these events: 'In the spring of 1789 there were horse races held at Vincennes, the Duc d'Orléans racing his mounts against those of the Comte d'Artois. Returning from the last of these races with Madame de Valence in her carriage, we were passing the rue St Antoine when we found ourselves in the middle of the first popular gathering of the period: the mob that destroyed the wallpaper factory of that respectable merchant, Monsieur Réveillon. Only long afterwards did I learn the reason for this riot, which had been incited by money.

'As we made our way through the group of four or five hundred blocking the street, they noticed the Orléans livery Madame de Valence's servants were wearing, her husband being first equerry to the Duc d'Orléans. This roused their enthusiasm, and they stopped us and shouted "Long live our father, long live the Duc d'Orléans". I paid little attention to the shouts, but I remembered them some months later, when I had learnt more about the unfortunate Duc's schemes.

'The popular uprising which ruined Réveillon had been organised, I have no doubt, to bring about the downfall of this excellent man, who employed three or four hundred workers himself and created a great deal of business for the faubourg St Antoine. This is his story as he told it to me.

'When he was young, he was working, I don't recall in what trade, in the faubourg, where he has always worked. One day, coming home after work, he met the father of a poor family, a worker like him, who was being taken to prison for non-payment of the *mois de nourrice*. This man was desperate at having to leave his family to face even worse poverty in his absence. Convinced that Providence had arranged the meeting, Réveillon ran to the nearest *brocanteur*, sold his tools, his clothes, all he had and paid the man's debts, so the father could rejoin his family. From that moment, he told me, his success began: "I have made my fortune, I have four hundred working for me, and can dispense charity with ease."

'He was a straightforward and fair man, loved by his workers. Since the evening of that terrible day when his machines, his stock and his shops were burnt and destroyed, I do not know what has become of him.'

In fact, Réveillon sought protection and support among those he had served, and who had helped him – the Crown and the police. He sought shelter in the Bastille as a voluntary inmate. But the warning shot did not rouse him to action. Unable to face the ruin of his reputation, he quit public life completely: correspondence was his only contact.

Réveillon let out the factory and the outbuildings in 1791, though he sold the plant. The only other step he took was to claim, with his usual perseverance, another gold medal to replace the one that had been stolen from him during the riot. In 1792 the Assemblée Nationale agreed to his request: 'Decree of the Assembly, 14th May 1792, being the fourth year of freedom, that this medal be given to J.-B. Réveillon, as a replacement for the inventor's prize he had received from the Crown in 1786, for his service to the art of paper-making, which prize medal was stolen from him during the looting of his home, on 28th April 1789.'

Réveillon lived quietly with his wife in their rooms in the rue des Bons-Enfants. He had witnessed the end of the Ancien Régime and was to see also the Directoire, the Consulat and the beginning of the Empire: he died on 17 September 1811.

Figure framed by a garland of flowers. J.-B. Réveillon. French, 1785. DTM.

Falconry. Designed by J.-B. Réveillon and printed by Jacquemart and Bénard. French, 1795. DTM.

Trophy, ribbons, garlands and birds. J.-B. Réveillon. French, late 18th century. Follot coll.

Rustic scene in grisaille surrounded by garlands. J.-B. Réveillon. French, c. 1780. Follot coll.

The importance of Réveillon's work

Paradoxically, no actual invention can be put down to Réveillon himself: he was never an artist like Papillon, for example. But even if he never wielded the burin or the brush or operated a press himself, he did know how to bring together the best designers and technicians of his age. It is therefore quite right that the papers from his workshops should bear his name. Because of his taste, and his reputation, he was able to make wallpaper an integral element in interior decoration, with the same status as tapestry, upholstery or leather. After Réveillon, wallpaper was used for itself, not as an imitation of something else, as it had previously been.

The originality of Réveillon's works is equalled by their beauty. He may have made free with other people's technical innovation such as paper in rolls, tempera printing, block printing and wove paper: the number of accusations made against him of infringing others' rights is most telling. But all such techniques he rapidly improved to a level of perfection: his paper was solid and strong, the printing clean and the colours fixed. Réveillon also owed much to the sureness of his taste: his flocked papers are among the most beautiful ever produced in France. He also made perfect imitations of textiles from Nantes, and Alsace, and *toiles de Jouy*, as well as copies of Indian cottons and Lyons silk. His panels with arabesques and foliage, taken from classical models, were a splendid innovation. The large and elegant designs, printed on a clear background colour (pale green, corn yellow, sky blue or soft pink, for example), could be over six feet long. Some of these designs needed up to twenty-four different blocks, and were of a quality and subtlety of engraving rarely surpassed.

These masterpieces may in some cases dazzle us with their technical virtuosity, by their decorative abundance and by their brilliant colours. But imagine a whole room decorated with such flamboyance; the excess of ornament would create a certain sense of unease. Even the best possible floral designs, impeccable arabesques and superb *grisaille* do not, together, make up a perfect design. One of the limitations of Réveillon's work is that it has so many varied sources of inspiration.

Just as Réveillon's fame eclipsed the achievements of his predecessors, so it has overshadowed the excellent work done by his contemporaries and competitors. From a modern viewpoint, it is quite clear that he was not the only wallpaper maker in late eighteenth-century France, but his talent, his exciting life and his sucess have made him the best known. History, however, had its revenge: most of Réveillon's fortune was in *assignats* issued by the governments of the Revolution, later seriously devalued. The paper they were printed on was made at Courtalin.

After the Revolution

Official wallpaper

It is of course difficult to calculate with precision the effect Réveillon had on other paper makers in Paris, though there is no doubt that he was a powerful influence on his contemporaries. There were about fifty workshops in Paris at the time, on which information is scanty. While their names and addresses can be found in contemporary directories, it is not possible to differentiate between manufacturers and merchants.

On the principle that the best must be made by the best, arabesque papers of good quality that do not have a maker's mark are most often attributed to Réveillon. But the only definite method of attribution is by consulting the maker's stamps fixed to the back of papers, or the samples of each paper which were by law deposited with the Tribunal de Commerce. All these officially deposited papers are kept in the print room of the Bibliothèque Nationale in Paris, but have at present been withdrawn from view, in order to restore them and make microfiche copies. It will not be possible to see the collection for some considerable time, and even the authors of this book were not able to photograph it.

While the shock of the French Revolution did not interrupt the production of wallpapers in traditional styles, it did create a new theme, that of the Revolution itself. The Phrygian cap and the red, white and blue cockade were added to the iconography of wallpaper, which thereby became a form of propaganda. One of the many reasons why the new rulers of France wanted wallpaper to their taste was the number of new offices that had to be quickly redecorated: the rooms for the Assemblée, the Committee of Public Safety, the tribunals, administrative departments and ministries of the Revolution.

Wallpaper makers in Paris were equipped to put new designs into production quickly at little extra expense. The required subjects were liberty and equality and the struggle against enemies of the constitution, both within and without. As ever, the ancient world provided the model. 'The traditions of every dead generation bear down upon the spirits of the living', wrote Karl Marx in *The 18th Brumaire of Louis Bonaparte* 'and even when the living seem to be trying to change themselves and the world, and to create anew, that is to say in exactly such revolutionary periods, that the living, like cowards, look back to the past, whence they borrow titles, words of command and even costumes, so as to appear on the stage of history disguised by the past, and with familiar lines . . . So it was with the Revolution from 1789

Apotheosis of a military hero in the year IX of the Revolution. Jacquemart and Bénard. French. BN.

Revolutionary paper with republican symbols framed by tricolour ribbons, and wreaths. French, late 18th century. Musée Carnavalet, Paris.

Trophy with cockerel. Imitation bas-relief medallion designed by Evariste Fragonard for Jacquemart and Bénard. French, 1800-10. Bibliothèque Forney, Paris.

Liberté, Egalité. *Revolutionary paper of about 1792, reprinted by stencil in 1935 for the Café Procope and in silkscreen in 1975 by Nobilis. Musée Carnavalet, Paris.*

Frieze with a landscape medallion in the style of Joseph Vernet. French, early 19th century. Bibliothèque Forney, Paris.

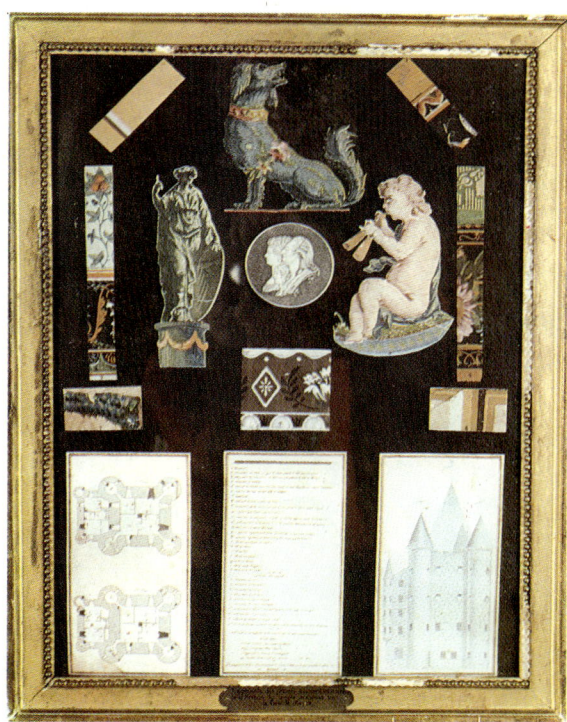

Fragments of paper from the Temple prison in Paris. French, late 18th century. Musée Carnavalet, Paris.

Frieze with a trophy. Dufour. French, c. 1800. Bibliothèque Forney, Paris.

Death to Tyranny. *Revolutionary paper in three colours and imitation bronze on a blue ground. French, c. 1792. Musée des Arts Décoratifs, Paris.*

Mortuary decoration in sepia on black. French, late 18th century. Follot coll.

to 1814, which wore first the costume of the Roman Republic and then that of the Roman Empire.'

So the classical world was the source for the Lictor's trophies, for the axes and rods, for the images of Brutus bringing down tyranny, for Liberty in a Greek cap and for the tablets engraved with the rights of man. *Grisaille* papers imitated Greek and Roman bas-reliefs. Gone were the refined pastel shades of the past: the colours for the new subject-matter were bold, as a reminder of the manly and martial nature of the times. Thus wallpaper became the mouthpiece of the Revolution, used for the first time in the service of an ideology. For the first time also, wallpaper was used to decorate municipal and public buildings. This new development increased the popularity of wallpaper considerably, and started a tradition that was to continue for many decades. Important national events were henceforth to be commemorated by new wallpaper designs.

While the new leaders of France were establishing their authority, the ordinary citizen continued to buy papers in the old styles, with designs of flowers, chintzes and arabesques. Flock and Chinese papers were still being made. The official iconography could hardly be used in private homes, but the adoption of wallpaper in public buildings did have an effect. Wallpaper was no longer the poor relation of other decorative materials, but had a role of its own. The Revolution was of value to both the manufacturing and retailing sides of wallpaper. The number of businesses grew from fifty in 1789 to sixty-seven in 1803 and to ninety-six by 1811.

Jacquemart and Bénard

What a splendid association of names! Pierre Jacquemart lived in the magnificent *hôtel* built by Jabach,[1] where he ran a drapery business. The *chevalier* Eugène Balthasar Crescent Bénard de Moussinières was head of the legal department in the Hôtel des Fermes and a member of the Comité de la Révolution, which gave him access to orders placed by the republican administration. The two of them borrowed 500,000 *livres* with which to buy Réveillon's business: given the size of the acquisition the price was not unreasonably high.

What had been the royal manufacturer now became the republican one. Jacquemart and Bénard had a virtual monopoly on official orders, not only for decorating the new offices of the Revolution but also for redecorating the town houses of the departed nobility, now taken over for public use. The factory at the Folie Titon employed two designers, who were responsible for creating an annual collection of new designs, and an architect

Overdoor. Bowl of fruit on a marble base designed by J.-L. Malaine for Hartmann Riesler. French, before 1802. MISE.

Design for a wallpaper that was produced by Jacquemart and Bénard in 1798. Musée des Arts Décoratifs, Paris.

Overdoor. Rustic landscapes framed with laurels and musical emblems. French, c. 1785. Follot coll.

Chinoiserie paper. Designed by Pillement for J.-B. Réveillon. French, 1780. Follot coll.

Overdoor. Parrots, flowers and fruit in a wicker basket on a blue ground. Designed by J.-L. Malaine for Zuber. French, 1795. DTM.

The Three Graces. *Decorative panel by Zuber. French, 1803. Zuber coll.*

who planned the decorations for public spectacles in Paris and in the provinces. The staff also included seventy children, aged between eight and fourteen.

The business seems to have been in financial difficulties in 1799, but was able to put its affairs in order, probably thanks to a number of private commissions, which compensated for the lack of public ones. A contemporary report confirms the beauty of the papers produced, which imitated perfectly the design and appearance of all sorts of textiles, from brocades to fine linens. In 1800 the firm took out a patent for the manufacture of a cambric lawn paper, but the patent was later contested by Chenevard and Pernon in Lyons, who had already been using the technique for two years, and also by Hartmann Riesler in Alsace and other manufacturers in Paris. Jacquemart and Bénard completely mastered architectural and sculptural effects, and those imitating the grain of woods such as mahogany and bur-walnut.

With the Consulat, business improved: the pace of economic life quickened, supported by the Peace of Amiens in 1802 which made export sales possible once more. The factory became bigger, in response to the continuing flow of official orders. Fashions also changed with the times: the Egyptian style was now in vogue, adorned with the trophies of victory. When the Empire succeeded the Consulat, Jacquemart's son and Bénard produced a flock paper with the Emperor's portrait framed by the symbols of imperial power. The cockades and cockerels were replaced by bees, all rather heavily gilded. The new imperial palaces at Fontainebleau, St Cloud and Rambouillet were also sources for valuable orders. Once when Napoleon was visiting Fontainebleau to inspect the work of decoration, he thought he saw a wall covered in fine silk, and was astonished to find it was a paper by Jacquemart. At the height of his anger, in front of the architect responsible for the work, Leroy, the Emperor shouted 'I have the means to pay, surely!' Nonetheless Jacquemart got the commission to decorate the rooms made ready for Princess Marie-Louise's arrival in 1810.

Not surprisingly, the end of the Empire put the business into difficulties, but it revived with the Restauration. Louis XVIII's coat of arms is found on Jacquemart's paper, and he was responsible for the decorations at the coronation of Charles X. The firm continued until the reign of Louis-Philippe, finally closing in 1840. It had been the offical supplier of four kings, one republic and one empire, a record of considerable economic and political enterprise. On the creative level, the firm preserved the artistic inheritance of the eighteenth century, adding to it new decorative ideas. The *grisailles* and gilded designs were an innovation, as were flocking and distemper printing. The firm tried to rival the huge sheets made by Dufour and Leroy and by Zuber. But these younger competitors, and the development of a wider market and new techniques, were to have a fatal effect. With the end of Jacquemart, the last of the grand old men of wallpaper disappeared.

Arthur and Robert

The firm of Arthur, established in 1772 on the quai Conti in Paris, is reckoned one of the capital's oldest and most important. Arthur later linked his business to that of Grenard, moving the workshops to the Chaussé-d'Antin where, by 1784, they were employing two hundred workmen. Their fame can be judged by the fact that all the guidebooks insisted that the factory be visited (though first place went of course to Réveillon). The novelty lay in the arrangement of the factory: the different workshops for block making, painting, gilding and printing were on separate floors, not in a continuous single storey as before. It is also possible that the firm had a room set aside as a showroom for their collection. There one would have found papers imitating 'fabric embroidered with flowers' (according to Mrs Cradock's *Voyage in France 1783-1786*) or sculpture in *trompe l'oeil*, architectural details, gilt or panelled wainscots, floral panels and arabesques on a white ground. Arthur's work can be distinguished from Réveillon's by its splendid handling of monochrome subjects, often introduced into huge architectural compositions and multicoloured panels of flowers, which were specially attractive. Here we can detect the hand of Malaine, who was a flower painter for the Gobelins and later chief designer for Zuber. The delicacy of his designs shows how skilled the engravers were, especially as all the blocks would have to be cut from hardwoods.

In about 1789 Arthur's son Jean-Jacques took over the business; Grenard retired and his place was taken by the paper merchant François Robert. Despite the factory in the rue Louis-le-Grand holding a royal commission, young Arthur became a dedicated revolutionary and a fervent Jacobin. As the commissar for the Temple, where Louis XVI was imprisoned in 1792, he had an important function in Robespierre's hierarchy, and when 'the Incorruptible' fell to the guillotine, Arthur was soon to follow. The Revolution did not spare many wallpaper makers: Arthur, Grenard, Cietti, Guérin (a former associate of Réveillon), all members of the Commune, died on the scaffold. The papermen Jean-Démosthène Dugourc and Etienne Anisson-Dupéron published the following announcement: 'Genuine republican wallpaper, made from original designs and suitable for administrative offices, public buildings and private rooms, is available from the "Manufacture républicaine", Hôtel

Hoche. *Jacquemart and Bénard. French, c. 1798. DTM.*

Frieze of putti. Grisaille on black with blue and white border. Late 18th century. Follot coll.

Frieze with fountain and swans. Jacquemart and Bénard. French, 1812. Follot coll.

Imitation earthenware tiles. Blue cameos on a white ground. Late 18th century. Follot coll.

Allegorical figure in Greek dress. Grisaille on a brown ground. One of a series of mythological subjects by Arthur and Robert. French, c. 1788. Follot coll.

Trompe-l'oeil paper. French manufacture, before 1800. Bibliothèque Forney, Paris.

The Centaur. Grisaille on a brown ground. Arthur and Robert. French, 1788. Follot coll.

Longueville, place du Carrousel. Ask for Citizen Dugourc'. Even so Anisson-Dupéron, a former director of the royal printing works and the son of a family of booksellers and printers, was executed, which led Dugourc to announce in the March 1793 *Journal de Paris*: 'Would our fellow citizens please note that our new manufacture of republican playing cards does not make wallpaper of any sort and there is no connection between us and the workshop at the Hôtel Longueville, place du Carrousel . . .' To keep one's head, one had to forget one's colleagues.

Robert carried on the business alone, opening a shop in the place Vendôme. The firm was still active up to 1804. What is noticeable in Arthur and Robert's work is the development of engraved work. Their large monochrome pieces, whether panels or screens or overdoors, led directly to wallpaper's most special achievement: the panoramic paper.

Panoramic or landscape wallpapers

After the succession of technical achievements that marked the eighteenth century, Réveillon's flamboyant work and the Revolutionary papers, wallpaper underwent a final transformation as the medium for a new genre of decorative art. It became panoramic.

Until now it has been claimed that panoramic papers were developed as a result of two other discoveries, of which much was made in late eighteenth-century Paris: the 'panoramas' in the boulevard Montmartre, and the spectacles created by Carmontelle. In fact, panoramic papers were produced before either of these famous inventions, though the inspiration for them all lay in illustrating the great literary and intellectual movement which painting was to emulate.

It was in the early nineteenth century that the word 'panorama' was first adopted by experts on wallpapers, and it has since become the accepted term. However, in view of the fact that we now know panoramic papers to have existed before the 'panoramas', we consider that a more suitable term might be 'landscape papers'.

The panoramic paper originated in British topographical drawing and painting of the eighteenth century, and its development makes a fascinating story.[2] Early examples were sketched or painted onto flat surfaces, but it was Robert Barker (1739-1806), an Irish portrait-painter living in Edinburgh, who first conceived the idea of painting on a cylindrical surface when he produced a view of the entire city from Carlton Hill. Patented in 1787, the large circular painting was exhibited in Edinburgh and in London at 28, Haymarket. Barker's next

Chinese panorama. Printed in sepia. Attributed to Desfossé, and perhaps after an Oberkampf toile de Jouy design. 1815. DTM.

Detail.

panoramic work was *London from Albion Mills, Southwark*, exhibited in the capital from 1792. Other artists were attracted to panoramic painting: in 1799 Robert Fulton, the American painter and inventor, acquired an import licence to introduce Paris to this new fashion. The licence was passed on to another American, who opened two rotundas in 1801 near the boulevard Montmartre. In one was a panorama showing the monuments of Paris and in the other the seige of Toulon. They proved to be popular attractions, and the French National Institute of Science and Art soon concluded that the panorama was useful and inventive and deserved encouragement.

Carmontelle's system, in which a large landscape was displayed by unrolling a transparent frieze in an optical viewer, was a development of older systems, such as the 'Catoptricon' developed by Johannis Zahn in 1685 and other seventeenth-century optical viewers of which so many instances have survived. The example described in the *Oculus Artificialis* at Erfurt is a hexagonal box divided by internal mirrors. The subjects are painted on the outer sides of the box, on ground glass, with peepholes to let in the light. The reflections of these subjects in the mirrors give the magical impression of filling the box. When the box is placed on a turntable, the spectator sees an imaginary landscape unfold before his eyes.

Louis Carrogis (1717-1806) who called himself Carmontelle, was a playwright, architect and landscape gardener. He was responsible for the Parc Monceau in Paris, a garden of illusions always in harmony with nature. He himself wrote (in his account of the Parc Monceau published in 1799) 'Nature changes with changes of place and season, so let us vary the setting, so that we forget where we are. Let us make a reality of what the most skilled painters only offer us in decoration – the choice of all seasons and all places.' Carmontelle's panoramas included views of Monceau, Raincy and of other Parisian gardens and parks.

The return to nature

This movement that grew in importance throughout the eighteenth century, culminating in Romanticism, had an effect on all the arts. The first signs of the movement can be found in Milton's *Paradise Lost* and, in France, in the Abbé Delille's translation of the recently discovered *Georgics* of Virgil, while Daniel Defoe's *Robinson Crusoe* is a later example. Jean-Jacques Rousseau, however, was the writer who made the theme his own, affirming his invincible belief in the excellence of nature. In *Julie ou La Nouvelle Héloïse* (Amsterdam, 1761) he wrote 'In that splendid solitude time as well as place have been brought together in a more than *human* magnificence.' This idea was developed in Berna-

The Festival of the King, at the Tuileries.
Jacquemart and Bénard. French, 1818. Carlhian coll.

The Grotto at Posillipo. *Overdoor after Piranesi. DTM.*

din de St Pierre's *Paul et Virginie* where an atmosphere of gentle melancholy tinged with exoticism suggests an escape from the world. This image of nature as peaceful and elegaic, wherein the only traces of man are the ruins of a gigantic architecture, can be seen as a major force in the paintings of Nicolas Poussin and Claude Lorraine. In the eighteenth century the taste for ruins was passed on by Piranesi to Hubert Robert, who brought these two strands together. Marguerite Yourcenar puts it that 'painters such as Pannini and engravers like the Bibiena family began before Piranesi or at the same time as him to construct these compositions in which real elements were subtly interwoven into a world of dreams.' (*Sous bénéfice d'inventaire*, Paris, 1962.) The pictorial aspects were to take on more important aspects. Hubert Robert was not the only painter to learn from the Italians that 'an architectural painter needs must be equally skilled in decoration, experienced in all aspects of design, as ready to dash off a *trompe l'oeil* perspective as to design a theatre set, lay out a garden or stage the whole decor for a court masque. For such an artist easel painting is a hobby: his preference is for a larger scope, be it decorating a gallery or a salon, or setting a series of imaginary landscapes in all their detail into a blank wall' (Lévèque, *L'univers d'Hubert Robert*, Screpel, Paris, 1979).

The earliest painted subjects that relate to panoramic wallpapers date from 1799, when the architect Louis Le Masson 'made a drawing, after nature, and to 15 *pieds* [just under 5 metres or 16 feet] in size, showing a general view of Rome and the Campagna, the Appenines and the sea. The view, taken from the terrace of San Pietro ai Monti, had been made in fifteen sections each at a different angle, so as to describe a complete circle. The original watercolour captures the effect of the setting sun, one of the splendours of Italy.' This close relation to the panoramic paper was made only twenty years before the opening of the spectacles in the boulevard Montmartre. This general view of Rome was very well received, as *L'Atheneum* tell us: 'on behalf of the King, the Comte d'Angevilliers, the governor of Rambouillet, asked for the picture to be painted by M. Robert in one of the two rotundas of the dairy.'

From these realistic views Hubert Robert was to develop fictitious panoramas, by placing together buildings or monuments that were in truth distant from each other both in space and time. He began his Roman views in 1777, and in 1785 was to paint the monuments of France, bringing together a number of physically distant elements into the imaginary landscape of a single canvas. But if the landscape was invented, the architecture was not.

At the 1788 Salon he exhibited a *View of Rome* and a *View of Paris*: each painting consisted of a gathering of the most famous monuments of each city. This reconstruction of urban topography was made possible by his skill as a designer: by reconstructing real sites he created imaginary landscapes.

The return to nature did not just influence pictures: it made itself felt in reality, with a fashion for gardens. The philosophy of the noble savage could achieve concrete form in a garden, and many cultured men were to plan them. In France, for example, there were the parks at Raincy and Monceau by Carmontelle, Bellanger's 1799 gardens at Bagatelle, the garden for the Marquis de Girardin at Ermenonville, Hubert Robert's own park at Méréville and Soufflot's *nymphaeum* at Chatou. Other examples are the 'wilderness' at Retz for M. de Monville and La Garenne Lemot at Clisson. This long series of gardens modelled on English landscape gardens and strewn with ruins replaced the splendid floral *parterres* with their exact geometrical patterning created by Le Nôtre and others. Such informal gardens in England showed an Italian influence, but in France they went by the name of 'jardins à l'anglaise'. Elsewhere in Europe they were called 'natural gardens'.

Strolling players in a square in Burgos. Part of a wallcovering in sepia on yellow. Royal manufacture. 1828. DTM.

Landscape as decoration

It only remained to bring these landsapes of fancy indoors, actually into houses. This need was met by panoramic papers, which, like the earlier tapestries, filled wall space with a huge backcloth of garden and landscape (sometimes more than forty-five feet long). Writing in *Traverses 5-6* (Editions de Minuit, October 1976) on the subject of 'Gardens as opposed to Nature' ('Jardins contre nature') the critic Jurgis Baltrusaïtis gives us the key to this secret garden: 'It is the setting for an escape into the Arcadia of antiquity, or the paradise in the wilderness of the first members of mankind, it is the solitude of the theatre or the festival. Festivals ... show us to what extent it is a fairyland.' This fairytale quality is doubly present in panorama papers, which create the illusion of an illusion.

These landscapes in wallpaper represented a completely new conception of interior decoration. They used the complete extent of the walls, save where interrupted by vertical openings such as windows and doors, to create a continuous decoration. The last strip joined up with the first, so there was no chronology to the scene presented. The vertical interruptions allowed for some changes of setting – from groves of trees to buildings, for example – without breaking the rhythm or continuity of the whole ensemble.

The earliest designs included boldly painted scenes to increase the sense of depth, and carefully executed skies (Zuber's imperceptible gradations of colour made him the master of this effect) added to the impression of infinite space within two dimensions. Only exceptionally would such land-

Screen. Street scene at the time of the French Revolution. The far right panel is based on an engraving, The Arrival of the Replacements *(BN). The street musician (3rd from right) is based on a Boilly print. Before 1800. Carlhian coll.*

scapes show real places. One exception is Pignet and Paillard's 1852 subject *Paris-Rome-Londres* where each city is depicted from an adjoining wooded hill. This steep viewpoint creates an odd, almost Chinese, perspective.

More often than not, the space is completely redefined within each section of the whole. This organization of space was already in use at the end of the eighteenth century for screens, which were often decorated with printed landscapes. For example, a screen in the Carlhian Collection, which can be dated to the last decade of the eighteenth century, has a basic design of clouds with grass and rocks in the foreground, and this is found on each of the seven parts of the screen. The basic green tints are repeated for fore-, middle- and background, and the middle ground is divided into two sections, one for architecture and one for people. A landscape paper from the Directoire, called *The Garden of the Palais Royal* uses the same repetitive structure: the views are framed by arches of white flowers. The real and invented are here well mixed. The monumental door gives onto several sections of the famous public promenade of the Duc d'Orléans, but also included, perhaps for their 'strong allegorical and symbolic content', are all sorts of other constructions – trellises, obelisks and kiosks. The *Garden of the Palais Royal* would seem to be the first example of a landscape paper. It is printed in *grisaille* on a blue background, using both techniques simultaneously. An overdoor of 1786, attributed to Arthur and Robert, seems to have been designed in the same spirit. It shows a sphinx under a weeping willow, an island with an ancient temple, a watermill surrounded by poplars, a wooden bridge, a church in the Italian syle, a fortress (probably the Castel Sant Angelo, in Rome) on a rock, and a lighthouse. A shepherdess and her sheep, a drover, two fishermen, a traveller whose wife and child are perched on the back of a donkey, and a sailing boat in calm water complete the scene.

These three examples are fore-runners of landscape decoration. In the nineteenth century, two French manufacturers were to compete for the market of such papers: Jean Zuber from Rixheim in Alsace and Joseph Dufour at Mâcon. They produced work of equal quality, but quite differently designed and made.

The Zuber company

In 1790 the Dolfuss family business, an important manufacturer of Indian cloth at Mulhouse in Alsace, opened a wallpaper department. To help with this enterprise they had secured the services of J.-L. Malaine, an official painter at the Gobelins factory, who had worked with Arthur and Grenard. Himself an important designer, he was to pass this skill on to his young Alsatian pupils. Under his direction the business produced much admired work, with particularly fresh and bright colouring. The business also sold paper from Parisian makers, and from Ferrouillat (a Lyonnais) in Germany, and from Holland, Switzerland and Italy (see B. Jaqué, 'Les débuts de l'industrie du papier peint à Mulhouse, 1790-94' in *Revue d'Alsace*, no. 105, 1979).

Jean Zuber (1773-1835) began working for Dolfuss in 1791, then became his partner. The business took the new name 'Jean Zuber et Compagnie' in 1802. Zuber brought in the painter P.-A. Mongin, whose large watercolours, with strong blue tones, show elegant figures in courtly settings, combining actual sites with imaginary elements; poetic landscape was his speciality. Mongin was probably responsible for the *Bagatelle Gardens* as can be seen by comparing the large gouache of 1792 (formerly in the Cailleux Collection) and the four others from the sixth and seventh years of the Revolution, [3] which are a mixture of views from the Tuileries and Marly gardens. 'It seems that if the landscapist's original inspiration was Marly, he soon forsook his model... there are transpositions between the landscapes, mainly via Italian models.' (M. Mosser, 'Jardins de France', note 51 of exhibition catalogue.) These similarities are reinforced by looking at the work that Mongin did for Zuber, where the same poses, the same architectural elements, the same trees are repeated. A solution to the problem of dating and attribution lies in the decorative scheme, to our knowledge unique, which is conserved almost intact at the Château de la Ribeyre at Cournon in the Puy de Dôme. In one circular room is the *Bagatelle Gardens*, together with a vividly printed overdoor of mythological subjects (Orpheus playing his lyre, Hermes stealing cattle, and other figures). In the main salon the landscape of the *Town and Country Scenes* is linked to four overdoors from a *grisaille* series printed by Arthur and Grenard in 1785.[4] These *grisailles* were originally used in decorative panels framed with columns of false marble or floral towers by Malaine.[5] The landscapes and the overdoors are framed by large borders and matching friezes. Everything would suggest that the papers, *grisailles*, borders and friezes came from the same manufacturer. So one may conclude that the *Bagatelle Gardens* were printed by Arthur and Robert, between 1795 and 1802, at which date Mongin moved to work for Zuber, probably after an introduction from Malaine. This first version of an imaginary landscape can be seen as a test piece by Mongin, in the style he was to master. He always tried to include in his landscapes as many different aspects of nature as possible, and to maintain the poetic motif by making the figures as inconspicuous as he could.

Swiss Views. 16-sheet set designed by Mongin for Zuber. French, 1804. DTM.

In his *Swiss Views* of 1804, a sixteen-panel paper, Mongin rediscovered the picturesque and romantic qualities of Alpine scenery, already celebrated by the writings of Madame de Staël and described in contemporary guidebooks. Mongin created this fantastic garden on a grandiose scale from coloured reproductions: he had never been there himself. For his *Hindustan* of 1807 he used Thomas and William Daniell's *Oriental Sceneries,* redrawing them with the lakes and streams of European parkland. The flora and fauna and the costumes, real or invented, provided the exotic element. He went one better with his 1814 *Great Helvetia* for which he used a series of sketches taken during a trip to the Oberland in 1806: he noted that 'All the details have been drawn from studies taken from nature by the artist.' A description of *Italian Views* (1818) claimed that 'all the scenes and costumes are taken from the life': but the views show the most well-known ancient monuments peopled with figures taken directly from Pirelli's *Roman Scenes.*

Whatever the call of realism, the design of such landscapes made them into imagined ones. Mongin was also to display nature larger than life-size in his *Arcadia* (1811). This *grisaille* presents a happy and pleasing landscape, modelled on the epic style of V. Gessner's *Idylls,* and certainly the architectural details – temples, tombs, *tholi,* ruins — are found in reconstructions of antiquity. In 1821 he produced the twenty-five panels of the *Gardens of France,* a veritable catalogue of architecture and statuary from all periods in French history, placed in a setting dominated by water: fountains, jets and cascades, pools and streams are everywhere. This landscape is Mongin's greatest achievement, one in which he took the genre to its very limits. It was an unexpected success, and was frequently reprinted and amended. In 1836 the figures were redrawn, in 1849 the park became a Spanish one, peopled with 'Neo-Louis XIII Iberians'. The final flowering was in 1850, when the design was used as a background for *Telemachus.* 1825 saw Mongin's last major work, the six-panel *Distant Lands,* which contains no human figures, only a few trees – a poplar, a weeping willow, a pollarded plane tree against a background of pines – and two classical buildings as witnesses of man's passage. The choice of cameo tints gives an unreal effect, as of immortality: perhaps the artist's vision of a lost Eden?

Mongin's legacy was considerable. He left posterity an iconography suited to the medium, in that it was based on the use of repeated motifs, such as trees and architectural devices, which divided scenes while giving uniformity to the whole.[6] The *grisaille* paper *Views of Scotland,* for example, uses this technique: based on J.-M. Gué's sketches in

The Bagatelle Gardens. Designed by Mongin for Arthur and Robert. French, c. 1815. Carlhian coll.

108

A Hunt at Compiègne. *Panoramic paper by Jacquemart and Bénard. Carlhian coll.*

The Toilet of Venus. *Ceiling roundel by Dufour. Lithograph from the Maigret sales catalogue. Carlhian coll.*

Architectural details: portico, balustrade and garden. The same motifs are used in the Adventures of Aeneas. *Dufour and Leroy. French, 1820. DTM.*

The French in Egypt. *Panoramic paper designed by Deltil (the artist's signature is on the obelisk). Jacquemart and Bénard, French, 1816. Carlhian coll.*

Pair of overdoors. Arthur and Robert. French, c. 1786.
Follot coll.

Arcadia. *Design for a grisaille landscape paper by Mongin for Zuber (see opposite, below left). Ink and sepia wash on canvas-mounted paper. French, 1811. Zuber coll.*

Advertisement for Arcadia. *Zuber coll.*

Scotland, it illustrates Scott's poem *The Lady of the Lake* and has a Gothic *trompe-l'oeil* border and frieze as a frame. This is a very early example of the neo-Gothic style in wallpapers.

Deltil succeeded Mongin as Zuber's designer. His best-known works are the 1827 *Battles of the Greeks*[7] and his *Views of Brazil* (1829), both designed according to his predecessors' formula. There are also the *Views of North America* (1834) which formed the basis for the 1852 *War of American Independence*. Zuber produced another twenty-five landscape papers between 1804 and 1850, and so successful were they in the American market that for several years the firm had an agency over there. Even recently, when a set of *Views of North America* was found in an old house, it was re-installed, on Jacqueline Kennedy's initiative, in the Oval Room at the White House.

As the panoramic paper developed, the idea of depicting an organized garden became less central. Trees and flowers retained the interest of Zippelius, Ehrmann and Fuchs, new designers who in 1844 created *Isola Bella* and, in 1848, *Eldorado*. The latter is a technical *tour de force* printed in 192 colours from 1,554 woodblocks. It was a chef d'oeuvre of panoramic papers, but remained, probably because of the very high costs involved, unfinished (the first and last panels of the paper do not match up). The thirty-three panels that were designed would have needed 3,642 woodblocks. *Eden* was designed by Fuchs for Desfossé. It would have been the final triumph of an interest in nature that first came to the fore in the eighteenth and early nineteenth centuries, and portrayed nature as all-powerful, unrestrained and innocent of contact with man. This undiscovered and undiscoverable region is God's own garden, Eden before Adam and Eve.

The Dufour company

Zuber's greatest rival was Dufour, who published his first panoramic paper, *Sauvages de la mer Pacifique* in 1804.[8] This paper was designed by Jean-Gabriel Charvet (1750-1829) after engravings in eighteenth-century travel books. (That the natives

are wearing the flowing robes of the Consulat can be attributed to contemporary rules of decorum.) Though the design is divided by clumps of trees such as cottonwood and palm, as in the *Gardens of France*, the whole is not up to Mongin's standards of beauty, poetry and breadth of vision. The backgrounds are sketchy, the trees slight, and only the numerous and colourful figures create any hint of charm. But, as Joseph Dufour explained in an accompanying booklet, the wallpaper also had an educational purpose. 'We felt that it would be worthwhile to bring together into one convenient form this multitude of peoples separated from us by the expanse of oceans. Thereby a cultivated man, who has read the accounts of travellers and is aware of the history of exploration, on which our work is based, can, without even leaving his room, find himself in the presence of these people, and see their lives unfold around him . . . . So a mother can give her daughter living lessons in history and geography, teaching her to make better use of her education. And even the trees and flowers will serve as an introduction to botany . . .'

In 1806 Dufour showed this work at the Fourth Public Exhibition of Products of French Industry. The Jury's report commented that this wallpaper, whose subjects were derived from Captain Cook's voyages, was the most curious to have been produced in that medium. In France extravagant notions of the South Seas were influenced by Neoclassical fashions. After Cook's death in 1779 Joseph de Laborde built a Doric temple as a

Overdoor. Classical decoration and motifs in imitation of bas-relief. DTM.

The French Garden. *Panoramic paper in 25 sheets by Mongin for Zuber. French, 1821. DTM.*

Arcadia. *Lithograph from Zuber's sales catalogue. Designed by Mongin for Zuber. French, c. 1850. Zuber coll.*

The Battle of Austerlitz. *Panoramic paper in 30 sheets by Jourdan and Villard. French, c. 1814. Carlhian coll.*

Detail of The Battle of Austerlitz.

Eldorado. *Panoramic paper designed by Zippelius for Zuber. Detail. French, 1848. V&A.*

Grenadier after the Battle.
Overdoor. Zuber. French, 1823. DTM.

Eden. *Panoramic paper designed in 23 sheets by Fuchs for Desfossé and Karth. French, 1861. Carlhian coll.*

Right: Niagara, Seen from West Point, New York. Sheets 1-10 of Deltil's North American Views *(32 sheets in all). Lithograph from the Maigret sales catalogue. Zuber. French, 1834. Zuber coll.*

Below left: Famous Hunts. *Sheets 8-16, by Deltil for Zuber. French, 1831. Zuber coll.*

Below right: Icy Seas. *16 sheets from Ehrmann and Schuler's* Lands of the Earth *(31 sheets in all). Lithograph from the Maigret sales catalogue. Zuber coll.*

Ceiling paper with coffering. Lithograph from the Maigret sales catalogue. Desfossé. French. Carlhian coll.

Flore. *Decorative scheme. Lithograph from the Maigret sales catalogue. Desfossé. French. Carlhian coll.*

monument to him at Méréville. In his booklet Dufour's descriptions are laden wth classical references and in this respect compare with the ecstatic account of Tahiti given by De Bougainville, the explorer to whom he gives mention.

Dufour set up shop in Paris in 1808, in the rue Beauvau. He employed Xavier Mader, an excellent designer and skilled engraver, who was to make the business's reputation. He created the *Gateways of Athens* (1808), *Cupid and Psyche* (1816), a *Gallery of Mythology* (1824) and *Greek Festivals* (1824). These are all paper pictures in *grisaille* based on subjects in Greek mythology: in scale and format they are like panoramic papers. The best of them is undoubtedly *Cupid and Psyche*, which is based on La Fontaine's fable. The story of Psyche had also inspired pictures by Gérard and Prud'hon as well as sculptures by Canova and Pradier. The models for Mader's design were the works of Louis Laffitte (1770-1828) who won the Prix de Rome in 1791, was a draughtsman in the Cabinet du Roi and showed four *Psyche* subjects in the 1817 Salon, and Merry-Joseph Blondel (1781-1853) who had won the Prix de Rome in 1793. He was the official designer for Louis-Philippe's Palais de la Couronne and two sketches for *Psyche* are known by him.

Christophe Xavier Mader came from Nantes, where his family, originally from Alsace, were dyers. After creating for Dufour this splendid series of *grisailles*, he began in 1823 to work as his own master in the rue de Montreuil. He produced excellent flock papers, and died in 1830. His widow went into partnership with his former apprentice Delicourt, a successful venture which at one point had over 150 employees. Later Delicourt also became independent, and in 1838 Jules and Alexis Mader took over the business, which was sold to Desfossé in 1851.

Mader's achievement for Dufour was to redesign and expand the range of subjects, which finally numbered about 1,500. His excellent work bears witness to his study of modelling and effect. By the subtle use of sepia with white highlights, Mader was able to brighten the architecture, clarify the backgrounds and give life to the figures in his designs.

After Mader left Dufour, the business carried on producing panoramic papers. Jean Broc (1771-1850) was brought in as designer. He created a *grisaille* paper of *Paul et Virginie*, 'the work of that good man and cultured and sensitive author Bernadin de St Pierre'. This large-format paper of thirty sections, in cameo tints, is both graceful and interesting. The Dufour and Leroy catalogue for August 1824 asks 'What purer source could we draw on? The fine taste and exquisite style of the author has inspired our painter to the utmost in his task. The real character of the original is brought to you in our series of pictures, that recount the whole

Fragment of paper with a classical design by Mader for Dufour. French, 1825. Follot coll.

The Miser, M. de Pourceaugnac, Dandin.
Three panels by Mader illustrating scenes from Molière. Dufour. French, 1825. DTM.

The Toilet of Psyche. *From* Cupid and Psyche, *engraved in grisaille in 26 sheets by Mader, after the paintings of Louis Lafitte and Merry-Joseph Blondel. Dufour. French, 1816. DTM.*

Detail from a proof for Cupid and Psyche.

story of Paul and Virginie. The storm that is Virginie's doom is presented in wallpaper in a novel and magical way: the terrifying and desolate scene will pierce the heart of all who see it, and will win the admiration of artists and connoissseurs.' The sentimental and naturalistic quality of the novel is well conveyed by the rich flora and disturbed atmosphere of the paper, which follows the original narrative closely.

Two other series, probably by the same designer, soon followed: *Telemachus in Calypso's Isle* in twenty-five panels in colour, based on Fénelon, and *Antenor*, also in twenty-five panels, based on *Les Voyages d'Antenor en Grèce* by Etienne de Lantier (1734-1826). These delicately coloured compositions have all the charm of Italianate gardens, with architectural features such as colonnades, fountains and triumphal arches in a Mediterranean setting with wind-blown palm trees. *Rinaldo and Armida*, a coloured landscape in thirty sections designed in 1828 after Tasso's *Gerusalemme Liberata* and *The Incas* (1826) based on Marmontel's work both retell epic stories in imaginary settings. Once again we find European and foreign motifs confused. Tasso's crusaders wear costumes derived from Hellenism via the late baroque, and the Incas have come straight from the opera stage. But imagined landscapes can tolerate such inexactness, and be more of a vehicle for reverie by refusing strict fidelity to detail.

It is not certain who designed all these decorative schemes. Despite Clouzot's claim, Mader certainly did not do all the designs for the historical pieces, as we can tell from a note in the August 1824 catalogue: 'As we were going to press, we saw the circular issued by Messrs Mader and Vennet which contains an assertion that needs correction. They claim that *for a period of thirteen years* Mader was Dufour's only designer. Without going into unnecessary detail, we must point out that, quite the contrary, Mader was never *our sole designer*. Monsieur Mader has too much refinement and modesty to wish to claim for himself even indirectly credit for work that was not the result of his imagination or effort.'

Later, in their 1831 prospectus Dufour and Leroy announced that 'we would particularly wish to draw your attention to the suite of coloured papers that we are now putting on the market, entitled *Rinaldo and Armida*.... We were assisted in this vast undertaking by the hand of a skilled artist, whose remarkable talent has added to the interest of a subject itself already rich in interest.' Surely it could not have been this one 'skilled artist' who created the whole sequence, from the *Italian Views* (including the 'Bay of Naples') up to *Orlando Furioso?*

Two other sources of inspiration for panoramic papers must be mentioned. Firstly there are the views of towns, which are closer to Hubert Robert's groupings of monuments than to true panoramas. For example, in 1815 Dufour published his splendid *Buildings of Paris* which shows side by side along the Seine the churh of St Sulpice, Notre Dame, Les Invalides, the colonnade in the Place Vendôme, the Arc de Triomphe, the Porte St Denis and the Palais Royal. The spectator is imagined to be on the opposite bank, where there are some tall trees. The same effect of real buildings in the wrong setting is found in Félix Sauvignet's circular *View of the Quay at Lyons* where the town's splendid private houses and public buildings are ranged along the river.

Then a military fad came upon panoramic papers. Influenced by war artists such as Gros, Gérard and Guérin, as well as by the official painter of both Republic and Empire, Louis David, designers began to portray the most famous passages of arms, the glorious moments of the Napoleonic legend. The best example of the style is Jourdan and Villard's *Battle of Austerlitz* which recounts in thirty-six sheets his famous victory over the emperors of Russia and Austria. The same taste led Zuber to produce his *War of American Independence* (1850).

In this short overview of panoramic papers we have only looked at some of the products of the two largest manufacturers. There are in addition a large number of other panoramic papers where the manufacturer cannot be identified. This is proof of

Paul et Virgine *(detail). After Jean Broc. Dufour and Leroy. French, 1823. DTM.*

the real popularity of the style, not only in France but also in North America, where Nancy McClelland has catalogued over 120 examples. French panoramic papers were not well known in Britain even after the removal of long-standing trading restrictions in 1825. They were much admired at the Great Exhibition of 1851, and Zuber's productions in the 1862 International Exhibition in London were praised for their general effect and fine technique, but the jury considered them alien to the true purpose of wall hangings. By this date the impetus given to the production of patterned designs by printing machinery was too strong for such elaborate decorations to be the concern of manufacturers.

The greatest period in the manufacture of panoramic papers was the first three decades of the nineteenth century, which witnessed the appearance of Mongin's *Swiss Views* (Zuber), *Cupid and Psyche* by Mader (Dufour) and Jacquemart and Bénard's *Hunt at Compiègne* after the painting by Vernet. Otherwise production was mediocre. At

Boats at Anchor in the Bay of Naples. *Sheets 11-16 of Views of Italy. Panoramic paper in 33 sheets. Dufour and Leroy. French, c. 1823. Musée des Arts Décoratifs, Paris.*

the 1855 Exposition Universelle, a pair of large wallpaper schemes representing *The Vices and the Virtues* were shown, the one based on sculpture by Clésinger (1814-83) the other on paintings by Thomas Couture (1815-79). One critic said: 'Our wallpapers can only ever imitate, copying the texture of tapestry in paper and the effect of oil paint with wool: nature will not support such travesties. This catalogue of folly ends up with wallpaper versions of the paintings of Couture.' At the same event Desfossé received a silver medal for his *Armida's Garden* and made it clear that he thought wallpaper could bring works of art to a wider public: 'Someone looking seriously at the whole matter could not but be struck by the distance between my own real works of art and the similar everyday products of other factories. I do believe that in linking such figures in the fine arts as Messrs Couture, Clésinger and Muller to my industrial processes I have created a new means of progress for our industry, in which art already plays such an important part.'

In effect, mechanization stifled inspiration, and quality declined into dull mediocrity as the woodblock engravers themselves disappeared. At the same time, the imaginary landscape was dropped from the repertoire of wallpaper design. However, in 1973 the Zuber factory started a new development by inviting contemporary artists to design decorative schemes. This initiative may renew the originality of wallpaper. Although modern houses and flats, even the second homes that so many people have, are often too small for wallpaper suites of thirty sheets, the keen interest in a return to a simpler life, concern for the environment and for ecology, and the taste for craft work are all favourable conditions for a renaissance of imagined landscapes in wallpaper.

American wallpapers

The seventeenth-century colonists of America led such hard lives that they had neither the leisure nor the taste for elaborate decoration in the home. Puritan settlers would scorn any display of colour or ostentation even of the simplest kind. In 1639 the Rev. Thomas Allen of Charleston was summoned before a court to be reprimanded for painting his house a lively shade. However, simple limewash decoration was applied directly, by stencil, to wall surfaces, overmantels, or to boards built into panelling by the settlers themselves or by journeymen artists. As the colonial social systems were crystallized and money began to circulate, so a place for the skilled artisan was created and domestic comforts and pleasing furnishings were introduced.

The earliest wallpapers in America were from England and France and became very fashionable, as can be seen from contemporary accounts and documents. 'Painted papers' were mentioned in a 1700 post-mortem inventory of Michael Perry, a bookseller and stationer of Boston. David Henchman of the same town recorded in his accountbooks of 1712 to 1714 sales of painted papers in quires and by 1730 the bookseller John Phillip was advertising in the New England Journal his stock of 'stampt paper in rolls for to paper rooms'. From the

1730s up to the War of Independence imports were constant, bringing with them easily transported surface coatings of the latest European styles; chintz and Gothic patterns, flock and Chinese papers all crossed the Atlantic.

Colonists were known to place specific orders with suppliers in London. In 1738 Thomas Hancock of Boston wrote to the stationer, Thomas Rowe, enclosing a sample of *chinoiserie* wallpaper which was 'all that is left of a Room lately Come over here, and takes much in the Town and will be the only paper-hanging for sale wh. am of the opinion may answer very well. Therefore desire you by all means to get mine well Done and Cheap as Possible, and if they can make it more beautiful by adding more Birds flying here and there with some Landskips at the Bottom should like it well. About three or four years ago my friend Francis Wilkes, Esq. had a Hanging done in the same manner but much handsomer, sent over here by Mr. Sam Waldon of this place, made by one Dunbar in Aldermanbury, where no doubt he or his successors may be found.' (C.C. Oman, 'English Chinoiserie Wallpaper', *Country Life*, 11 February 1953.) Other colonists such as Robert Morris, the affluent banker of the Revolution, in 1770 went so far as to order Chinese papers direct from Canton.

Domestic manufactures can be said to have begun in 1739 when Plunkett Fleeson, an upholsterer originating from London and Dublin, issued papers from his shop at the Sign of the Easy Chair in Chestnut Street, Philadelphia. His advertisements appearing in the Pennsylvania *Gazette* up to 1783 described American papers which were low in price and not inferior to imports; gilded or coloured papier mâché or raised paper mouldings for hanging were included in his stocks. On 12 December 1765, the Boston *Newsletter* noted that at a meeting of the Society for Promoting Art, the New York manufacturer John Rugar had produced several patterns from his own large stock of paper hangings. Ten years later Ryres and Fletcher announced their new American paper-staining factory in Philadelphia, a town that was to become the centre of wallpaper production in the eighteenth century. By this date only a small number of factories were established, but manufacturers facing competition from foreign imports were determined to undersell them by up to 20 per cent, offering home-produced papers of comparable quality, and in some cases more durable and better suited to the American climate.

Joseph Dickenson of Vine Street, Philadelphia, mentioned in 1786 in the *Independent Gazetteer* that 'flies and smoke operate to soil paper in common rooms if the goods are too delicate, to prevent which I have pin grounds that fly marks will not be perceptible upon and dark grounds which smoke will not considerably effect.' Dickenson could show

The Pleasures of Hunting and Fishing.
30 sheets in grisaille after Carle Vernet. French, c. 1820. P. des Ligneris coll.

a patriotic and forceful style of advertising as in the Pennsylvania *Packet* in 1787. His papers were cheaper than imports and 'notwithstanding some falacious reports propagated by foes to this country that paper cannot be made equal to European, I am determined to prove the contrary and am willing to show colour for colour, paper for paper cheaper than can be imported from any part of Europe.'

Whatever the growth of native wallpaper manufacture, it did not at this stage pose any threat to imports. This report on commerce with Europe appeared in Brissot de Warville's *Nouveau voyage dans les Etats Unis de l'Amérique*, published in Paris in 1788, the year of his visit, and in New York in 1795.[9] Wallpaper was in universal use, giving 'a neat and agreeable appearance to dwellings' but rag paper was very expensive, the best production being confined to Pennsylvania at that time.[10] Lord Sheffield made a similar study and published his observations in Philadelphia in 1791. He reported that forty-eight paper-mills were operating in Pennsylvania, that the printing of books had in-

Panoramic Wallpapers   1. General Themes

Date	Maker	Title and notes
1790-1800	Arthur and Robert	*The Bagatelle Gardens* (first version, for overdoor).
	Unknown	*Garden of the Palais Royal*.
1797-1800	Arthur and Robert	*Town and Country Scenes* (an example can be found in the USA).
1804	Zuber	*Swiss Views* (designed by Mongin: 16 sheets in 95 colours from 1,024 blocks).
1804	Dufour (Mâcon)	*Natives of the Pacific* (designed by J.-G. Charvet. 'Based on the discoveries made by Captain Cook, de La Perouse and other travellers, and comprising a coloured landscape printed onto 20 sheets').
1806	Zuber	*Hindustan* (designed by Mongin and based on Thomas and William Daniell's *Oriental Scenery*, London, 1795-1808).
1808	Dufour	*The Gateways of Athens* (grisaille paper in 16 sheets).
1811	Zuber	*Arcadia* (designed by Mongin and based on Gessner's *Idylls*, grisaille paper in 20 sheets).
1813-14	Zuber	*Swiss Views* (designed by Mongin from sketches on the spot; the later engravings were used also for *William Tell*).
1814	Jacquemart and Bénard	*The Hunt at Compiègne* (in colour, after Vernet).
1815	Unknown	*Chinese landscape* (sepia monochrome paper in 20 sheets, after a *toile de Jouy* by Oberkampf).
c. 1818	Unknown	*The Seasons* (grisaille paper in 16 sheets, now in the Museum of Fine Arts, Boston).
1818	Zuber	*Italian Views* (designed by Mongin in 20 sheets).
1818	Zuber	*Antique Monuments* (including Roman scenes after Pirelli).
1818	Jacquemart and Bénard	*The Festival of the King at the Tuileries* (In colour, after Boilly).
c. 1820	Unknown	*The Hunt* (grisaille paper in 30 sheets, after Vernet).
1821	Zuber	*The Gardens of France* (designed by Mongin in colours on 25 sheets; in 1836 the designs were used for *Characters in the Style of the Day*, in 1849 for *Spanish Garden*, and in 1850 for *Telemachus*).
1823	Dufour	*Paul et Virginie* (designed by Jean Broc and based on the novel by Bernadin de St Pierre, grisaille paper in 25 sheets).
1823	Dufour	*Italian Views* (grisaille paper in 33 sheets, heightened with body colour, showing Amalfi, Tivoli, the eruption of Vesuvius and the Bay of Naples, which was also the subject of Prévost's panorama at the Boulevard de Montmartre).
1820-5	Unknown	*Venetian Scenes* (or *The River Banks*) (grisaille and sepia paper, after Vernet).
1823	Dufour	*Telemachus in Calypso's Isle* (25 sheets in 85 colours from 2,027 blocks, and based on Fénelon).
1825	Zuber	*Distant Lands* (designed by Mongin in 6 sheets: versions in grey, yellow and sepia – the last without the figures).
1825	Jacquemart and Bénard	*The French Landscape* (designed by Hippolyte Lecomte, in colour).
1826	Dufour	*The Incas* (30 sheets in colour, based on Marmontel).
1827	Zuber	*Scottish Views* (grisaille paper in 32 sheets, after J.-M. Gué's sketches and Sir Walter Scott's *Lady of the Lake*).
1827	Dufour and Leroy	*Antenor* (25 sheets in colour, based on Etienne de Lantier's 1797 *Voyage d'Anténor en Grèce et en Asie*, 1797).
1828	Dufour	*Rinaldo and Armida* (30 sheets in 71 colours from 2,386 blocks, based on Tasso's *Gerusalemme liberata*).

1829	Zuber	*Views of Brazil* (designed by Deltil in 30 coloured sheets, after Eugène Ehrmann's lithographs for M. Rugendas's *Voyages pittoresques*. In 1848, the designs were used for a *Conquest of Mexico*, with handpainted figures in the background).
1829	Dufour and Leroy	*On the Banks of the Bosphorus* (25 sheets in colour).
1831	Zuber	*Landscape with Hunters* (designed by Deltil, in colour).
1832	Zuber	*Chinese Design* (designed by Zippelius, 10 sheets in colour).
1832	Unknown	*Orlando Furioso* (based on Ariosto).
1834	Zuber	*North American Views* (32 sheets in colour: used in 1852 for *War of American Independence*, in 223 colours from 1,690 blocks).
1837	Zuber	*Horse Races* (designed in colour by Deltil, 'just the right decoration for a country house').
1840	Lapeyre and Drouard, (successors to Dufour and Leroy)	*Italian Views* (large grisaille decoration).
1840-50	Pignet jeune and Paillard	*Roman Scenes* (30 sheets in grisaille: compare *The Discovery of America*).
1844	Zuber	*Isola Bella* (large exotic decoration, designed by Ehrmann, Zippelius and Fuchs on 18 sheets).
1845	Clerc and Margeridon	*Festival of Louis XIII* (in colour).
1848	Zuber	*Eldorado* (designed by Ehrmann, Zippelius and Fuchs in 192 colours from 1,554 blocks on 33 sheets).
1851	Delicourt	*Hunting* (in colour, after Desportes).
1852	Desfossé	*Dream of Happiness* (16 sheets in colour depicting a large landscape with Renaissance figures after Dunand).
1854	Desfossé and Karth	*Armida's Garden* (designed by Muller, in colour: floral and architectural decoration with frieze, including a winter garden and Flora's gallery).
1855	Zuber	*Lands of the Earth* (designed by Ehrmann and Schuler, in colour).
1861	Zuber	*Japanese Landscape* (or *Chinese Garden*) (designed by Poterlet, in colour).

Views of Asia. 12 of 30 sheets. Sepia on a yellow ground. c. 1820. Carlhian coll.

1861	Desfossé	*Eden* (designed by Fuchs; 23 sheets in colour from 3,642 blocks: the last great panorama, never finished).
1867	Atelier Hook	*Large Garden Decoration* (designed by Dumont, in colour).

2. Town Scenes

1815	Dufour	*The Monuments of Paris* (30 sheets in colour, based on Prévost's panorama in the boulevard Montmartre: the foreground figures are after Vernet).
1823	Félix Sauvignet	*Views of Lyons* (25 sheets in colour).
1852	Pignet jeune and Paillard	*Paris, London and Rome* (32 sheets in sepia).
1845	Unknown	*Panoramic view of Moscow from the Kremlin* (hand-painted by Baron J.K. Akali and shown in 'Trésors du Kremlin' exhibition, Grand Palais, Paris, 1979-80).

3. Mythological Subjects

1816	Dufour	*Cupid and Psyche* (grisaille paper in 26 sheets engraved by Xavier Mader after paintings by Louis Lafitte and Merry-Joseph Blondel).
1824	Dufour	*The Gallery of Mythology* (designed by Mader, grisaille paper in 24 sheets).
1824	Dufour	*Greek Festivals* (designed by Mader, grisaille paper in 30 sheets heightened with green and blue, comprising 6 subjects).

4. Military Scenes

1816	Jacquemart and Bénard	*The French in Egypt* (designed by Deltil, in 30 sheets).
1814	Jourdan and Villard	*The Battle of Austerlitz* (30 sheets in colour).
1827	Zuber	*Views of Modern Greece* (or *Battles of the Greeks*) (designed by Deltil, 30 sheets in colour illustrating the Greek fight for independence).
1829	Dufour	*The French Campaigns in Italy* (grisaille paper in 30 sheets).
1845	Pignet	*The Annals of Victory* (32 sheets in colour).
1852	Zuber	*War of American Independence* (32 sheets in colour; the background is from *North American Views*).

creased to a great extent since the Revolution and that the manufacture of paper hangings was carried on with great spirit in Boston, New Jersey and Philadelphia.

The war between England and the thirteen states, and the independence gained and confirmed in the Treaty of Versailles in 1783, decreased the level of trade between England and the United States to the benefit of the French who had supported the rebel colonists. In the 1790s William Poyntell of Philadelphia offered to print bespoke patterns in any colour at three days' notice but was equally happy to advertise in 1795 the sale of over 4000 pieces of elegant French paper, landscapes and fireboard decorations. Arabesque papers were to find favour, and legend has it that Martha Washington planned to decorate a room at Mount Vernon with a set of these in honour of the Marquis de Lafayette. To her disappointment, her guest arrived before the paper was delivered, so General Washington, Lafayette and his aide-de-camp set about hanging the paper themselves. On another occasion Washington, in a memorandum in his own hand, gave an upholsterer directions for making flour paste for wallpapering and a method of smoothing out wrinkles in the paper.

When Washington died in 1799, a Boston wallpaper manufacturer, Ebenezer Clough, prepared a dignified memorial publication in blue, grey, white and black showing personifications of Liberty and Justice mourning on either side of a pedestal bearing the inscription 'Sacred to Washington'. An example of this hall or stairway decoration has been preserved in the extensive wallpaper collections of the Cooper Hewitt Museum, New York. Ebenezer Clough was thought to have given a copy of this paper to each State governor in 1800 and he added a patriotic note to his publicity for it: 'As the above attempts to perpetuate the memory of the Best of Men, it is hoped that all real Americans will so encourage the manufacture [of wallpaper] that manufacturers may flourish and importations stop.'

In the early years of the nineteenth century the influence of French designs nevertheless prevailed. Asa Smith of Baltimore printed fluttering Pompeian figures and garlands of flowers and ribbons in the popular style of the First Empire, while in 1813 Moses Grant in Boston offered fancy landscapes and views which avoided too much 'sameness' in the design. On the other hand a French manufacturer published a stylish wallpaper specifically for the American market around 1813. This commemorated the first important naval victory of the War of 1812 in which the *Constitution* captured the British frigate *Guerrière*. The engagement in 1812 is pictured in a vignette, and the American captain Isaac Hull is shown in a portrait medallion after a painting by Gilbert Stuart. A portion of this topical paper is held by the Cooper Hewitt Museum.

By 1817 shipments of panoramic and pictorial wallpapers from France were eagerly received. In that year the New England Palladium announced the arrival at James Fosters' shop in Boston of the newest subjects, including the monuments of Paris, the voyages of Captain Cook, English gardens, views of Switzerland, Italy, Hindustan, the Ports of Bordeaux and Bayonne, Grecian Arcadia, etc. From the start the market for these colourful decorations was a brisk one, to the point that the firm of Zuber in Alsace issued papers representing the War of American Independence and views of North America. In her important publication of 1924 the American wallpaper historian Nancy McClelland gave a full account of the large numbers of French scenic papers preserved at that date in historic homes of the East Coast, a remarkable collection, considering that scarcely any found their way into buildings across the English Channel.

The financial outlay in engraving vast numbers of wooden blocks for these decorations was often beyond the means of even some of the French manufacturers who, as an alternative, chose to paint sheets of paper with simple landscapes. No outlines were printed, and tempera colour was applied with a wide sweep of the brush. These primitive but effective reproductions were exported to America,

Britannia enthroned among Corinthian columns, arches and urns. Paper from a house at Haddam, Connecticut. Block-printed on joined sheets in black and white on a blue ground. Zechariah Mills. North American, c. 1794. Cooper Hewitt coll. Gift of Jones and Erwin, Inc.

Bandbox with cover. Block-printed on joined sheets, in orange, white, grey and light brown distemper colours, and in green, brown, black and yellow colours with glossy finish, on a light blue ground. Mounted on cardboard. Rim covered in border paper. Putnam and Roff, Hartford, Connecticut. North American, 1823-24. Cooper Hewitt coll. Gift of Mrs Frederick F. Thompson.

where the idea was copied. McClelland recorded the existence of a charming rustic scene and a landscape with the first railroad in a house in the High Street of Salem, Massachusetts.

As the nineteenth century progressed, so technical improvements were sought. Following a tour of London, Paris and the Zuber factory in 1839, the manufacturer Josiah Bumstead instigated a number of improvements in his Boston factory in order to compete sucessfully with imports and to keep pace with new fashions in such stock-in-trade items as borders, flocks and wallpapers imitating fabrics. Recent discoveries have shed light on the prevalent styles of the period. A sample book containing twenty-nine patterns of about 1823 and bearing the mark of Janes and Bolles of Hartford was recently presented to Old Sturbridge Village. Collections of bandboxes, fireboards and window shades covered with wallpaper fragments are now preserved by the Cooper Hewitt Museum, the Shelburne Museum, Vermont, and the American Museum in Britain at Claverton Manor, Bath. The cardboard bandboxes were covered with left-overs of simple blockprinted wallpapers and can often be dated by their newspaper linings. Attractive designs commemorated American heroes and historic events, and primitive early nineteenth-century papers displayed exotic scenes, buildings, forms of transport and a whole range of animals, birds and flowers. (The term bandbox is derived from the original function of small oval boxes to contain men's collar bands and was extended to include larger examples.)

By the end of the eighteenth century the United States had attained a high degree of commercial self-sufficiency. Although labour-saving machinery was being used in Britain by the 1970s it was not until after the War of 1812 that Americans made the first steps from artisan labour to factory systems. John Howell and Son, the most successful Philadelphia firm of wallpaper manufacturers, founded in 1790, was the first establishment to import from England and put into production a steam-driven printing machine in 1844. This firm and one other from the same city represented American production at the Great Exhibition in London in 1851. For this event Jean Zuber as a member of the jury compiled international statistics for an official exhibition report; he noted that the American industry supported 1300 workers. Expansion was inevitable, and the 1860 census showed that twenty-six factories were in operation. A similar exhibition of manufacturers and art was held at the New York Crystal Palace in 1853. As industrialization progressed, so the centre of wallpaper manufacturing shifted from Philadelphia to New York.

Notes (pp. 76-126).

1. Everhard Jabach (1610-95) was a famous financier whose collection of paintings and drawings was bought by Louis XIV and formed the basis of the royal collections. His magnificent house in the rue St Merri, Paris, which was demolished in the nineteenth century, stood where the Pompidou Centre is now.

2. H.J. Pragnell, *London Panoramas of Robert Barker and Thomas Gertin*, London Topographical Society, no. 109, 1968.

3. These four gouaches, signed and dated, are on sized paper and measure 63 x 83 cm (approx. 24¾ x 32½ inches). Private collection, Paris.

4. The series includes illustrations on the following themes: Pyramus and Thisbe, Apollo and Daphne, Iphigenia Condemned to the Regions of Hell, Pygmalion and the Statue, The Offering to Pan, and Orpheus Charming the Animals (after the works of Van Loo, Delafosse and Fragonard).

5. A complete set decorated the walls of a country house at Dampierre-sur-Salon, Haute-Saône. An inscription in red chalk, found underneath one of the panels, indicates that they were hung in 1789. These papers are now in an American collection.

6. Bernard Jacqué, in 'Papiers peints panoramiques et jardins. L'oeuvre de A. Mongin, chez Zuber et Cie 1804-1827', *Nouvelle de l'estampe*, no. 1, 1980, was the first to make an aesthetic comparison between the French garden and panoramic papers.

7. In a later edition *The Battles of the Greeks* lost its original characters, as the event was no longer topical.

8. Dufour wrote an explanatory booklet to accompany this paper, with the same title (Moiroux, Mâcon, Year XIII, 1804-05). A copy is held by the Municipal Library in Mâcon, and extracts appear in English in Nancy McClelland's *Historic Wallpapers*.

9. Brissot de Warville (Jacques-Pierre Brissot, 1754-93), a French politician and journalist, was particularly interested in promoting the rights of coloured people. As a member of the Girondin party, he was executed during the Revolution.

10. 'If there is a commercial product in which Europeans need not fear any competition, one which assures all European manufacturers profitable business, it is paper making.' (Brissot de Warville, *Nouveau voyage dans les Etats-Unis de l'Amérique*.)

The best study of early American production is still that of Nancy McClelland (in *Historic Wallpapers*).

CHAPTER FOUR
Grandeur and decadence

Technical and artistic refinements in France (1815-30)

In France, these years were characterized by a perfection of technique, as manufacturers continuously sought to improve production methods. Papers were of better quality, and inks and colours more varied and striking. In this search for perfection, Zuber took over the paper mill at Rappenviller where in 1830 Amédée Riesler succeeded in producing paper on continuous rolls. The technique had been devised in 1799 by Louis Robert who was working for Didot St Léger at Essonnes, but through lack of industrial and financial support in France his invention was first exploited by the English. The strength of paper was considerably increased by this method, so that production of wallpapers on mechanical presses became possible. At the same time Zuber's chemical laboratory produced new colours and inks; working with the chemists Leffler de Berne, Thénard and Rigault, Jean Zuber perfected the tints chrome yellow, Prussian blue and green. In 1820 Michel Spoerlin devised a tinting technique, similar to that used for sky effects, which made it possible to change from one colour to another during the course of printing the same motif. This made it possible to print the whole range of the spectrum, and almost op-art effects were achieved by using increasingly stylized floral designs. Several years later Zuber perfected printing with aligned ink-trays, which allowed him to print strong colours side by side without any intermingling. The tartan patterns he created were imitated by many other manufacturers. By 1830 craftsmanship in wallpaper had reached a climax that later production could not match; the subtlety of these papers disappeared with the uniformity of machine production.

Everyday papers were enough to guarantee the income of manufacturers, who turned more and more to producing papers that imitated other materials by *trompe l'oeil*, such as textiles, from pleated or embroidered cloths and heavy draperies to the lightest muslins, woods like mahogany, rosewood and lemonwood, marble in the form of pilasters, capitals or panels, and other architectural details such as bas-reliefs, gilt friezes, and trophies. At the peak of their excellence these techniques played with matte and gloss effects: 'we have found the secret of giving papers the appearance of those materials which most delight the eye: the softness of wool, the flat shine of cotton, velvet or satin, the shimmer of silk, the grace of embroidery. No longer will wallpaper have a flat and lifeless surface: it will follow the graceful folds and draperies of the material it imitates.' Thus wrote Sébastien Lenormand in his *Manuel du fabricant d'étoffes imprimées et du fabricant de papiers peints* (Roret, Paris 1830).

As to borders, there was a profusion of possibilities – acanthus or palm leaf, ribbons or subtle drapery – in distemper and flock, enlivened by shadow and highlight.

Dufour and Leroy's 1831 catalogue admitted: :'it would be quite useless to try and list all our novelties. We will limit ourselves to bringing to your attention our prismatic and Persian designs, with flowers in different scales, our new wainscot and firescreen papers, or our borders, for which this year the choice available is considerably wider than usual. Now that we have also started producing the new glazed satin, our decorative schemes will be all the more noticeable and remarkable.'

The Jacquemart and Bénard factory, for its part, offered velvet papers with flowers heightened with gold, and overdoors and firescreens in bronze and

Feathers. Dufour and Leroy. French, 1812. Follot coll.

Paper imitating stretched fabric. Mauve on grey with green points. 1812. Follot coll.

Greek key design created for a French manufacturer. 1830. Bibliothèque Forney, Paris.

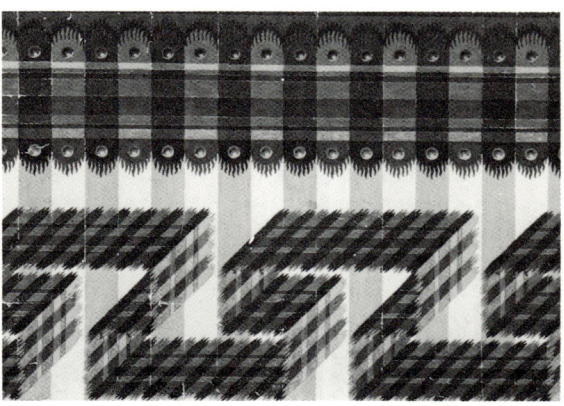

grisaille, designed by such famous names as Jean Broc, Evariste Fragonard, Guérin and Cogniet. Dauptain, of the rue St Bernard in Paris, produced satin finishes and cameos in polychrome and monochrome that were much admired. He was the first to create the interiors in imitation Gothic, Renaissance or 'Pompadour' styles which were characteristic of the reigns of Louis-Philippe and Napoleon III. Other manufacturers in Paris and in the provinces were equally successful, but the end was at hand: the reign of Charles X brought to a close the most brilliant and elegant era in wallpaper. The inheritance of the great eighteenth-century creators was wound up, as the woodblock gave way to the machine.

The industrial age and the great exhibitions

In the early years of the nineteenth century the British wallpaper industry was at a low ebb: heavy taxation, trading restrictions and a paucity of good design stood in the way of progress. Stylistically, wallpapers were comparable to French productions of the period, but lacked their fine technique. In his lecture on the history of paper hangings delivered to the Royal Institute of British Architects in 1839, the decorator John Gregory Crace commented on current issues, proclaiming the poor state of design in Britain as opposed to that of Europe. There artists arranged the colours themselves and directed the printing, thus producing fewer but better designs. Another decorator, Mawer Cowtan, addressing the Decorative Art Society in 1844, complained that design was not held in high enough regard; wallpaper printers and block cutters were generally paid more than artists.

However, the progress of industrialization in Britain was gaining momentum, and every kind of technical innovation was sought to speed up mass production. Louis Robert's invention of machinery that could produce continuous lengths of paper was introduced into England by John Gamble. He patented and developed it in association with the brothers Fourdrinier, the London stationers who gave their name to a machine that was put into production in 1805. The benefits of it were finally realized after 1830 when the excise authorities permitted the use of continuous paper for printing wallpaper. Calico printing had been mechanized in the late eighteenth century, and now aspiring patentees strove to modernize wallpaper production methods, adapting engraved plates and cylinders or rollers.

The steam-driven, rotary wallpaper printing

machine, which was adopted universally by mid century, was first used by C.H. and E. Potter of Darwen in Lancashire. In 1839 Charles Potter, aided by his foreman Walmsley Preston, attempted to print wallpapers on textile machines using engraved rollers. But experiments with metal 'surface' rollers on which the pattern was left raised, as in block printing, were more successful. After further improvements were made in applying colours and drying the rapidly printed festoons of paper, comercially acceptable wallpapers were put on the market by the Potter brothers in 1841.

The expanding industry was to be encouraged by reductions in the duty on paper in 1836 and the abolition in the same year of the paper-staining duty. Output was increased tenfold, and the population at large could now enjoy the latest productions of the machine age. Wallpapers were presented as such in the exhibitions of art and industry. In 1849 the Society of Arts in London presented the 'Select Specimens of British Manufacture and Decorative Art', in which the manufacturers Crace, Horne and Jeffrey, William Woollams and Townsend and Simpson were represented.

The competition with French imports was gradually revived after the removal of trading restrictions in 1825, and at the Great Exhibition of 1851 there were displayed belaboured wallpaper panels, simulated pilasters and pictorial papers which were clearly attempting to rival the luxurious French papers of the Second Empire. Class 26 of the exhibition was reserved for wallpaper, papier mâché and tapestry. Block-printed reproductions of Old Master paintings and a 24-foot frieze depicting the Elgin marbles in *trompe l'oeil* were among the more novel entries. Cheap machine productions were no less impressive, papers from Heywood, Higginbottom and Smith of Manchester were printed in twenty colours from fourteen rollers.

In effect the glittering display showed that industrial progress had outpaced the theory of design. In the mid nineteenth century manufacturers had little interest in correcting this, and consequently machine-made articles were often overloaded with meaningless ornament. As early as 1839 the Art Union had warned, in relation to the French, that through 'the non-employment of artistic skill on our part we find ourselves considerably in the background. Machinery will not do all'.

The debased artistic tastes encouraged by such vigorous commercialism were attacked by the architect and writer Augustus Welby Northmore Pugin. He condemned contemporary Gothic patterned papers in which caricatures of pointed buildings were repeated from skirting-board to cornice. Pugin designed wallpapers using medieval themes, such as *Tout vient de Dieu*, printed for J.S. Cooper by Mawer Cowtan and *Rose and Lily*, one of several papers intended for the new Parliament

Stylized flowers in frames. Owen Jones. English, mid 19th century. V&A.

Gothic paper. Woodblock-printed. English, c. 1840. V&A.

Stylized flowers. Owen Jones. V&A.

1. Horse-racing scenes. Details of a machine-printed paper. English, mid 19th century. V&A.

2, 4. Hunting and fishing scenes. English, c. 1870. V&A.

3. Commemorative wallpaper for the 1862 International Exhibition, South Kensington. Machine-printed. English. V&A.

5. Hunting scenes. English, c. 1870. Bibliothèque Forney, Paris.

buildings and printed in 1848 by Scott, Cuthbertson and Co. These patterns adhered to the strict principles of design Pugin had himself laid down: that wallpaper should be flat and two-dimensional and each object must be 'honest in construction and fit for its purpose, to give true pleasure'.

Pugin's ideas were later supported by Ruskin and the architect and designer Owen Jones, whose influential *Grammar of Ornament* (1856), clarified styles of decoration over the centuries and in different countries. His own wallpaper designs were, like Pugin's, flat, unobtrusive and dignified. Henry Cole, a civil servant and reformer, also played a part in improving popular taste by issuing a magazine, *The Journal of Design and Manufacture* (1849-51), in which Owen Jones, Digby Wyatt and the painter Richard Redgrave offered advice to manufacturers and advocated a fresh approach to design. From 1847 Henry Cole had himself run his own firm, Summerly's Art Manufactures, producing objects of everday use to improved designs. He had been involved in planning the Great Exhibition and subsequently became Principal of the School of Design in South Kensington.

Numerous publications wrote of the shortcomings of the wallpaper industry. In his book of 1852, *Curiosities of Industry*, George Dodd suggested that the public would welcome a reformed principle of design in decorative patterns as opposed to the absurdities found in current paper hangings. At the Great Exhibition British manufacturers had been overshadowed by the French; it was E. Delicourt who won the Gold Medal. Even in 1861 John Stewart, a critic for the *Art Journal*, accused the British of petty meanness in their attitude to design. The French, he claimed, were still more enlightened in this respect. Robert Smith replied in articles published in the Manchester *Examiner* and *Times* in March 1861. Defending the manufacturers, he protested (a little unconvincingly) that heavy taxation had restricted the range of their production, but that they could boast of such talented designers as Owen Jones and James Huntington, whose elaborate floral and architectural patterns were purchased by many firms in London and Manchester. John Stewart had the best of the argument, and the industry in time became more receptive to new attitudes.

Both criticism and guidance were offered to the general public by Charles Lock Eastlake in his *Hints on Household Taste in Furniture and Upholstery* of 1868, a publication which found a parallel in Emile Cardon's *L'art au foyer domestique* of 1884. Metford Warner, the director of the London firm of Jeffrey and Co. and himself a pioneer in wallpaper manufacture, invited many progressive architects and artists, including Eastlake, to design wallpapers for his firm. Eventually wallpapers were raised to artistically informed standards, and the industrial

Circular ceiling paper. Machine-printed. English, c. 1850. V&A.

Ironwork grille. Block-printed. Designed by Thomas Willament (1786-1871). English, 1830. V&A.

Muse. Grisaille paper. French, 1850. Bibliothèque Forney, Paris.

Floral wallpaper. Machine-printed by C.H. and E. Potter, Darwen, Lancashire. English, 1849. From The Journal of Design, *April 1849.*

La Favorite. Leroy. French, 1860. Bibliothèque Forney, Paris.

Paper with undulating floral pattern. The first paper to be printed on a cylinder steam press outside Britain. Zuber. French, 1850. MISE.

exhibitions of the latter part of the nineteenth century showed signs of progress and new inspiration.

The union of art and industry

France did not escape the movement towards the industrial and machine age. As in England, the result was a complex relationship between the two, from which art, needless to say, did not emerge as master. It was in this era that the bourgeoisie became the new arbiters of taste, with the aristocracy following behind. However, the bourgeoisie had a keen desire to acquire the marks of nobility, and took pains to imitate the great styles of pre-Revolutionary France, from Gothic to Louis XVI. This interest in the arts became broadly based, as industrialization made art objects available to a much wider section of society. In 1867 F. Ducuing wrote: 'I have said that in our era art has had to become an industrial product, as in effect, taste and luxury became the prerogative of the less leisured classes. But art loses nothing by this change. Rather, art can gain infinite resources thereby, to the same measure that art has gained by becoming the handmaiden of science.'

Although wallpaper had been taken up by the aristocracy in the eighteenth century, it now lost favour with the nobility and upper classes. But its use became widespread amongst the middle classes. In the luxurious private houses of the nobility that 'style of wealth, bastard child of all styles' as Zola called it, reigned, and the *tapissier* gradually gained control of interior decoration. Damasks and velvets, silks and other rich stuffs covered the walls, fell in heavy folds around windows and doors and covered furniture with quilting, edges and trimmings.

The major towns in France were the scene for a veritable frenzy of urban redevelopment. In Paris, under the Baron Haussmann's guidance, large collectively owned blocks sprang up, which Victor Hugo described as wardrobes. To meet the demand of this new construction, wallpaper makers tried to improve their techniques. Once continuous-roll paper was available, the pace of development grew.

Friezes of flowers and ribbons around a panel of embroidered tulle and lace, from Mulhouse. French, c. 1835. MISE.

Large trompe l'oeil paper imitating gathered drapery. Zuber, French, early 19th century. DTM.

Right, from top to bottom:
Two advertisements in wallpaper. Block-printed by Paulot and Carré. French, c. 1828. Follot coll.

Border with passementerie. Designed by Mader for Dufour. French, 1810-20. Bibliothèque Forney, Paris.

Border with drapery and floral garland. Designed by Merrii, 1815-20. Bibliothèque Forney, Paris.

Frieze with flowers and white and gold palm-leaves on a bronze ground. Follot coll.

Fireguard. The only known use of prismatic colours for a figurative subject. Zuber. French, 1831. MISE.

Crystal Palace. Paper commemorating the Great Exhibition. Heywood, Higginbottom and Smith, Manchester. English, c. 1851. V&A.

Oriental scenes. Printed on yellow in sepia with white highlights. French, c. 1830. Halard coll.

*Paper in graduated colours designed by Fritz Zuber.
French, 1824. MISE.*

*Figured rosettes on a prismatic ground.
Designed by Julien for Fritz Zuber.
French, 1826. MISE.*

Paper imitating lacework. Printed in white on a cinnamon-coloured ground on continuous paper. Designed and engraved by Koechlin Ziegler, Mulhouse, for Zuber. French, 1831. MISE. This paper was shown at the National Exhibition of Industrial Products in 1834.

*Frieze, border and paper. Co-ordinated design by Zuber.
French, 1813. MISE.*

Paper commemorating the 1878 exhibition at the Trocadéro, Paris. Nobilis coll.

Monuments of Paris *(The Porte St Denis, the Tour St Jacques, the Obelisk and St Sulpice). Lithograph from the Maigret sales catalogue. Desfosse. French, 1857-58. Carlhian coll.*

Left: **Hunting scenes.** *Swiss, 1860-70. Nobilis coll.*

Right: **Everyday scenes.** *Swiss, 1860-70. Nobilis coll.*

Left: **The Bivouac.** *Swiss, 1860-70. Nobilis coll.*

Right: **The Mexican War.** *Swiss, 1860-70. Nobilis coll.*

Armida's Garden. *Designed by Muller for Desfossé and Karth. French, 1864. Musée des Arts Décoratifs, Paris.*

Roses. *Paper imitating tapestry, by Guillou-Dumont. French, 1870. Bibliothèque Forney, Paris.*

Floral bouquets. *A naturalistic paper by Jules Riottot. French, 1845. Bibliothèque Forney, Paris.*

The Empress Eugénie. Designed by Guérite for Zuber. Musée des Arts Décoratifs, Paris.

Sad Pierrot. Gouache study by Thomas Couture for Desfossé's series The Vices and the Virtues *(detail). French, 1855. Musée des Arts et Métiers, Paris.*

Two greyhounds. Wallpaper in trompe-l'oeil imitating a framed painting, c. 1860. Follot coll.

Large flower arrangement. Zuber. French, c. 1860. MISE.

Friezes of pelmets and valances. 1860. Nobilis coll.

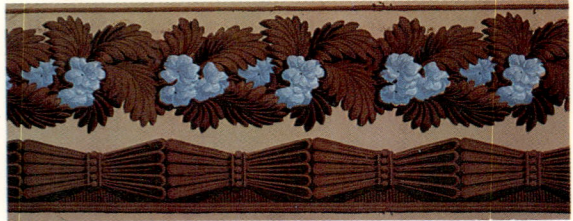

Sphinx and canopic vase. Guillou Wagner. French, 1860. Bibliothèque Forney, Paris.

Frieze of lace with ribbons. 1850. Nobilis coll.

Frieze of drapery. Mid 19th century. Halard coll.

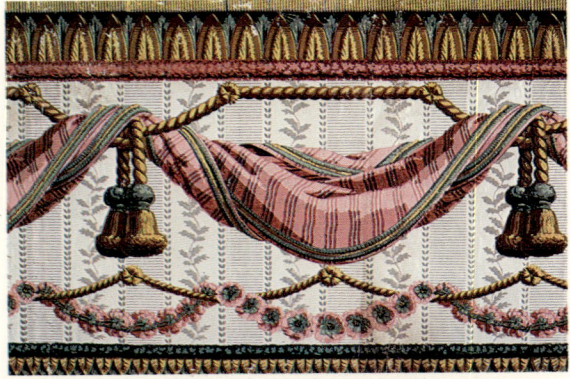

Bouquets of roses in frames against a wooden background. 1880. Nobilis coll.

Pheasant and flowers. c. 1860. Nobilis coll.

Imitation brocade paper. 1850. Nobilis coll.

The first roller-printed design, from a copper-plate engraving, was produced by Zuber in 1829, using a horse-powered machine. In 1843 Isidore Leroy took out a patent for cylinder relief printing, with the ink fed from a continuous blanket. In 1847 Zuber installed the first steam-powered press, purchased in England, together with a charging machine with continuous dryer. His firm at Rixheim was at the head of technical developments. The invention in 1858 of gravure made matte and coated effects possible. In 1863 Paul Balin patented a process invented some years before by A. Saegers, which made it possible to emboss papers cold, using a fly-press. This process of mechanization increased production considerably, and manufacturing costs fell, enabling large stores and shops to offer a wide choice of fashionable papers at reasonable prices.

The firm of Turquetil, founded in 1853, produced papers solely for the mass market, with low-priced designs in various styles and often using a figured paper called 'Gobelin'. Isidore Leroy made Gothic, Renaissance and Moorish papers. In 1867 he produced his *Alhambra* design, writing 'I tried by linking machine and woodblock techniques to produce a unified effect that would characterize a new idea in wallpaper design.' (*Note pour MM. les présidents et membres du jury*, exhibition of 1867.) Zuber also followed the trend: while continuing to produce luxurious block-printed papers, he also introduced Gothic and Rococo designs.

In the end, the precision of machine production became so compelling an idea that mathematical accuracy was the ultimate goal. In this shift of values the craftsman felt disgraced if his handiwork did not match the exactness of the machine. Thus the aesthetic ideas of the time, typified by an absence of individual style and the search for inspiration in the work of the past, gradually came to terms with the machine. Wallpaper had been an art of *trompe l'oeil*. Now it was one of sham appearance: sham tapestry in botched Renaissance style, fake Gothic architecture, 'Louis-XIV-style' imitation velvet.

The principle that it is better not to make in one medium something which can be better made in another does not extend to industrial production, which has the capacity to match things perfectly. As Charles Blanc wrote in his *Grammaire des arts décoratifs* (1886), 'The genius of this profession ... is that it can in one operation give a simple piece of paper or card not only the sheen of silk or satin ... the thick substance of drapery or the glaze of ceramic finishes, but also the grain of fabric, the texture of old tapestry, crochet or Genoese velvet, the deep embossing of Spanish leather, the regularity of brocade and even the swell and curve of upholstery.'

With the increasing poverty of creative inspiration after the 1860s, men such as Mérimée began to think that the Industrial Revolution needed industrial artists, trained in schools like the Ecole des Beaux Arts or the Académie. Some proposed the opening of new schools in the major industrial towns in the provinces. Originally the craftsman had been trained in his father's studio, who had in turn been taught by *his* father. The craftsman was also both designer and maker. But industry was employing workers who were only makers, and who needed design training. This problem led to a number of interesting initiatives.

In 1858 the Société du Progrès de l'Art Industriel was founded, becoming in 1863 the Union Centrale des Beaux-arts Appliqués à l'Industrie. It was made up of industrialists (Turquetil represented the wallpaper makers), critics and artists, with the architect Guichard as president. The Society organized exhibitions and lectures, conferences and competitions, and founded a museum and a library.

In Great Britain critics and reformers were not alone in condemning the undesirable effects of industralization. In 1836 William Ewart, Chairman of a Parliamentary select committee on art and industry, reported that the provision of art schools, libraries and galleries was the only way to extend the principles of design among the manufacturing population. In this spirit, objects were selected from the Great Exhibition of 1851 to form a study collection of decorative art in the new South Kensington Museum. From 1855 it was available to schools of art.

Because of its belief in the unity of production, from design to finished object, the French Union Centrale was able to foster a generation of craftsmen to replace those that the earlier dichotomy had expunged. But unfortunately this alliance of art and industry was only to produce dull imitations of the past. This was the era of the designer 'huddled over the treasures of the Cabinet d'Estampes, bent on finding a new masterpiece therein', as Balzac puts it in *Le cousin Pons*. Renaissance, Gothic, Chinese, Arab and eighteenth-century styles were all worked over, of which Fleury Chavant's *Dessinateur de papiers peints* is a sad illustration. Out of this ocean of mediocrity, only the stream of naturalism retained a freshness of inspiration.

Pompeian-style pilaster and frieze design. Lithograph from the Maigret sales catalogue. Desfossé and Karth. French, mid 19th century. Carlhian coll.

The floral motif

The most memorable feature of the decorative style of the nineteenth century is the floral motif, which was regularly used in furnishings, in painting and in dress. This interest in flowers as decoration was the continuation of the naturalistic movement which originated in the eighteenth century and which gave rise, among other things, to landscape wallpapers. In addition, there was now a growing interest in scientific knowledge, which led to the publication of many books on botany, and which is exemplified by the work of Joseph Redouté (1759-1840). He was Marie-Antoinette's private tutor and the official painter to the Jardin des Plantes. His two series of engravings, *Les roses* and the *Choix des quarante plus belles fleurs tirées du grand ouvrage des liliacées* were frequently reprinted and were a major source of reference for designers and painters throughout the nineteenth century.

Early in the century Malaine had designed for Zuber panels and overdoors with roses and arrangements of flowers. Armfuls of flowers also appeared on the furniture, which was made of papier mâché or lacquer and inlaid with mother-of-pearl or gilt. This fashion first started under Louis-Philippe and continued until the Second Empire. Flowers covered porcelain (such as Sèvres), fabrics and wallpapers. The flowing crinolines of the ladies, like masses of pink and white petals swaying in waltz time, gave the impression that the rooms of the period were peopled with flowers. On wallpaper, whether hand- or machine-printed, roses and peonies abounded, gently climbing walls or forming beribboned friezes and graceful wreaths. In 1865 the artist Guérite created for Zuber the portrait of the Empress Eugénie in a frame of natural flowers. The cool beauty of the monochrome portrait is enlivened by the rich garland of roses, peonies, wistaria and lilac, the whole a gracious symphony of pink and blue. Muller made for Desfossé *Armida's Garden* and the *Galerie de Flore*, two huge compositions where the luxurious abundance of flowers is offset by stark stone statuary, while Ehrmann, Fuchs and Zippelius created a heady floral bouquet for their 1848 paper *Eldorado*.

Every manufacturer scattered flowers freely on his wallpapers. Garlands of roses, bunches of wild flowers, bouquets of poppies, lilacs and roses were everywhere. The rich blooms of peony and eglantine, set against a background of greenery, patterns of narcissus, acanthus and brightly coloured iris made a happy contrast to dull, imitative designs. This carpet of flowers, designed in the same spirit as the Indian fabrics which themselves had inspired wallpaper, was an original design motif, quite separate from the servile imitation of the past.

Roses on a black ground. English, 1840. V&A.

Vase of flowers. Designed by Zippelius for Zuber. French, 1860. Zuber coll.

PART TWO
The industrial age

This period extends from the second half of the nineteenth century until the First World War. It saw the birth in Europe of a powerful movement towards a fresh treatment of natural motifs, started by the work of William Morris. Called Art Nouveau (*Modern Style* in France, *Jugendstil* in Germany) this movement created a new iconography that broke with classical forms, and ended in the almost abstract formalism of the Bauhaus. Wallpaper was affected by this new iconography, while remaining at the same time, alas, the vehicle for the tired repetition of past designs. The avant-garde was buried under mass production devoid of real creativity.

Larkspur. *Designed by William Morris. English, 1872. (A polychrome version was made in 1874 and the design used for a chintz in 1875.) The accompanying frieze is of later date, probably c. 1900.*

CHAPTER ONE
The last great styles

William Morris, a new spirit in wallpaper

As throughout Europe, England experienced in the nineteenth century a passion for the rediscovered romanticism of the Middle Ages. Under the influence of Pugin, Gilbert Scott, William Burges, Alfred Waterhouse and the ideas of John Ruskin, buildings were invaded by pinnacles and gables, gargoyles and buttresses. The English and French Gothic architecture of the twelfth to the fifteenth centuries was the major source of inspiration, but German, Venetian and Spanish models were also used.

This renewal of interest in the Gothic, which lasted only for a generation, was not a retrogressive attitude, nor nostalgia for a lost age. Like Viollet le Duc in France and Ruskin in England, William Morris found in the Middle Ages a model for changing society and fighting against the ugliness of the modern world. He dreamed of an era when the craftsman could create in contentment objects for all to use, when art would not be the preserve of an elite but the common pleasure of everyday life. He did not want art to be only for some people any more than education be only for some or freedom only for some. He asked that art be 'art by the people and for the people . . . a joy for the creator and the user' (*Collected Works*, London, 1910-15).

Morris's Red House at Bexley Heath in Kent, built by his friend Philip Webb in 1860, is a reworking of older vernacular styles in a very free way that prefigures functionalism. All the furniture and decoration was designed by Webb and Morris, and members of Morris's family circle. The son of a middle-class family, this poet, artist and reformer took his socialist ideas as principles, and without being a revolutionary either in his actions or his work opposed the mass production of the industrial age: 'It was its use and abuse that moved his hatred: the spectacle of the machine . . . destroying men while it made things, regardless of use or beauty.' (Watkinson, *William Morris as Designer*, London, 1979.)

Morris, Marshall, Faulkner and Co., his first business (which later became Morris and Co.) was set up in 1861 and made fabrics, tapestries, furniture, tiles and wallpaper, using craft techniques wherever possible. Morris himself mastered the technique of using vegetable dyes and spent four months studying weaving so as to learn all the techniques involved. The works produced by the firm never strained the relationship between material and decoration: flat surfaces got flat decoration. There was no imitation of other materials or fake three-dimensional effect.

Before Morris's time there had already been a reaction in England against the overblown naturalism of Victorian decoration and the unattractiveness of industrial production. Henry Cole and his followers had insisted, in a somewhat doctrinaire fashion, on the 'flatness' of design so as to ensure that ornament be abstract rather than imitative. Morris was never so dogmatic. His designs have a breadth and richness, nourished by the originality and freedom of his inspiration. His wallpapers were a reaction against the flat, stylized patterns, based on historic ornament, such as those designed by Owen Jones. Morris renewed the decorative vocabulary of his time, re-introducing nature with a surfeit of flowers and foliage. His well-known wallpaper, *Daisy*, printed by Jeffrey and Co. in 1864, exemplifies his simple and naturalistic style.

Flock paper. Designed and woodblock-printed by Pugin for Lord Gough at Lough Cutra Castle. English, c. 1845. V&A.

Dado-filling-frieze paper. Designed by Christopher Dresser for Jeffrey and Co. English, 1874.

Original design by Philip Webb for the gesso panelling and painted plaster frieze in the Green Dining-room at the V&A, which may well have influenced the design of wallpaper in three parts (dado, filling and frieze). English, 1866-67.

From 1864 onwards Jeffrey and Co. printed in woodblock all Morris's wallpapers. The director of the company, Metford Warner, was one of the most important figures in the wallpaper industry. He asked numerous artists to design for him, including William Burges, E.W. Godwin, Albert Moore, Christopher Dresser and Brightwen Binyon. Morris had been a friend of Burne-Jones since university, and had links with Dante Gabriel Rosetti and the Pre-Raphaelites. All these people worked for Morris's firm. In his search for the past Morris used the talents of Rosetti and Burne-Jones in designs for stained glass, and Burne-Jones also designed tiles and tapestries for him. Paradoxically, their taste was individual and refined while Morris himself was appealing for a popular art, free from aesthetic elitism.

From Morris's considerable output we are here only concerned with his wallpapers.[1] His catalogue lists forty-nine papers for walls and five designed as ceiling papers. Almost all his papers use motifs of flowers, fruit and foliage, either in continuous graceful patterns (as with *Queen Anne, Jasmine, Vine, Acanthus, Pimpernel, Poppy, Lechlade*) or organised in loose bunches on a background of grass or foliage (as in *Daisy, Lily, Powdered, Lily and Pomegranate*.) Other designs had large curling ribbons of flowers (as with *Fruit or Pomegranate, Trellis, Venetian, Indian, Spray, Daffodil, Grafton, Wild Tulip, Norwich, Hammersmith, Pink and Rose, Flora, Chrysanthemum*). The design of ceiling papers presented Morris with a particular problem, as he was very concerned that the design be totally two dimensional, with no suggestion of relief or perspective. This effect was reinforced by the dark designs being set against clear, light backgrounds, without shadows and in perfectly symmetrical arrangements. Morris did admit, however, that he had designed the ceiling papers against his will, preferring fresco, stucco, beams or even simple white paint for ceilings. He thought that a room entirely covered in wallpaper, ceiling and all, would be an 'unbearable box'.

William Morris's influence, spread by what he wrote as well as by what he produced, was considerable not only in England but throughout the world. In 1890 he founded the Kelmscott Press, which specialized in fine typography and printing. In architecture Morris influenced the development of the Domestic Revival movement of Philip Webb and Richard Norman Shaw, who built the first garden city, Bedford Park, on the outskirts of London in 1875. This new interest in private housing involved architects and designers in domestic planning, which was very valuable for the wallpaper business.

Art Nouveau

The Arts and Crafts Movement, inspired by Morris, was to have a strong effect on English design. At the same time, after the 1870s, a Japanese influence began to be felt, which can be detected in E.W. Godwin's and Christopher Dresser's wallpapers as well as in many other products in imitation Japanese embossed leather. These two tendencies which might seem to have nothing in common made an important contribution to the Aesthetic Movement of the 1870s and 1880s which was to lead to Art Nouveau, particularly in the case of Bruce Talbert. He won a gold medal at the International Exhibition in Paris in 1878 for his sunflower papers, which were widely imitated and copied.

English manufacturers also specialized in paper for children's rooms, often designed by the illustrators of children's books, of whom the most important was Randolph Caldecott. In addition there were Kate Greenaway whose graceful, feminine drawings have a typically British charm, Mable

Pink and Rose. *Designed by William Morris. English, 1890. Reprinted by Sanderson.*

Acanthus. *Designed by William Morris. English, 1875. V&A.*

Myrtle. *Designed by William Morris for an embroidery in 1875 and printed posthumously as wallpaper by Morris and Co. English, 1896. V&A.*

The Atmy. *Frieze by Shand Kydd Ltd. English, 1896.*

The Months. *Design by Kate Greenaway for a nursery paper. Printed in copperplate by David Walker. English, 1893. V&A.*

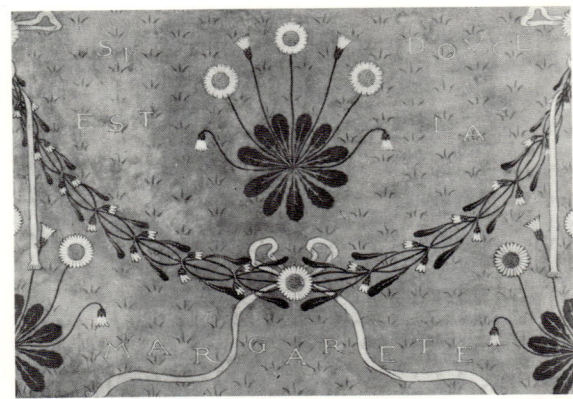

*Si douce est la Margarete.
Designed by Walter Crane.
Exhibited at the Philadelphia
Centennial Exhibition, 1876.
English, c. 1875. V&A.*

*Ceiling paper to accompany
Si douce est la Margarete.
Designed by Walter Crane for
Jeffrey and Co. English,
c. 1875. V&A.*

*Flowers and foliage. Designed
by Arthur Mackmurdo for
the Century Guild. English,
1884. V&A.*

Lucy Atwell who made her reputation after 1910 with her drawings of naive little figures of children and animals, and last but not least Walter Crane who became after 1875 the most popular of wallpaper designers.

Walter Crane (1845-1915) was a splendid book illustrator whose work delighted adults and children alike. He could never decide for himself between the decorative arts and painting in the grand manner – his work in the latter could be called pompous in its treatment of a troubled symbolic world. His finest achievements are his purely graphic creations, which are crammed with people, animals and flowers. In his essay 'On Wallpaper' he re-affirms, as did Morris, the need for design to be purely two dimensional and constructed in such a manner that it could stand repetition and matching-up easily. One of his first woodblock prints, *Si douce est la Margarete,* got a special mention at the 1876 Philadelphia Centennial Exhibition. It was clearly inspired by William Morris's *Daisy* and was a great success. Here Crane treats his floral theme with great simplicity, placing the delicate stems of the flowers on an ochre ground. *Margarete* is a complete design in three parts, with a frieze, white lining paper and ceiling paper. This arrangement, called Dado (the dado-filling-frieze formula) was much adopted in the last quarter of the nineteenth century and the firm of Jeffrey and Co. published a series of different types which won prizes at the 1873 Albert Hall fine arts exhibition. Although there were many machine-made papers in evidence, fine block-printed ones were given due prominence, especially nursery papers.

Crane also designed extremely subtle co-ordinated papers for walls, friezes and ceilings. He preferred light and symmetrical designs, evoking more dynamic and exaggerated forms than his friend Morris had done. As first president of the Art Workers' Guild in 1884 and of the Arts and Crafts Exhibition Society founded in 1888 he was able to spread his ideas throughout America. He exhibited in Vienna and in 1900 had a great success in Hungary. At the Turin exhibition of 1902 he was awarded the title of *Commendatore* for his work. His drawings in homage to international workers' solidarity earned him the name 'the artist of socialism': in these drawings a mass of happy people march together into the sunlight towards a better world.

On his return from the USA, Crane and his wife, who was a great source of inspiration to him, moved into a new house which he decorated, as Morris had done, with papers of his own design.

One of the most notable figures in the new movement was the architect and designer Arthur Heygate Mackmurdo (1851-1942). Even though he had travelled through Italy with Ruskin studying Gothic and Renaissance art and architecture,

St James's. *Designed by William Morris for the Throne Room and Wellington Room at St James's Palace. English, 1880. V&A.*

Grafton. *Designed by William Morris. English, 1883. (Note the stencil effect.) V&A.*

Right: Colombine. Designed by A.F. Vigers and block-printed by Jeffrey and Co. English, 1901. V&A. (Compare William Morris's Black Thorn of 1892.)

Far right: Daisy. Designed by William Morris in 1862 as part of a series with Pomegranate and Trellis for Morris, Marshall, Faulkner and Co. who tried printing them from zinc plates. The papers were finally printed by Jeffrey and Co. under Metford Warner's supervision. English, 1864. V&A.

Block-printed paper. Designed by A.F. Vigers. English, late 19th century. V&A.

Block-printed paper. Designed by A.F. Vigers. English, c. 1890. V&A.

Watercolour design for a monochrome paper by Lewis F. Day. English, 1891. V&A.

Field of flowers. Designed by C.F.A. Voysey. English, 1901. V&A. (Compare Walter Crane's Si douce est la Margarete.)

classical art was never his inspiration. In 1882, in emulation of Morris, he founded the Century Guild, a co-operative producing furniture and household objects, fabrics and wallpaper.

Mackmurdo's designs unite the natural inspiration of Morris with an abstract and sinuous linear quality close to Japanese calligraphy, which anticipates the Art Nouveau style. This decorative effect is seen in the title page of his 1883 book on Wren's city churches and in the typography of *The Hobby Horse*, the journal of the Century Guild. This style was extended into wallpaper, where the elegant designs often portray an imaginary flower, part tulip, part chrysanthemum and part flame. The same mixture of naturalism, almost abstract form and Japanese influence is found in the painting of Mackmurdo's friend James McNeill Whistler, who decorated the famous Peacock Room to enhance F.R. Leyland's porcelain collection.

If Morris's art can be defined as nature stylized, Mackmurdo's goes a step further: his fluid line with its gentle waves and undulations like grass or foliage hovers on the edge of abstraction. Though on the Continent of Europe this gentle line was to be the central motif of a new aesthetic in decorative art and architecture, England paradoxically moved towards straight-line forms. So for Mackmurdo the curve was but one stage in his development, soon behind him. By 1886 all trace of sinuosity had gone from his wallpapers and fabrics in favour of a purist, angular straight-line style which was also evident in his designs for the Guild's stand at the Liverpool exhibition. In 1904 Mackmurdo gave up design work to concentrate exclusively on promoting his social and aesthetic ideas. He is important as the link between Morris, who attacked the ostentation and heaviness of Victorian taste, and Charles Francis Annesley Voysey, the rising star of English architecture and decoration for two decades after 1890, of whom the architect Henri van de Velde wrote: 'it is as if spring arrived all of a sudden'.

Voysey (1857-1941) designed papers and fabrics in a style much influenced by Mackmurdo – the same strength of motif, the same sinuous line but to a softer rhythm. For the supporters of Art Nouveau in France, organic and naturally found form replaced intellectual form. Gallé, for example, inscribed above the door of his studio: 'Our roots are in the heart of the wood, in the moss on the banks of the stream'. But for Voysey the process was one of reason: he realized that a return to nature was a return to the source, but from that source a selection, based on a serious analysis, must be made. Natural forms must be reduced to simple symbols. Voysey assimilated instantly Mackmurdo's tendency towards a linear abstraction in architecture, and his designs became more spacious. This can be appreciated in the reconstruction of one of his interiors in the Geffrye

The Shallop Design
Designed by C.F.A. Voysey for Essex and Co. English, 1901. V&A.

Cereus. *Designed by C.F.A. Voysey for William Woollams. English, 1886. V&A.*

Flowers. *Designed by Lewis F. Day and block-printed. English. V&A.*

The Owl. *Designed by C.F.A. Voysey for Essex and Co. English, 1896. V&A. Also produced as a woven fabric by Alexander Morton and Co.*

Flowers and foliage. Designed by H. Wilson for Jeffrey and Co. English, 1894. V&A.

The Orchard. Designed by W.J. Neatby for Jeffrey and Co. English, c. 1904. V&A.

Design by C.F.A. Voysey. Blue bird, yellow flowers and green branches on an ochre ground. English, 1891. V&A.

Museum, London, which combines wallpaper with a wide white-painted frieze.

Morris, Mackmurdo and Voysey were all founder-members of the Art Workers' Guild, and another notable figure in the Guild was Lewis F. Day. This excellent but conservative designer was responsible for making printed papers with floral motifs, both stylized and natural. The names of Heywood Sumner and Alan Francis Vigers should also be mentioned, as should the Silver Studio whose wallpapers were some way from the precepts of the Arts and Crafts Movement, but all of which were, up until the First World War, one of the most distinctive and easily recognizable products of British industry.

Young America

British industry was the model here. The first printing machine was imported into Philadelphia by John Howell in 1844, and another, with multiple colour printing, followed two years later. The famous English firm, Jeffrey and Co., who had printed papers not only by William Morris but also by Lewis Day and Walter Crane, opened an office in New York. A great deal of interest was aroused by Oscar Wilde's lectures in the United States on the renaissance of interior decoration and the rebirth of craftsmanship. This interest contributed to the setting-up, between 1876 and 1916, of various societies to encourage design. Morris's influence was again at work in the first exhibition of pieces by Tiffany,[2] whose two-dimensional designs were inspired by Arts and Crafts ideas. These theoretical movements hardly concerned the buying public, who continued to prefer papers inspired by the past, together with the perennial bamboo motif. Around 1890 the architects Hunt[3] and Sullivan[4] brought in a range of new ideas that broke with the past, and the young Austrian architect Adolf Loos[5] learnt much from their work during his trip to Chicago in 1893. An ornamental style already influenced by floral motifs was naturally receptive to Art Nouveau. Designers and architects worked together to produce large integrated designs.

Bing noted, 'in the interior decoration of country mansions, the old habits of colonial line and an influence from England, where there has always been a tradition of rural building', and that American art was aware of practical needs ('electricity has brought in a new era, and the new country knows it'). The American people 'could act without having behind them any past at all. Having learnt and appreciated all the secrets and techniques of earlier times, they could create for themselves without reference to former method.'

Goethe made the same point at the beginning of the nineteenth century:–

> Oh America: yours is a more fortunate land
> than our old continent.
> You have no tumble-down castles
> Or suchlike ruins.
> In times of trouble
> You are not brought down
> By useless memories or futile quarrels.

Alfred Loos had the same impression: 'Happy the land where there are no laggards and no plunderers – only America enjoys that fortune.' Bing was also aware of this in wallpaper: 'Another decorative art form that is today very successful is that of wallpaper. A large number of makers – in the states of New York and Pennsylvania alone there are more than twenty – create papers in excellent and particularly modern taste: their liberality of design and clear colouring makes them the equal of English production and a salutary lesson to our French manufacturers'. In this context we could mention the York Wale Paper Company P.A. and the M.H. Birge factory, which was certainly the largest manufacturer before 1900 and specialized in imitating leather with sparkling bronze effects. We have come a long way from Brissot de Warville's comments a century before. Bing adds: 'Where, alas, has that time gone, when Parisian wallpapers dominated the markets of the world?'

In this great democratic movement, was it to be the machine or the craftsman to bring art and beauty within the reach of all? America had her own reply, according to Bing: 'There seems to be a principle that the machine is the inevitable enemy of art – and the time to fight such preconceived ideas is now. Given an original design of quality and that it is carefully and sensibly prepared for multiple repetition, the machine can be a force in public taste' (*La culture artistique en Amérique*, Paris, 1896.)

Block-printed paper by John D. Sedding (1838-90). English, 1885. V&A.

Original design for bamboo filling. Designed by E.W. Godwin for Jeffrey and Co. English, 1872. V&A.

The Vine. *Designed by Heywood Sumner (1853-1940) and woodblock printed by Jeffrey and Co. English, 1893. V&A.*

Artistic influences in France

After defeat in the Franco-Prussian war of 1870, which the bourgeoisie laid firmly at the door of the imperial regime, the France of the Third Republic turned towards 'the modern'. The new generation believed wholeheartedly in the industrial and machine age: ironwork and the new discovery of electricity quite went to their heads. Thanks to this magical new lighting, walls were looked at in a totally new way.

The Belle Epoque also witnessed the 1900 International Exhibition in Paris. On the banks of the Seine the guest countries put up pavilions that were real palaces, symbols of the pride and wealth of each nation. Victorian England built a reproduction of Kingston House, constructed on a metal frame. The newer styles were shown alongside the revival ones, all expressing British comfort; one example of this eclecticism was the rare Worcester porcelain shown in a splendid Chinese cabinet. The pavilion of Kaiser Wilhelm's expanding Germany was correspondingly opulent. The United States took as a model the Pantheon in Rome, though the décor was poorly researched. (The magazine *L'Illustration* regretted that the Americans had not shown any of their new style mansion houses.) France's contribution was also built of iron, though the designs, as audacious as any Gothic arch, were concealed behind a classical façade. These buildings were the Grand Palais and the Petit Palais, near the Champs Elysées, the work of the architects Deglane and Girault. As for the decorative arts, the exhibition represented a stalemate: the conservative tradition was as strong as ever and the Art Nouveau style had yet to win over all the critics.

In the latter camp, mention must be made of one individual, Samuel Bing (1838-1905). A Frenchman born in Hamburg, he moved to Paris in 1871 where he ran a shop called Art Nouveau. He showed furniture and objects by all the leading designers in the new style. He was also responsible for a wave of orientalism, by showing genuine objects that he had brought back from his trip to China and Japan in 1875. In 1893 he undertook a study trip to the USA at the request of the French government. His report, *La culture artistique en Amerique,* from which we have already quoted, was published in 1896. In it Bing defended the machine, which could become 'an important factor in the development of public taste. By means of the machine, a unique and inspired idea can be made to spread infinitely the joy of pure form.' America was a new country, without the burden of a past. This lesson in modernity Bing put to work at once by showing his furniture *in situ* without the paraphernalia of traditional connoisseurship. At the 1900 exhibition the uncluttered style of his shop was reflected in his contribution. 'The modern home', he said, was in search of 'a rigorous and necessary simplicity'. Bing continued to support this revolution in the decorative arts, which was to lead Le Corbusier to say that 'in 1900 the match was put to the fire.'

Octave Mirbeau wrote: '. . . now nothing is straight, nothing at right angles, nothing is true. Everything rounded has gone square, everything square rounded: I mean that nothing is square, round, oval, nor oblong nor triangular, not vertical, not horizontal. Everything turns round, in and out, up and down and out of true. There are nothing but garlands in varnished bronze, astragals in stained wood, multi-coloured faience ellipses, arches in burnt sandstone, panelling in figured leather, friezes of untidy waterlilies and furious peacocks, sunflowers perched on moulded pedestals like parrots on a pole . . . Flat thin caterpillars are coiled around our keyholes, tadpoles climb and slither in viscous waves over doors and windows, edges and drawers. Fireplaces become bookcases, bookcases screens, screens wardrobes and wardrobes sofas. The electric light can glare from floor or ceiling: the lightbulbs are fashioned into nightmare beasts and dream flowers. The light hops and skips, two-steps and quicksteps: a regular St Vitus's Dance. The furniture looks drunk . . .' (*Des Artistes*, Paris, 1922.)

A small number of designers created for a discerning elite those papers in pale and gentle colours that made Colette comment, when visiting the very modish home of Yvette Guilbert: 'I'd rather be spanked in public than sleep in a cream cake like that.' Nonetheless the English style gradually won over public taste. In Alfons Mucha (1860-1939) France found their own contributor. He put himself heart and soul into designing 'Art Nouveau to the point where the furniture would go Bing if you touched it.' (P.J. Toulet, *Les tendres ménages*, 1923.) In 1901 Mucha contributed to *Les combinaisons ornamentales* and the following year set out in his *Documents décoratifs* a vocabulary that fabric and wallpaper designers were to use. The friezes and papers that Mucha himself designed were inspired by flowers such as poppies and waterlilies, whose petals turn and twine in uneven patterns. This bold approach had an immediate and vital effect on European architecture. Henceforth internal and external architecture had to be one with the decorative scheme.

So Gaudí[6] in Spain, Horta[7] and Van de Velde[8] in Belgium and Guimard[9] in Paris were as much decorators of volumes and spaces as they were designers of buildings. In this they were at one with the great traditions of the past and anticipated the synthesis of the arts (the 'great work') that Gropius hoped for from the Bauhaus.

Paper imitating toile de Jouy. *Printed in copperplate. French,* c. 1900. Nobilis coll.

Hector Guimard was the driving force behind what can be called the first 'housing scheme'. He was much impressed by a visit in 1895 to Horta's Tassel house, and in particular by the stairway, where a design of underwater plants climbed the walls in a whiplash movement. He decided to change his plans for the Castel Béranger, a housing block near Auteuil which he had designed the previous year in a neo-Gothic style. He changed the architecture, exposing the internal workings of the building, to make daily and family life easier, more comfortable and pleasanter. He even designed the kitchen fittings. It was a great success. Visitors to the show apartments were enchanted by the unified decorative scheme in which doorknobs and fireplaces, stair-rails and carpets, and of course wallpapers, were conceived as a totality. The wallpapers all used the same design but with a different colour scheme for each apartment. The motifs eschewed realism, so as not to conflict with displays of real flowers; the underlying tones of yellow, violet, grey and white went together perfectly.

But Guimard's papers were exceptional. A few manufacturers tried 'something in a modern line' by lifting designs from art periodicals, but most interior designers turned their backs on such papers, which were debased by being crudely imitated for fabrics, and chose instead plain background colours and friezes stencil-painted with animal and genre scenes by artists such as Maurice Denis[10] and Boutet de Monvel[11].

This style lasted until the First World War. The pre-war generation, sensing the coming disaster, tried to snatch all they could from life and find the maximum of new experiences. Paris was the centre of a creative maelstrom. The beginning of the new century saw the birth of Fauvism and Cubism as well as the discovery of Negro art, movements whose real force only became apparent fifteen years later. In 1910 France heard the first echoes of Expressionism from Munich, but the 'barbarian invasion' really began with the Ballets Russes in 1909. Bakst's costumes and sets with their unusual shapes and colours were an inspiration to the decorative arts.[12] Paul Poiret reluctantly admitted that 'like many French artists I was impressed by the Ballets Russes and would not be surprised to find that they had some sort of influence upon my work. But it should be quite clear that I was already at work and had made my reputation before M. Bakst ever appeared.' (*En habillant l'époque*, 1912.) Poiret, the famous couturier who revolutionized women's dress, was also a flamboyant patron of the arts, mixing with famous artists such as Dufy[13], Van Dongen[14] and Dunoyer de Segonzac[15]. He also travelled to Germany and Austria where he met Josef Hoffmann, director of the Wiener Werkstätte, the architect Hermann Muthesius and the painter Gustav Klimt, whose portraits of fashionable Viennese ladies, often painted full length against opulent oriental backgrounds, must have influenced him. Through his friends the Freudenbergers he visited the most modern flats and houses in Berlin, and in Brussels he saw the Palais Stoclet that Hoffmann had built, a total creation from its architecture down to the ties to be worn by its rich industrialist owner.

Returning to Paris, Poiret's thoughts were only of interior and furniture design, though he did not accept the strict dogmas of Hoffmann's teachings. He opened a school for the decorative arts, the Atelier Martine, named after his daughter. Here children of twelve and over followed their own inclinations in designing fabrics, floor coverings and wallpapers, which were notable for their freedom of design, spontaneity and fresh colours. Several of the papers were printed by Paul Dumas. Poiret then opened a workshop in the rue de Clichy where Dufy engraved a series of woodblocks for a bestiary, which he then gave to the industrialist Bianchini to print. Poiret felt cheated, and so his workshop was closed. He felt discouraged by the lack of public understanding of his ideas.

In his article 'Arts décoratifs' written at the time of the 1912 Salon d'automne, André Véra suggests that the new generation will have none of Impressionism, *japonisme* or *chinoiserie*, pale tints in wallpaper or the taste for nature. They put their faith in science and demand an art for the elite. They support artists that their contemporaries reject – Baudelaire, Renan, Cézanne. 'This change of heart by the intelligentsia will favour a decorative style that is particularly architectural.' Houses, as well as furniture, were not to be made up from different parts or diverse sources: they were to have a deliberate simplicity. Sombre tints were rejected in favour of clear colours, in line with the serious intent of the whole. This proposal and these notions underline the interaction of all the arts, of which wallpaper is a constituent part.

From Jugendstil to Bauhaus

With a climate often severe, and its austere traditions, Germany had preferred until the beginning of the nineteenth century to use leather or cloth to cover walls, these being harder wearing and longer lasting than paper. During the first part of the century the strict principles of the bourgeois Biedermeier period had held back innovation, despite the theories on colour and surfaces put forward by Gottfried Semper (1803-79) in 1841. A professor of architecture at the academy of fine arts in Zurich, he designed Richard Wagner's theatre at Bayreuth. He brought back from a visit to Italy and Sicily the notion of polychrome wall decoration that was developed from antique examples.

But, as throughout the rest of Europe, the Germans soon found it necessary to safeguard certain national traditions in order to counterbalance the ugly anonymity of industrial products. They took to heart the new notions proposed by Ruskin and Morris in England. In 1896 *Pan*, a quality magazine on art and design, carried an article on art in the English house and the following year Muthesius[16] publicized the ideas of the Arts and Crafts Movement: later he was to organize exhibitions of English furniture. The magazine *Jugend*, flagship of the new Jugendstil, invited the English artist Walter Crane to design a cover for one of their first issues. So there were close links between Germany and Britain at the end of the nineteenth century.

Otto Eckmann, who in 1894 had given up painting to concentrate on the applied arts, made a number of designs for printers in which an exuberant floral motif, close to English models, is prominent. For the firm of Engelhardt in Mannheim he designed a series of twenty-five papers whose names – *Crocus, Mountain Violet, Agapanthus, Maple, Chestnut, Dandelion* – bring Morris's papers straight to mind. *Fasan*, a typically Jugendstil design, was inspired by the call of a pheasant.

Hans Christiansen, who designed papers for the firm of Iven in Hamburg, tried to exclude figurative forms altogether, keeping only an undulating linear design. In his papers a curling line moves in waves between friezes that echo the same motif. The titles that he chose, such as *Memory* and *Nostalgia* illustrate his desire to escape reality.

Walter Leistikow, Bernard Paulik, Max Lenger, Paul Brück and Margarete von Brauchitsch all helped wallpaper in Germany towards an Art Nouveau style. Leistikow worked for the firm of Adolf Burchardt in Berlin, Pankok for the Enkhausen Brothers in Luneburg, and Brück and von Brauchitsch, along with other artists, provided designs for Ernst Schütz in Dessau. This company received a gold medal at the 1900 Paris exhibition

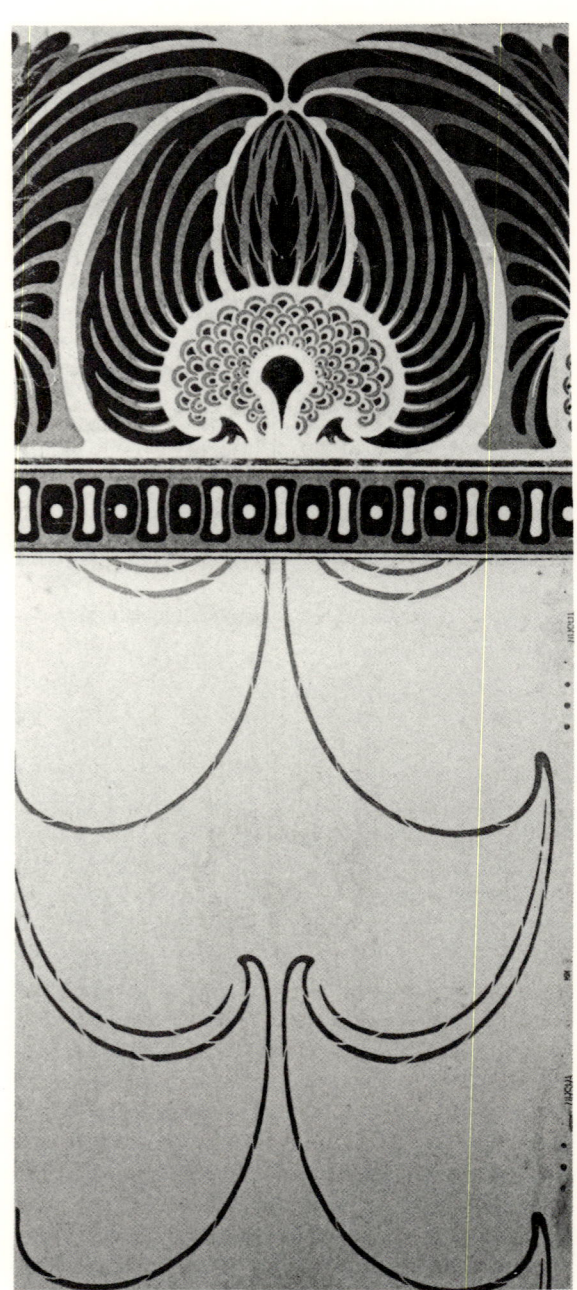

Fasan. *Designed by Otto Eckmann, in olive green on yellow. German, c. 1900. DTM.*

for its imitation leather and velvet papers, acknowledging the quality of their product and its modern design.

The designer Peter Behrens (1868-1940) founded the Werkstätte für Kunst in Handwerk in Munich in 1897: he was an enthusiastic supporter of Jugendstil but later a Constructivist. His designs were inspired by William Morris.

Not surprisingly Great Britain provided the reaction to the dynamism – we might say animism – of Art Nouveau. As we saw, Mackmurdo's design for the Century Guild's stand at the Liverpool exhibition of 1886 was all straight lines, and Charles Rennie Mackintosh, a leading member of the Glasgow School, began to design in a rectilinear style after 1897. He had a considerable influence in Europe, but his ideas were particularly well received in Austria. There the ground had been prepared by Joseph Maria Olbrich who in 1897 founded, with Klimt, the Vienna Secession, a group of artists opposed to the official art of the time.

The new movement found an organizer in Josef Hoffmann, who in 1903 set up the Wiener Werkstätte. These studios put into practice Morris's craft theories in a rigorous but inventive way. Hoffmann's theories, known as the Quadrat Hoffmann, were so radically different from usual practice in architecture and the applied arts that they were the basis of a real revolution.

Since Hoffmann saw architecture as a total art that embraced furniture and interior design, he himself was not indifferent to wall decoration. In 1912 he created an unusual design, *Prism*, a wallpaper that uses alternating straight lines as if for the shafts on a series of columns. Despite the general tendency of the time towards industrial production, Hoffmann believed that in the case of fabrics and wallpapers the different technical processes should be undertaken by the artist himself or under his supervision at least. Any notion of social purpose is forgotten: for him the decorative arts are luxury products, made to embellish the daily lives of a select few. This notion is fully embodied in the house that he built in Brussels for the coal baron Stoclet, but – sadly for the history of wallpaper – the walls of this pleasure dome were covered with rare marbles, tinted granite or gilded mosaics designed by Klimt.

The wallpapers produced by Dagobert Peche (1887-1923) for the Wiener Werkstätte linked Hoffmann's theories to traditional floral motifs, which were here restricted by the need for a rectilinear form. In some cases, such as *Antinoüs*, the design is simplified to a bare outline, in others the colour scheme is reduced to monochrome: in *Reed* the vivid design and uniform colouring create a vibrant effect that is a metaphor for wind over grass. Peche worked in Vienna for the Max Schmidt company, then in 1914 in Cologne, where he was

Tulips. *Designed by Joseph Maria Olbrich, in yellow on a blue ground. Austrian. DTM.*

Grey flowers on a yellow ground. Designed by Dagobert Peche and produced by the Wiener Werkstätte. Austrian. 1913. DTM.

Floral motifs. Printed in green and sepia. French, c. 1900. DTM.

The Rambler Rose. *Designed by George Walton for Geoffrey and Co. English. V&A.*

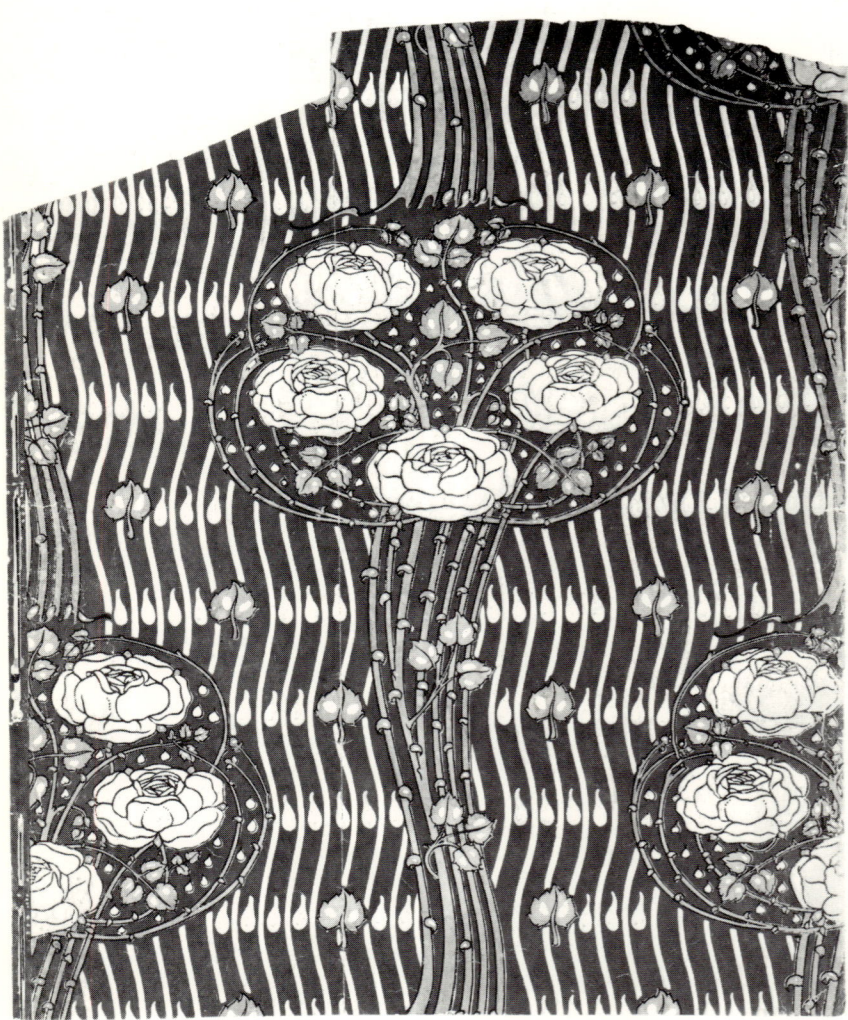

when war broke out. From 1918 to 1919 he worked in Zürich. Returning to Cologne, he designed for the firm of Flammersheim and Steinmann papers in increasingly geometrical designs that are close to Cubism. Peche was one of the great designers of his day. Though his design vocabulary was always modern it was never restricted by particular artistic dogmas: he retained an originality of invention and freedom of inspiration.

Adolf Loos's rejection of Art Nouveau went even further: proclaiming that 'any decoration is a mistake', he insisted on plain white walls, thus prefiguring the theories of Le Corbusier, whom he met often in Paris in the 1920s. Such theories, of course, did not help the development of wall decoration.

The movement towards simple form, which in Austria was essentially aesthetic, became in Germany a social force. The credit for this must go to the architect and all-round designer Richard Riemerschmid (1868-1957), who from 1912 to 1924 was head of the arts and crafts school in Munich. He created a number of solidly tasteful designs, suitable for industrial production at reasonable prices, an idea that was to be later the cornerstone of the Bauhaus. His refined taste, which can be seen in his designs for furniture, fabrics and wallpapers, is close to the elegance of Viennese production, despite a deliberate tendency towards functionalism.

Functionalism: the key word at last. The opposition of 'function' and 'decoration' had, for a time, a disastrous effect on wallpaper, at least on wallpaper in its traditional forms. The imitation of different materials, the great series of panels and the splendid floral themes gave way to a much blander paper, which became merely a coloured background. This explains Le Corbusier's excitement at visiting the Deutscher Werkbund in Germany, where Peter Behrens, Joseph Maria Olbrich and Paul Bruno were all working. This experimental workshop of the avant-garde was a paradoxical ensemble, as its aim was to make three almost irreconcilable disciplines work together: those of the artist, the craftsman and the industrialist – an 'alliance of the deadliest enemies' as Muthesius called it in 1914. Although the Werkbund's exhibition in Cologne a few months before the outbreak of war was apparently not the success expected, their ideas created the notion of an industrial aesthetic, which we now call industrial design, and which had a crucial influence on the Bauhaus. As Gropius himself admitted, 'their idealism gave us birth.'

The Bauhaus grew out of the School of Arts and Crafts headed by the Belgian architect Henri van de Velde in Weimar, but was given its true form and direction by Walter Gropius in 1919. Its influence has continued until today both in architecture and in all the applied arts. All kinds of different workshops – for furniture, metalwork, household

The Fairy Garden. *Designed by Walter Crane for Jeffrey and Co. English, 1890. V&A.*

Design for a wallpaper by A.H. Mackmurdo. English, c. 1884. V&A.

May Tree. *Frieze by Jeffrey and Co. English, 1896. V&A.*

Watercolour design for a wallpaper by Lewis F. Day. English, 1890. V&A.

Design for wallpaper for the Castel Béranger by Hector Guimard. French, 1896. Musée des Arts Décoratifs, Paris.

Wallpaper for the Castel Béranger by Hector Guimard. French, 1896. Bibliothèque des Arts Décoratifs, Paris.

Wallpaper for the Castel Béranger by Hector Guimard. French, 1896. Bibliothèque Forney, Paris.

Design for frieze for the Castel Béranger by Hector Guimard. French, 1896. Bibliothèque des Arts Décoratifs, Paris.

The Squire's Garden.
Designed by C.F.A. Voysey
and machine printed. English,
1898. V&A.

Ceiling paper by Walter
Crane. English, 1895. V&A.

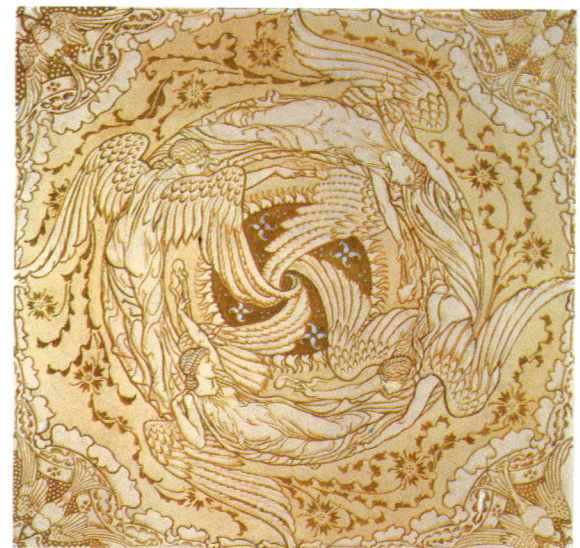

Two papers for Queen Victoria's Diamond Jubilee.
Designed by C.F.A. Voysey, for Essex and Co. English, 1897. V&A.

Reconstruction of a decorative scheme designed by Voysey with a large white frieze. English. Geffrye Museum, London.

Relief paper imitating leather. Designed by Paul Balin. French, c. 3890. Collesson coll.

Floral frieze by G.F. Jackson. English, 1907. Halard coll.

'Cathedral'-style paper c. 1900. Nobilis coll.

Roses. Atelier Martine. French, 1912. Bibliothèque Forney, Paris.

objects, ceramics – had a place in what Gropius called the 'great work', the creation of a complete environment 'by all and for all'.

The mural workshop, headed by Wassily Kandinsky, was a source of important theoretical experiment, but the small number of commissions meant that the body of completed work is slight. Large coloured surfaces became features in their own right. 'Colour should be an element in architecture and a means of defining space. Our wallpaper, more often than not of a single colour, was the result of experimentation in the mural workshop.'

The architecture of glass and steel proposed by Gropius and his followers, notably Wassily and Hans Luckhardt in Berlin and the Viennese architect Richard Neutra in Los Angeles, undoubtedly killed new creativity in wallpaper. The few avantgarde designs, whether machine- or hand-printed by some brave entrepreneurs, did not have a great success. But there is no doubt that at the same time the traditional kinds of wallpaper – fake leather and cloth, floral designs, neo-Biedermeier – attracted a bourgeois public who still preferred the grand and pompous style that had been celebrated in all its glory at the 1900 exhibition.

Post-war reconstruction plans, despite the economic pressures of the 1920s, increased the level of production of low-priced papers. Some manufacturers used artists as designers, or formed links with art schools, as with the Krefeld group led by Gerhard Kradow, a pupil of Paul Klee and Kandinsky at the Bauhaus. Several studios merged to form the VERKA association (Verband Kunstgewerblicher Ateliers), and provided makers with designs somewhat above the usual dull level.

Stripes and branches. Designed by Dagobert Peche for the Wiener Werkstätte. Austrian, c. 1923. DTM.

Notes (pp. 143-64).

1. William Morris also designed thirty-seven chintz patterns, which were printed by Thomas Clarkson from 1868 and by Thomas Warde in 1875. These two printers attempted to rediscover the use of vegetable dyes, for the sake of their beautiful hues and harmony with nature. The limited variety of such dyes was a corrective to the superficial styles caused by the superabundance of chemical dyes.
2. Louis Comfort Tiffany (1848-1933), son of Charles Louis Tiffany (founder of the jewellery firm Tiffany and Co.), himself founded an interior design firm in 1879, but gained greater fame for his patented hand-made iridescent *favrile* glass.
3. Richard Morris Hunt (1827-95), was an American architect and interior designer who worked in France and Switzerland.
4. Louis Henry Sullivan (1856-1924), an American architect of the Chicago school, was an innovator whose importance was recognized only after his death. The

Branches. Designed by Dagobert Peche. Austrian, 1925. Nobilis coll.

Chicago Auditorium (1886-90), the Guaranty Building in Buffalo (1894) and the Carson, Pirie and Scott store in Chicago (1899-1904) constitute his major work. Frank Lloyd Wright was one of his pupils.

5. Adolf Loos (1870-1933) was a pupil of Otto Wagner and adopted a style which denied any ornamentation, the effect being entirely due to fine materials and the juxtaposition of various planes.

6. Antoni Gaudi y Cornet (1852-1926) was the greatest and most daring Art Nouveau architect. His major works are the Casa Vicens in Barcelona (1878-80), the Palacio Güell, Barcelona (1885-89), the chapel of Santa Coloma de Cervelló (1898, unfinished), and the Sagrada Familia cathedral in Barcelona (1884-1926).

7. Victor Horta (1861-1947) was a Belgian architect who used much decorative ironwork in his designs, as exemplified particularly by the Hôtel Tassel in Brussels (1892). His other works include the Hôtel Solvay (1895-1900) and the Maison du Peuple (1896-99), also in Brussels.

8. Henri van de Velde (1863-1957), a major figure in European Art Nouveau, was an architect, interior designer and designer of jewellery and ceramics. Samuel Bing commissioned him to design rooms for his shop L'Art Nouveau. He became director of the School of Arts and Crafts in Weimar in 1904, appointing Walter Gropius as his successor in 1919.

9. Hector Guimard (1867-1942) was the major Art Nouveau architect in France. Besides the Castel Béranger, he was responsible for many of the entrances to the Paris Métro (1899-1904).

10. Maurice Denis (1870-1932) was a co-founder of the Nabis, who rejected the naturalism of Impressionist works in favour of an emphasis on subject matter. Denis' paintings follow his own theory in that they are 'flat surfaces covered with colours'.

11. Louis Maurice Boutet de Monvel (1851-1913) created brightly coloured paintings in a naive, highly finished style.

12. Léon Bakst (Lev Samoïlevitch Rosenberg, 1866-1924) was a Russian painter and decorator who revolutionized stage design.

13. Raoul Dufy (1877-1953), a painter, engraver and designer who under the influence of the Fauves aimed to render form by means of colour. He also made several designs for textiles and ceramics.

14. Cornelius Kees van Dongen (1877-1968), was a Fauve society painter.

15. André Dunoyer de Segonzac (1884-1974) was a painter and engraver who illustrated many books in a bold and vivid style.

16. Hermann Muthesius (1861-1927) was later to become the champion of art in industry. As Superintendant of the Prussian Board of Trade for Schools of Arts and Crafts he gave a highly controversial lecture on the backward-looking nature of German craft and industry, which led to the formation of the Deutscher Werkbund.

Lozenges. Designed by Dagobert Peche for the Wiener Werkstätte. Austrian. DTM.

CHAPTER TWO
Contemporary wallpapers

With contemporary wallpaper we encounter a problem in that we are looking at an art form in continual change. Although some recent designs certainly deserve a place among the classics, most modern decorative ideas seem to be linked to changes in fashion. An individual judgement is therefore almost impossible, because of the absence of any standard as a reference. In addition to these aesthetic problems, we must allow for the severe burden of economic events on modern wallpaper production. Despite each country's maintaining its own traditions, changes in the world economy have led to the formation of international groups producing uniform products. Other changes have made it possible for wallpaper makers to produce some papers in huge quantities, certain of a large market. Such makers, less constrained by the laws of economics, can encourage independent artists' designs which will help wallpaper avoid the ever-present risk of dreariness.

The new German school

In the years after the First World War German manufacturers continued to produce the traditional gentle designs in soft colours, mainly printed on wood pulp or grained paper for a textured effect. These manufacturers, who also produced some new designs, included Pickaërt and Sieburg with their flocked papers, Rasch, and Auswahl Verlag Cadi in Munster with velour papers. On the other hand, lovers of the past, church restorers and so on, kept up the traditional methods of woodblock printing, for example Julius Henbus in Frankfurt. At the same time the reconstruction programme in Germany led to a need for new wall decoration and a complete break with the past.

In 1956 the La Marburg company perfected a technique for preset rolls, and in 1960 the Rasch firm, based at Bramsche near Osnabrück, made a particular name for itself by issuing a series of papers in collaboration with the Bauhaus. Ten years later the same firm published a collection of 'art papers' designed by artists of international standing such as Peynet, Salvador Dali, Letizia Cerio and Elsbeth Kupferoth, who had all worked with wallcoverings before.

But it was only in 1974 that the wallpaper industry encountered a 'revolutionary change' – to use the words of W. Eitel, director of the La Marburg company. The business, now a large commercial enterprise, had been in 1845 a simple wholesaler and only began manufacturing paper in 1879. At the time of writing, the new factory, built between 1945 and 1949, employed six hundred workers in its seventy workshops, and their designers worked closely with designers of fabrics and furniture. The discovery that La Marburg launched in 1974 (and which was quickly taken up by other large manufacturers) was called, very aptly, 'Second-generation Wallpaper'. If we had to distinguish between these papers and traditional imitative or flocked papers, we could say that they, too, sought to give the impression of a material, but by using a foam base. The expanded foam 'Profile Vinyl' had a third dimension compared to the earlier flat vinyl wallpapers, which because of concerns about safety and odour never really caught on in Germany. The contrast between the matte relief and the gloss base gave an optical effect enhanced by the play of shadow and changing light on the surface. Another development by La Marburg in 1956 was the application to the paper surface of woven threads. Nowadays such expanded foam wall-coverings are always on a paper base but the decorative effect is still achieved by various uses of vinyl.

Being an industry in which technology is all important, wallpaper making in Germany has now almost entirely gone over to photogravure printing, which allows for up to twelve separate inkings.

This is true of Bammenthal, a firm which also has a branch in France. It is a large family firm, run by Roland Ditzel, a major innovator and technician, together with his brother and Ernst Huebner. These second-generation specialists, having had enough of traditional wallpaper and paste, in 1976 launched a pre-pasted paper that could be stripped easily. The technique was taken up by other companies, including Borges, Rasch and Pickaërt and Sieburg but had only a limited success. Most professionals did not realize the importance of the new method, and the buying public, as market research has shown, only thought of putting paper up when buying. But this has not deterred Bammenthal, who are biding their time.

The fashion for designs of small, charming motifs was as much of a success in Germany as it had been in England, France, America and Sweden. Most manufacturers published new collections with suitably evocative names, all using soft colours and small elements in well co-ordinated but ultimately unoriginal designs. Elsbeth Kupferoth, whose designs were much in demand, did a series called *V.I.C.* (very important collection) for Bammenthal. The eight designs should, she said, 'harmonize as if they were parts of the same picture'. She used stripes and splashes, marks like coloured crayon, often on relief paper, in fresco colours and imitating various fabrics.

The *Cottage* collection by Pickaërt and Sieburg was a group of papers all covered with flowers like embroidery. Their most recent designs, *Tiffany Vinyls*, have a very Art Nouveau flavour, they co-ordinate and are washable. Another collection, the *Tiffany Gallery*, is on paper with a cloth finish and has a distinctive design of small floral motifs. Children are not forgotten: a series of papers especially for them has simple designs of dogs, cats and rabbits, even cowboy boots.

In 1980 Borges[1] published their *ISI* collection, a series of variations on small stylized flower and bird designs, which co-ordinate with fabrics. Bed- and table-linen and cushions were available to match, and the collection included, for the first time in a long while, a frieze paper. Young designers such as Canei worked on vivid new papers with small geometrical patterns. She wrote that 'excited by the sight of woods and plants and trees and by the variations of some colours between warmth and cold, I wanted to create wallpapers to embody this atmosphere in which light played such an important part'.

Design 706. *Frank Lloyd Wright for F. Schumacher and Co., New York. North American, 1956. V&A.*

La Marburg tried the experiment of using a designer, Yanasch, who is a writer and painter, story teller and bear trainer (his last collection was called *Bear's Kisses*). But such diversions should not obscure the real strength of German manufacturers: their considerable technical expertise. Research into new materials for wall-coverings is a continuing activity, for example, in the need for non-flammable papers (in which Germany seems more involved than any other country), which could lead to wallpapers being made on a glass-fibre base.

New work in America

Shortly after 1900 Worley, a designer for Birge, created a number of Art Nouveau designs with sparkling effects in a wide range of colours. Until the First World War America was to concentrate on the exuberance of Art Nouveau motifs.

In the 1920s contemporary activity and events were the source of inspiration for American as well as for English designers. The discovery in 1922 of Tutenkhamun's tomb prompted an Egyptian style that was very successful. Decorative friezes and panels were also in vogue. Donald Deskey, who was responsible for all the interior design at the Radio City Music Hall in New York chose a paper called *Nicotine* for the smoking room. Here, strong, brown-tinted motifs were laid out against an aluminium background like the pieces of a jigsaw puzzle.

Although the Paris 1925 exhibition catalogue makes no mention of an American contribution in its wallpaper section, in 1939 the Cooper Hewitt Museum in New York mounted a major exhibition for the bicentenary of the first American wallpaper manufacture. The exhibition contrasted mass production with the spirit of craftsmanship. A concern with hand-made work emerges in the fact that Nancy McClelland imported landscape papers by Zuber and Mauny from France and also in the designs of Mary Robertson, Hall and Proetz and Lin Tissot, whose papers were all woodblock-printed by Katzenbach and Warren Inc. in New York. There were also copies of Chinese papers such as Mrs Torrance's *Morning Glory* and *Yellow Lily* and *Country Life and the Hunt* designed by Charles Burchfield for the Birge company.

After the Second World War American manufacturers continued to make copies of old documents, or borrowed motifs from France, England and China, but these designs were not appropriate for new forms of housing such as skyscrapers. Frank Lloyd Wright, whose houses were designed to harmonize with their surroundings, was aware of this problem and turned his hand to designing wallpapers, mainly using a system of small geo-

Plaid and patchwork paper.
F. Schumacher and Co., New York.
North American, 1952. V&A.

Montauk. *Nursery paper.*
North American, 1930. V&A.

Design 602. *Frank Lloyd Wright for F. Schumacher and Co., New York.*
Hand-printed from the Taliesin Line. North American, 1956. V&A.

metrical elements. Other designers such as Jack Denst in 1968 used purely graphic elements in their attractive compositions.

In 1967 the Boutique Américaine opened in Paris. It was run by Juliette Mathis, who had been approached by American manufacturers when she was the agent for the Boussac company in America. Billy Manzon, a young designer who joined the shop in 1972, has confirmed to us the effect that Mylar papers had on their Parisian clientele and on interior decorators who had lost interest in wallpaper.

These metallic wallpapers were a spin-off from the space programme. NASA created the new material itself while researching protective coverings, and American designers had the idea of silkscreen printing on it. Jean Vigne's *NASA* paper is based on a superb photograph of the lunar landscape. He wrote to NASA asking permission to use it and received a telegram a few days later: 'OK for authorization for wallpaper. Good Luck. NASA'.

The cinema and the illusionistic effects of Hollywood sets have played a large part in forming American taste in wallpaper. For a large section of American society, even the well off, who do not own pictures, wallpaper is the most important decorative element. Americans change apartments, which are most often rented, relatively frequently, and being less conservative and more open to shifts in fashion than Europeans, also change their wallpaper, often asking an interior designer's advice. In addition they feel it important not to have the same paper as their next-door neighbour, so sometimes have papers printed in their own choice of colours. The expense of such 'hand-printed' papers, however, restricts them to the wealthy.

American wallpapers, with their flamboyance, life and colour, have sometimes shocked European taste, but one can never accuse them of dullness. They were created for a society whose life-style and idea of living space is different to Europe's.

The themes are the same, the treatment different: co-ordinated designs combine elements a European would never have dared juxtapose. Birds and flowers abound, but are large and brightly coloured; exotic motifs such as banana leaves are life size. But there are also extremely subtle greys and pastels, *pointilliste*, 'tachiste' and batik papers, and ones in Chinese, Japanese and Egyptian styles. All these are 'hand-printed' (what Europeans would call screen-printed). The panoramic papers are relatively simple in inspiration and execution – exotic beaches for travel agents, landscapes and views for a Western style – but there are some particularly elegant ones for skyscrapers in a Chinese style by Ilonka Karasz.

The Resources Council was set up in 1958 to form closer links between designers, architects and clients, and moved in 1976 into a twenty-floor building in Third Avenue. It is an immense showroom for everything pertaining to interior design and fittings, from antiques to lighting to flower arrangements, and there is a large wallpaper section displaying the work of the major manufacturers, which has to be bought from retail outlets. We have come a long way from the seventeenth century.

Coromandel. *Philip Graf Wallpapers Inc. North American.*

Macao. *Designed by Saloomey for Charterhouse Designs. North American, 1977.*

*Neoclassical-style papers.
English, 1914. Halard coll.*

England: old and new themes

The period between the wars in Great Britain was one of almost complete sterility and lack of invention. The same phenomenon could be found on the Continent of Europe, but Britain's insularity made matters worse. The creative impulse seems to have come to a standstill before the First World War; thereafter manufacturers concerned themselves almost exclusively with technical problems and the quality of the finished product, for example with perfecting the mechanical resistance of paper or the surface finish. Certainly Britain was well ahead of the field in certain aspects of production, having skills which made it possible to produce extremely expensive woodblock papers or reproduce old-fashioned flock papers to the designs of eighteenth-century masters. In this fascination both with industrial and technological progress and with master craftsmanship Britain slipped into nostalgia, forgetting how to create[2] and being content to re-use the famous and glorious designs of the past in an effort to avoid the horrors of the war years and the ugliness of the present.

The idea of the Dado at the end of the nineteenth century encouraged a revival of the frieze, and was caused partly by a shortage of paper. Manufacturers developed all sorts of designs for these limited spaces: landscapes, *chinoiseries*, scenes with children and floral patterns. The wallpaper was applied in strips several yards long, usually horizontally but sometimes vertically. This arrangement was convenient for the neo-Egyptian style brought into fashion by archaeological discoveries. Separate decorative elements, such as rows of lunettes, overdoors and octagons, suited the dado style. The Art Deco style was also adopted with considerable skill and grace. The Plain Porridge Papers corresponded to the white walls demanded by Le Corbusier and Loos in France.

Some companies, such as Sanderson, made satin papers with moiré and ivory effects, which had the cold luxury of a film set. The best examples are found in the work of Sanderson, Cole, Potters and John Line.

In British production since the Second World War the same tendencies can be seen at work as in the rest of Europe. This is due essentially to the increase in the ease of communications, the levelling out of local differences, and the regrouping of the economy by multinational companies. But Britain is still well ahead in the technical field, and British wallpapers, whether hand-, block- or machine-printed, have an undoubted quality. The one style where they are unparalleled is that of the floral pattern – proof of the lasting influence of

Provence. *Connaissance Fabrics. North American, 1978.*

Ticking Stripe. *Cole and Son. English, c. 1930. Reprinted 1981.* Wild Rose. *Frieze. English, c. 1890.*

Stipple. *Cole and Son. English, c. 1948.* Grapes. *Frieze. English, c. 1935.*

Paper by Woodson Wallpapers. North American, 1978.

The Cosmonauts. *Foucray. French.*

Cousin-Cousine.
Follot. French, 1979.

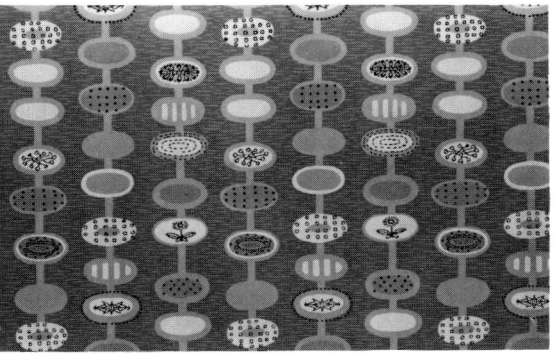

Silver Studios frieze. John Line and Sons. English, c. 1905. V&A.

Provence. *Designed by Lucienne Day.* John Line Limited Editions. English, 1959. V&A.

Morris, Crane, Day and Voysey. Except for Graham Sutherland, Edward Bawden, John Aldridge, Lina Lindsay and John Drummond, designers have looked to the past for inspiration, in particular to the work of William Morris, which has been a source for manufacturers in England and elsewhere.

The two firms of Cole and Sanderson each have an incomparable collection of engraved woodblocks, some of them extremely old. It is marvellous to find these blocks, properly catalogued and conserved and stored in long racks like rare books in an enormous library. The Cole collection is probably the most valuable in the world. Their oldest block is of an authentic Elizabethan paper found at Besford Court, which was reprinted to commemorate the 400th anniversary of the birth of Shakespeare. This paper has since found a continuing market, showing that it is possible to create a new paper from a detail of an old one, just as Cole did with *Sheep and Shepherd*, for which they used part of a design attributed to Jackson. Again using the resources of their splendid collection, the firm has published medallions and stripes from seventeenth-century decorative schemes or from the designs Frederick Crace used for the Royal Pavilion at Brighton. They also have the blocks for Pugin's designs for the new Houses of Parliament which were used during restoration. A large part of the collection consists of late nineteenth-century papers, and some of these well-known designs were reprinted at Sir Cecil Beaton's request for use on the sets of the film *My Fair Lady* in 1964, which contributed in large measure to starting a revival of Victorian fashion in England.

Another designer is Stephen Young, whom we met in his studio in Mortimer Street trying to match a shade of blue that Her Majesty Queen Elizabeth II particularly liked and wished to see used in a reprint of a Frederick Crace design. Mr Young told us that he had in the past recreated colour schemes from old drawings and designed wallpaper motifs from fragments in old houses. 'Sometimes', he added, 'I reconstruct and transfer to silkscreen designs from some blocks that are too badly damaged to repair. I also make designs by combining elements borrowed from different originals. The most important part of my task is the choice of colours, as a good design can be ruined by the wrong colour scheme.'

Cole does not only draw upon the past. For the Festival of Britain in 1951 the firm published papers designed by Richard Guyatt and Lucienne Day, then launched the first abstract papers by Guy Irwin and Eduardo Paolozzi, which were the beginning of a new direction. Unfortunately the designs were pirated and badly reproduced in cheap versions. The important quality of Cole papers is their perfect execution, to which can be added the unheard-of luxury of having a design 'personalized' on request.

Arthur Sanderson's career began in London in 1850, when he was importing the best French papers for his shop in Soho Square. In 1865 he moved to 52 Berners Street, and soon became a force to be reckoned with. Not considering his contemporaries' work to be of high enough standard, he opened his own factory in Chiswick in 1879. His three sons[3] kept up the prosperity of the firm, increasing the work force and employing new machines. Soon they bought up Wallpaper Manufacturers Ltd and the long-established firm of William Woollams and Company. As their collection of woodblocks increased, so did their success. In 1930 they took over Jeffrey and Co. and in 1940, when Morris and Co. went into voluntary liquidation, obtained all William Morris's woodblocks, which were the foundation of their successful 'hand-printed' collection.

Each year Sanderson produce 30 million rolls of wallpaper from their modern factory at Uxbridge, while the smaller factory at Perivale, built after fire destroyed the Chiswick one, is used for hand-, block- and screen-printing. Sanderson are undoubtedly the largest exporters of wall-coverings, flock papers and vinyls being particularly important. In 1962 their *Triad* collection, with co-ordinated papers, fabrics and carpets, was a particular success. Since 1958, some William Morris papers have been re-coloured and adapted for machine printing. The floral papers are the masterpieces of this collection and their inimitable charm rests untouched by variations in fashion.

Lace. Cole and Son. English, 1939. V&A.

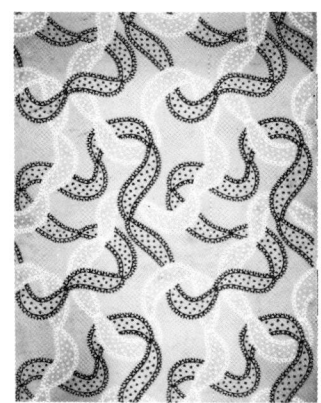

Triad. *From a Silver Studio design.* Sanderson. English, 1962.

Triad. *Nursery paper, from a Mabel Lucy Atwell design.* Sanderson. English, 1962.

Patchwork. *Laura Ashley. English, 1979-80.*

Among the success-stories of contemporary paper, mention must be made of Laura Ashley, who has evolved a delightful and quite British style. Bernard and Laura Ashley began silkscreening fabrics in a small way in 1953. In 1954 they printed their first Liberty-style design on a machine built by Bernard. Nine years later they set up a workshop in a disused garage, Laura designing, and Bernard perfecting the press. Their first successes were gardening aprons and dishcloths, and their first clothes appeared in 1966. Using factories in Wales and Holland Laura Ashley produced her first wallpapers in 1972-73. The London shop, opened in 1969, was the seal of success. Branches followed one after the other in different capitals – in Paris in 1974, for example.

A simple, almost rustic design has been their trademark. The wallpapers have co-ordinated patterns of small flowers, printed in a single pastel colour or reversed out, which gives an air of tasteful unity. Their success[4] is all the greater because the papers are modestly priced and appeal to a nostalgic taste. But times and styles change, and Laura Ashley now produce papers with geometric patterns and multicoloured stripes. One cannot let grass, or even small flowers, grow under one's feet!

Nor should we forget the carefully hand-printed products of Osborne and Little with their clear designs, nor the work of Tricia Guild, Victoria Coates, Sybil Colefax and John Fowler. A visit to the Designers Guild shops in London or Paris, started in the early 1970s by Tricia Guild, gives one a taste of a particularly British setting. In it walls and curtains, sofas, cushions and skirted tables are suffused with the same light. A closer look shows that harmony has replaced co-ordination. The wallpapers, printed from cylinder presses, and the screen-printed fabrics use geometric motifs or details of flowers, foliage or shells, in very soft pastel shades.

There are other British makers who produce work of quality, but we have tried to identify the most important influences in the contemporary scene. Who knows whether the future will also remember them?

Chartres. *Mary Fox Linton. English, 1980.*

Design 74. *Osborne and Little. English, 1978.*

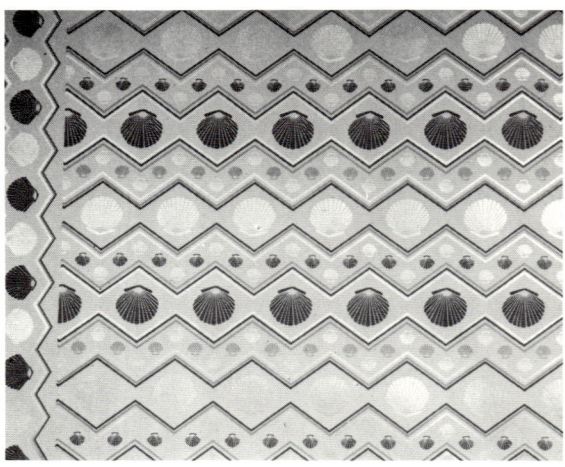

France between the wars

The survivors of four years of gruelling and deadly warfare had but one desire: to live life to the full. Attitudes became more liberal: women's hems and hair-styles got shorter. The *garçonne* – a new type of woman, popularized in the novels of Victor Margueritte – came into being, dancing in a cloche hat to a jazz band. And, like millions of others, went to the 1925 exhibition in Paris. The exhibition, which had been planned since 1914, was a celebration of the luxurious and the striking. The objects and furniture exhibited were made from the costliest and most precious materials: rare woods, sheathed in sharksin or inlaid with mother of pearl. The furniture, fabrics and wallpapers all conformed to the broken-line pattern. As Belleville and Bénédictus wrote in their report of the wallpaper section: 'These designs exploit surprise, the unexpected, contrast: the main motif is hidden by the structure, and yet seen clearly through it . . . the whole has a spectral quality . . . But the new ornament has great advantages, for it reflects a sense of decorative discipline that will educate industry. We are back to geometrical elements and angular forms, but with an independence from the rules of logic that out-does the most fantastic curlicues of the turn of the century.'

No more *trompe l'oeil*, no more naturalistic flowers. If wallpapers did use flowers in their design at all, it would consist of broken lines, its surface divided into patches. New forms drew their inspiration from the study of the atomic world newly revealed by science. Friezes became larger, and the borders and separate panels were now put against completely plain backgrounds. Walls that were sometimes decorated with stencil landscapes had their edges defined by a different design.

This return to a design based on panels made it possible in some houses to devise a scheme of separate elements in different combinations according to the size of each room. These elements would include friezes of foliage, a background paper, landscapes, architectural motifs or picturesque scenes surmounted by baskets of flowers, normally printed from blocks in two or three colours, with a different one for the background. (This use of few colours reminds us of Jean Cocteau's dictum that 'a poet always has too many words in his head, a painter too many colours on his palette'.) The woodblock technique meant that quantities printed could be small, whereas machine printing required a large first run.

Cubism and Orphism, as exemplified in the work of Robert and Sonia Delaunay and the Villon brothers, made unexpected new effects possible, thanks to wallpaper and furnishing fabrics. Colour created form, in smoky grey, violet, puce, orange,

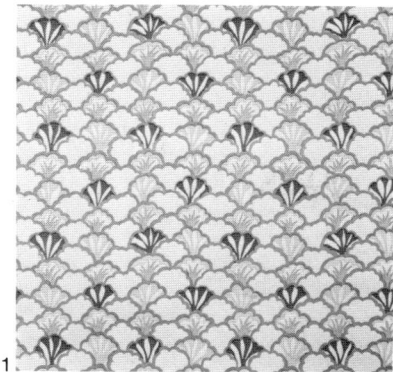
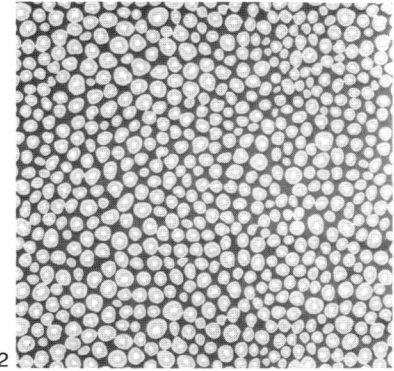

1, 2. Harmonics. *Designers Guild. English, 1980.*

3. The Fountain. *Designed by Paul Bril for Papiers Peints de France. French, 1919. Bibliothèque Forney, Paris.*

4. *Bouquet of roses, designed by André Mare for the Société Française de Papiers Peints. French, 1922. Bibliothèque Forney, Paris.*

5. Roses. *Manufacture Française de Papiers Peints. French, 1925. Bibliothèque Forney, Paris.*

6. *Vase of flowers. Atelier Pomone. French, 1925. Bibliothèque Forney, Paris.*

7. Siesta. *Atelier Pomone. French, 1925. Bibliothèque Forney, Paris.*

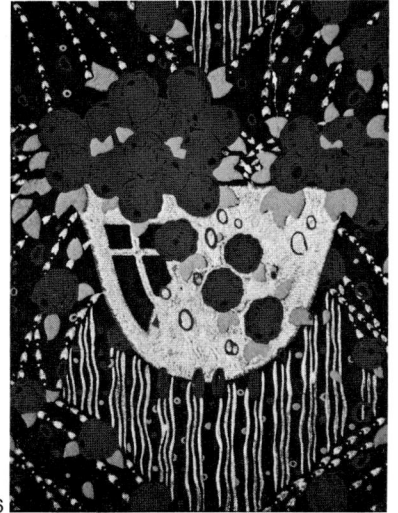

Harlequin. *Follot. French, 1925. Bibliothèque Forney, Paris.*

Flowers. *M.L.A. Reims. French, 1925. Bibliothèque Forney, Paris.*

Roses. *Ruhlmann. French, 1925. Bibliothèque Forney, Paris.*

tangerine, coral, pink, chocolate brown. Fashion demanded large areas of silk shot with gold on tinted backgrounds.

Some designers took over and renewed the old motifs from *toiles de Jouy*, others put their imagination to work on papers inspired by sports and games. But the critics only saw them as 'jazz as compared to music – flashy, violent and fierce'.[5]

The French wallpaper industry, which consisted of only a few manufacturers, intended their products to supply both national demand and foreign export. Wallpaper, according to the report of the fabric and wallpaper sections of the 1925 exhibition, was 'a material of wide application, which must please all classes of society and the taste of the widest possible public.' So papers with floral patterns, papers in the grand styles, updated and amended, were still produced in large numbers. Nevertheless, some makers turned to well-known painters and engravers for new ideas. Thus Paul Dumas produced papers and fabrics printed by relief cylinder gravure after designs by Dufy and the Atelier Martine, which contained oriental or Cubist elements, patterns of roses and leaves, splashes or purely graphic motifs with stripes predominating.

René Gabriel, whose ambition had been to be a woodblock engraver, opened a shop called Au Sansonnet in 1920, in the rue Solférino near the Seine, where he sold his own block-printed wallpapers. The designers Emile-Jacques Ruhlmann and Jean-François Leleu also tried to have their own fabrics and wallpaper printed, but without success. Public taste preferred the tapestries of Lurçat or *toiles de Jouy*. Leleu did not get his chance until after 1945, when the Follot company bought his work, and he got the splendid job of supervizing the décor of the great liners of the French merchant fleet.

The Galliera exhibition

The Musée Galliera in Paris had been holding exhibitions of decorative art since 1902, and in 1928 called on Henri Clouzot to mount a retrospective exhibition of French-produced wallpapers and fabrics to be shown together with contemporary material. André Groult, in the rue de Saussure in Paris, showed designs by Alix and Laboureur, as well as his own work. Grantil, whose workshops were in Châlons-sur-Marne, showed papers with animal and floral motifs, as well as children's friezes. Paul Gruin and his son Marcel used the designer Louis Riguet (who signed himself 'La Rose Moderne') and Baeschin. The latter also worked for the Hans company in the faubourg St Antoine: their flocked papers were much admired by visitors to the exhibition. Isidore Leroy employed the designers Henri Stéphany, Xima and Marcelle Ladeuil. Le Mardelé, in the faubourg St Antoine,

Tennis Players. *Designed by Lina de Andrada for Paul Dumas. Follot. French, 1925. Bibliothèque Forney, Paris.*

Arab Buildings. *Designed by Henri Stéphany.*
French, 1925. Bibliothèque Forney, Paris

Abstract paper designed by Primavera.
French, 1927-28. Bibliothèque Forney, Paris.

showed work by Jean Fressinet with such titles as *Opéra, Business* and *Folie du jour*. Ruhlmann, Süe, Mare and Suzanne Fontan showed work done for the Société Française des Papiers Peints: their factory was in the Oise region but there was a showroom in Paris in the faubourg St Denis.

Charles Follot, in the boulevard Diderot, offered wallpapers signed by the artist Bénédictus, who was well known for his designs for use on artificial silk.[6] He had the expertise to overcome the technical difficulties in adapting them to wallpaper, and his compositions contain mainly floral motifs, treated geometrically without too much clash of colour. Paul Dumas had the help of Houdin, who had designed *Forêt Vierge, Fleur Perdue* and *Jeux de Lumière*. The Société des Arts Graphiques Modernes in Nancy showed papers by Jacques Camus and Paul Colin, who was later to design posters. There was also the 'free work' shown by the Atelier Martine and the papers from the Primavera studio signed by Colette Guéden[7].

This renewal of interest in wallpaper appealed only to a few. The designs by artists were block-printed, could not be produced in large quantities and were therefore expensive. The industrial manufacturers continued to make papers in traditional or modern styles, the latter often inspired by contemporary design but rarely successfully. The general report on the 1925 exhibition explains this creative poverty: 'French wallpaper will win back its supreme position in the world market once every manufacturer has a creative director – we might say creative *dictator* – as well as technical and commercial directors.'

There was some reaction against the poor taste of mass-produced papers. In 1928 Adolphe Halard, whose shop Nobilis was in the rue Bonaparte, imported German, Austrian and British wallpapers of good quality, full of charm and freshness.

In the 1930s creativity was lost under conservatism and tedious repetition, caused both by the manufacturers themselves and by developments in architecture towards transparent, bare surfaces. Houses were opened out into landscape, walls pierced with bay windows to create natural panoramas. A few wooden screens, on runners or folding, sufficed to divide up spaces. Natural colours were the norm. This style, which was to become international, first appeared in the 'Esprit Nouveau' pavilion designed by Le Corbusier for the 1925 exhibition. The Stuttgart 1927 exhibition confirmed its success. This 'modern art' was easy to assimilate: its adoption by public enterprises lasted until after the Second World War. It was around this time that Le Corbusier made his famous remark: 'Get the Ripolin out: whitewash your walls and you yourselves will see better', which was quoted by several magazines. Wallpaper makers tried to follow the trend by printing papers with such a small pattern that they looked plain, as well as the traditional styles that still attracted a large public. But the gap between the theorists and the industrialists was widening. Louis Cheronnet signed the *Manifeste de l'Union des Artistes Modernes* demanding a functional programme: equipment was to replace decoration in the home, a 'clinical' style would offer the eye and the spirit rest after the strains of modern life. 'Where there is Art there is no call for decoration. The fittings of a house should show the personality of the inhabitant rather than his wealth or social position.' The Second World War did not heal this breach or reconcile the two camps, as André Véra lamented in 1941: 'Rather than designers on the one hand and workers in the arts on the other, would that there were just craftsmen, for the beauty of work and the peace of society.' ('Manifeste pour le renouveau de l'art français', *Urbanisme*, Orléans, October 1941.)

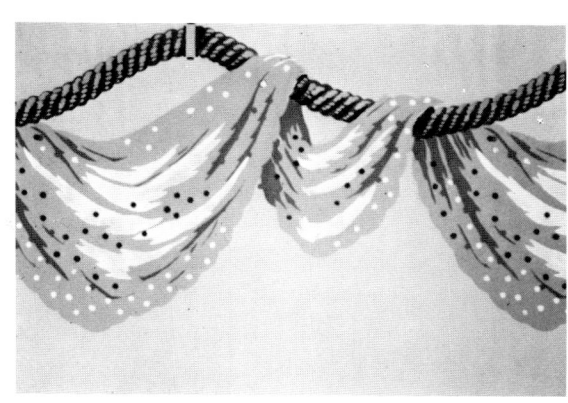

Le Malibran. *Frieze by C. Portel for Nobilis. French, 1936. Bibliothèque Forney, Paris.*

Frieze of drapery and roses. Hans company. French, 1930. Bibliothèque Forney, Paris.

Honesty. Isidore Leroy. French, 1930. Bibliothèque Forney, Paris.

April. *Designed by R. Gabriel for Nobilis. French, 1936. Bibliothèque Forney, Paris.*

The Altar of Friendship. *From a design dating from the French Revolution. Nobilis. French, 1937. Bibliothèque Forney, Paris.*

Drapery, *designed by C. Portel for Nobilis. French, 1936.*

France today

In 1945 there was much reconstruction to be done, so accommodation was built quickly and cheaply, without even plinths or mouldings as ornament, and which needed inexpensive and quickly applied wall-coverings. With a blast of publicity the wallpaper makers offered their solutions: false bricks and false stone, vermicelli papers. If in the past paper had misled the eye, now it was total deception. Flock papers came back, but in the same imitation styles that made them 'faked fakes'. Industry imitated the styles of the past from nineteenth-century models which were themselves imitations, and often with the wrong colours as well.

Cloth papers such as Duofibra, figured papers and plasticized papers were a great success. It was the age of plastic, that miracle material. Next was the turn of metallic papers, the descendants of those papers with metal powders that rusted with time. These experienced a great renewal.

With the 1960s, society at last shook off the spectre of war and beame in consequence avid for change. Economic expansion turned into frantic consumption. New styles disappeared the day they appeared, and this pattern of euphoric change went on. Industry responded to demand and the range of products increased.[8] A third major change in wallpaper opened up new means of expression.

Changes in print technology also took place, bringing silkscreen, collotype and photogravure to the repertory available (see Manufacturing Techniques, Chapter 2). At the same time, printing inks and colours changed radically. Besides the oil- and water-based inks, a whole new range was now available, in particular vinyls (polymerized hydrocarbon resins). They made the paper surface impermeable, and offered a wide range of matte and gloss effects. These possibilities were to make vinyls widely used. No longer at risk from damp, wallpaper could be used in bathrooms. Marks and stains could be washed off, so kitchens could also be papered instead of being tiled or painted. This transformed modern living spaces. Apartments were now much smaller, and some rooms, such as dining-rooms, had disappeared or been changed. The living-room now embraced both lounge and dining-room, or more often a 'dining area' crept into the kitchen, which in consequence was no longer just a work room. Similarly, the bathroom was no longer the dreary dressing-room it had been, but an independent room, where imaginative decoration could take wing. The makers of wallpaper perfected washable, hard-wearing and greatly varied papers for these needs. Papers for kitchens copied designs on tea cloths, or tiling, papers for bathrooms imitated marble or panelling. Another transformation was that walls became plain surfaces, without plinths or mouldings, cornices or rails. Paper no longer had to follow the shapes of panels or frames on walls. The new space available encouraged subtle designs in soft colours, or the use of natural materials so as not to overstrain or tire the eye. Thus a new product appeared in 1952, which many experts regarded as a wall-covering rather than a wallpaper. Appropriately called grass-cloth, this material combined a paper backing with a decorative surface of natural fibres. 'Could anyone dream of a more natural decoration, both simple and tasteful, to live, love and think in about the turbulent age we live in. . . . That is why these hangings go so well with any kind of furniture; as their decorative content is timeless, as many art but in the same colours, so that they could be alternated. This has given wallpaper a new direction: it has become a personal creation, which anyone can use to create their own environment. 'Everyone can share the dreams of cats and poets, and travel to the ends of the world without leaving his room.' (Vecquaud, catalogue of the Nobilis exhibition.)

'So we have come a long way from the strips placed in servile symmetry, the glaring motifs so persistently counted when one was ill in bed. There are still symmetrical patterns, but so much gentler, so much softer. And now when designs are vigorous or clash, there is more space around them.' So wrote Michel Dufet in 1953 at the time of the exhibition 'Les papiers peints et les décorateurs du XVIIIème siècle à nos jours' at the Musée Galliera.

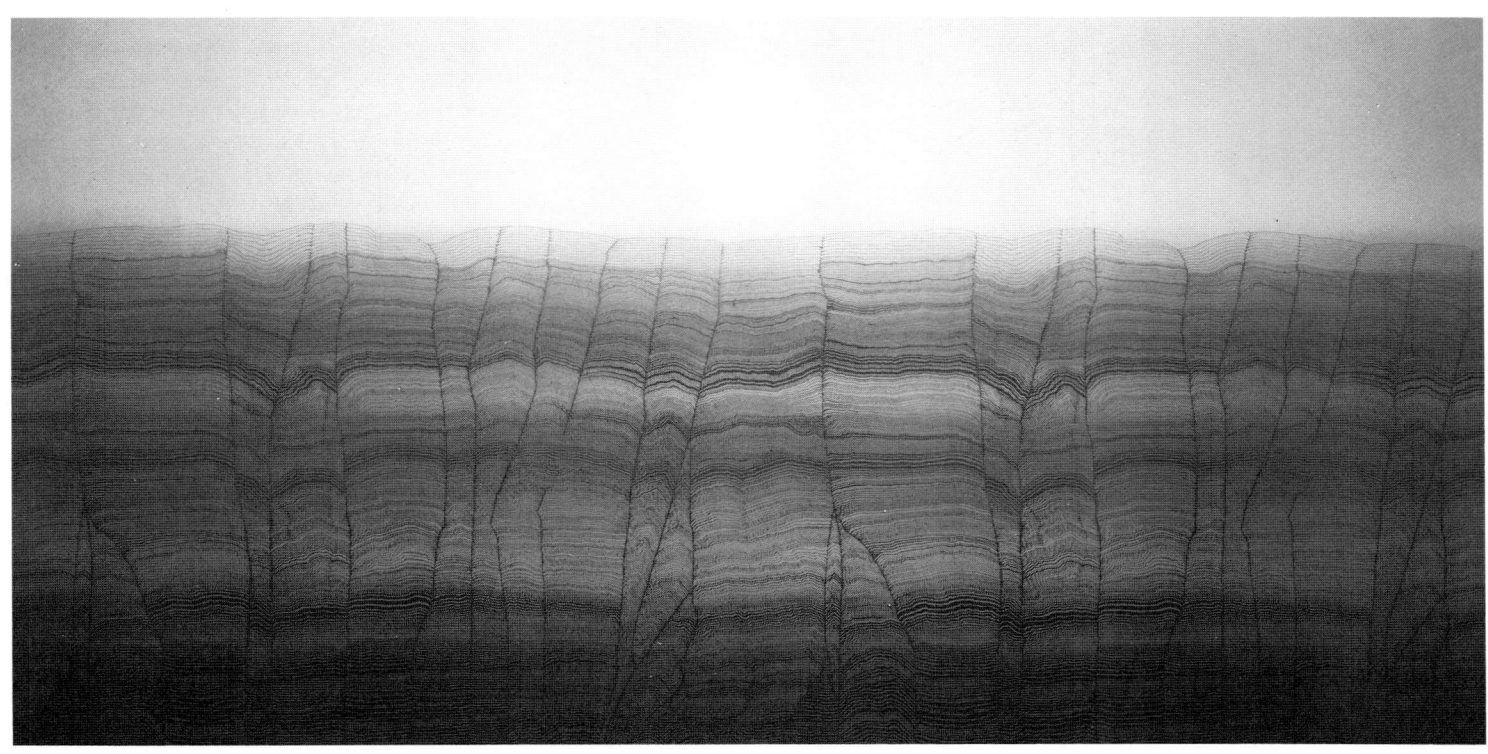

The Cliffs. *Designed by Alain Le Foll for the Zuber* Landscapes *series. French, 1977.*

lovers have realized, just as many collectors, museums and galleries have chosen this Korean paper to show to best advantage their collections, be they paintings, sculptures or fine furniture.' (Vecquaud, catalogue of the Nobilis exhibition.) This idea of timeless value and fitness without reference to one particular style was linked to the notion of craft and ecology, which itself stimulated the use of grass-cloth.[9]

In 1979 Nobilis published several new designs with a wide range of uses. The background is printed with a repeated motif or with a design (of bamboos, birds or flowers) over which the grass-cloth is laid so that the pattern can be seen indistinctly through the layer of fibres. The firm also produced grass-cloth papers with different designs,

This exhibition had the happy inspiration of getting the best interior designers to create décors with wallpapers both old and modern. Maubert used papers by Grantil, Dumas and Follot to create a *trompe l'oeil* of a window with a cast iron balcony. Carlhian suggested a series of planes by a decorative panel by Fumeron, screen-printed by Dumas, together with a bamboo trellis-work paper by Hans. Grellou combined papers by Zuber, Desfossé and Nobilis to recreate a *fin de siècle* atmosphere. Jansen used wallpapers by Mauny to create a complex bamboo pergola complete with urns of flowers, a baby chimpanzee and a white parrot on a perch. These examples show how eager manufacturers and designers were to find new uses, not necessarily conventional ones, for wallpaper. Pierre

L'Album de Zofia. *Designed by Zofia Rostad for ESSEF, 1980.*

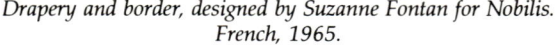

Drapery and border, designed by Suzanne Fontan for Nobilis. French, 1965.

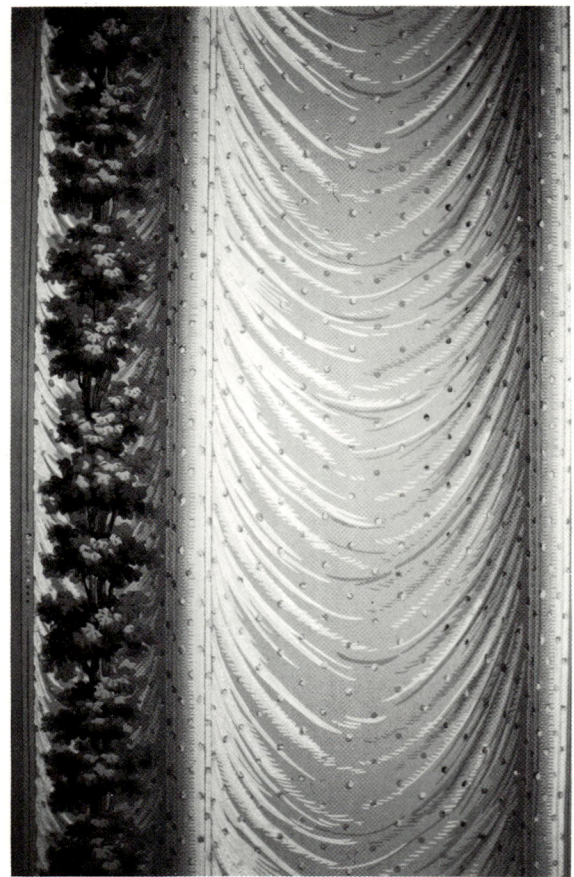

Motel, president of the Chambre Syndicale of French wallpaper makers, agreed with this: 'It is difficult to describe the incredible range of materials, colours and subjects available today. Different styles are reproduced: damasks and Persian work, drapery and upholstery and *toiles de Jouy*. Modern designs are in strong colours or pale pastels, in cretonne or in leather, figured or varnished, or stencilled, with varied backgrounds, and plasticized. And this material can be used in so many pleasant ways, all over a wall or in panels, to create contrast or heighten a decorative effect. Finally, for a relatively low cost, wallpaper can change any family's decoration, in a word to make walls live or, as Paul Valéry put it, make them sing.'

The exhibition at the Hôtel de Sens in 1966 was another turning point for wallpaper. Henri Béchard made a display of fragments of old papers – roses and bouquets of flowers – against a Chinese velour paper the colour of gold and a frieze by Leroy and Dumas: it was like peeping into a magic cabinet. In 1969 M. and Mme G. Fagu[10] organized an exhibition at the Palais Royal for Papiers de France, in which designers were invited to create wallpapers for their own imagined decorative schemes. Gaillard-Motel printed for Henri Béchard an octagonal paper, the first ever geometrical design to co-ordinate with a carpet. But this initiative did not get the support it deserved. A similar appeal was made by the president of the Union Centrale des Arts Décoratifs, Mr Eugène Claudius-Petit, in the catalogue for the exhibition 'Trois Siècles de Papiers Peints' organized by Yvonne Brunhammer and Madame Amic. 'For several months this museum will be a shrine for wallpapers, which will be displayed in all their original splendour. Of course this will provide a new source of interest for interior designers, but this celebration of a tradition nearly four hundred years old will also encourage manufacturers to find artists to design wallpaper worthy of the art of our time.'

In fact the manufacturers were feeling a distinct uncertainty, as shown by reports in the *Officiel du papier peint* in 1969. For other products with a mass market, industry was calling on a new kind of inventor – the designer. When even art was being industrialized as multiples, it was time for wallpaper to do something.[12] The new inspiration and pressure was to be found in the first American wallpapers being delivered to an antique dealer in the rue Bonaparte: they were to go on sale the next year at the Boutique Américaine.

Meanwhile manufacturers were producing low-cost papers in vaguely modern designs and with limited ranges of colour that would do for any shop, hair-dresser or laundry being modernized. To take a single case, 2,150,000 rolls of one paper (design number 5998 of the Verkindere company, trademark Decofrance) were sold between 1972 and 1975: one printing was of 160,000 rolls. Wallpaper was the mirror of its age again: the design was based on the shape of a television screen!

'This seasonal industry has much in common with haute couture, in that it reacts to fashion.' (G. Fagu, *Panorama de l'industrie française du papier peint*.) In 1971, in homage to the celebration of the 2,500th anniversary of the Persian Empire founded by Darius, fabrics and wallpapers in a Persian fashion were produced. Then there was a brief return to Art Deco styles. But in 1976 'rétro' became the range. The style was characterized by its inspiration from nature, its use of small motifs on pastel backgrounds[13] and repeated and co-ordinated elements. This charmed the public. The designs were re-worked in negative, ringing the changes between size of motifs and background in subtle ways, using fine designs based on the geometry of leaves and plants, with effects of cane-work, garlands of flowers, cross-graining. The market was swamped with new collections by young designers. Their antiquated and gentle charm, in such contrast to contemporary life, made these papers a refuge from harsh reality. 'Rétro' was reassuring, a reminder of the lost age of our grandparents, when man was nature's friend, an idea which was supported by the ecology movement. Paper was all trellis and vine, wistaria and tropical forest, ivy and bamboo, flowers and fruit... Manufacturers tried to catch up with the style by calling in designers, which led to a degree of uniformity between different collections.

In the 1979 and 1980 collections, nature was everywhere. Bouquets and bushes, birds and baskets of flower and fruit abounded. Even ceilings were invaded by arbours and bowers, and the newly popular friezes formed garlands on the walls. Some companies also tried *trompe l'oeil* designs such as stone, marble and wood from Inaltera, metalwork from Salubra and even heavy weaving from Follot and Crown.

Co-ordinates went very bold, especially in American collections where floral and geometrical motifs were sometimes linked. Textiles were of course still included here, sometimes co-ordinated with vinyl or lacquered papers, as with ICI's Vymura, or with oil-cloth, floor coverings or net curtaining. Co-ordinates are useful, in that they create a harmonious progression from room to room, and despite the vagaries of style (from stripes to splashes), co-ordinates surely will become the classics of modern wallpaper, to which every manufacturer will have to concede. As for papers in past styles, after the imitation of old documents the fashion seems to be passing to so-called Louis XIII and Louis XVI papers. There is some renewal of interest in flock papers, with both old and new designs, and for panels of three to six strips screen-

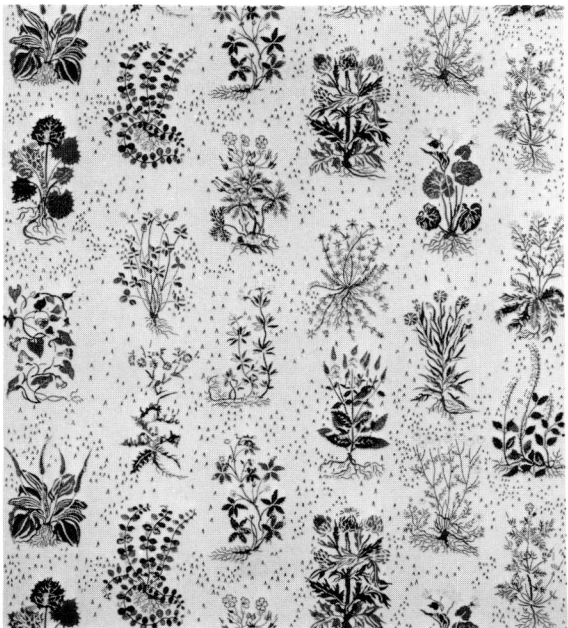

Flora Danika. *Designed by Bent Karlby for Dahls Tapetfabrik, Copenhagen. Danish, 1951. V&A.*

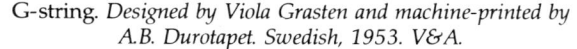

G-string. *Designed by Viola Grasten and machine-printed by A.B. Durotapet. Swedish, 1953. V&A.*

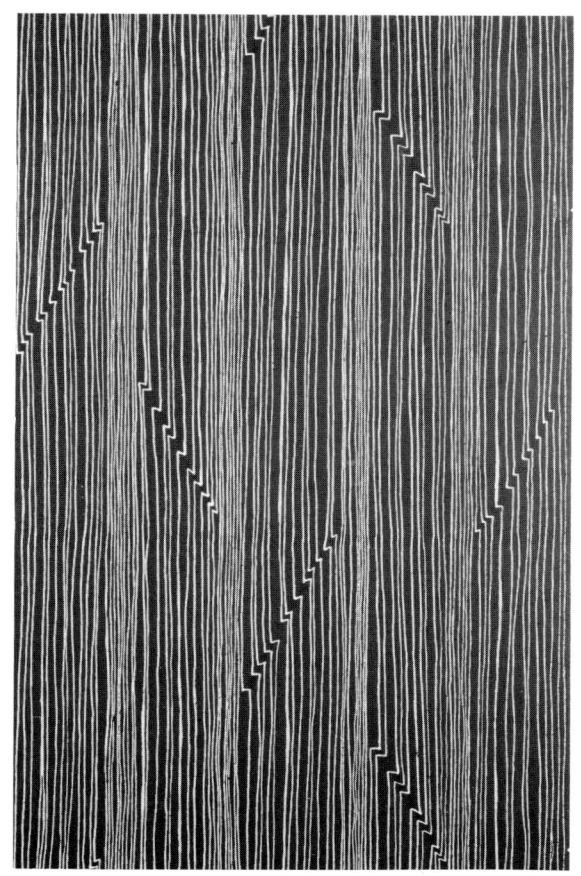

Floral frieze. Swedish paper designed for Les Dominotiers. 1980.

printed, notably the large panoramic papers by Zuber, which deserve the status of works of art. They restore wallpaper to its former place as a medium for dream and escape.

The amazing renewal of interest in wallpaper would not have been possible without two supporting developments. One is the great increase in the number of shops specializing in decorating materials, which offer a wide choice. One of the best known in Paris was the boutique of Madame Borgeaud,[14] in her hat and white gloves. Her sales line, known throughout Paris, was 'Je vous vois dedans!' ('I can see you in it!') These shops, whose stock is constantly changing, are the means of distributing to the public the new products advertised in the press. The second important phenomenon is the appearance of a number of 'publishers' who have transformed the production and marketing of wallpapers while still keeping in close touch with established manufacturers.

Publishers of wallpaper

In the modern world, marketing networks have developed considerably. Commercial competition has become very much fiercer, which has led to the formation of groups of manufacturers and has endangered small firms who cannot cope with soaring running costs. In the world of wallpaper the production of the maximum number of lines and the creation of larger ranges have bred a new species of professionals who can respond to these requirements without being tied to the costs and drawbacks of plant and factories. These are the publishers, whose role is to get manufacturers to produce the ranges that they design. For this they either call on their own staff or buy designs from freelance artists. While an artistic sense is obviously indispensable in a publisher (in the understanding of wall decoration a good design, for example, must look good from a distance and cater for the joins), technical knowledge is also necessary, so that he can cope with the constraints of printing and the problems arising from it.

The mock-up is worked and reworked, retouched and finally produced to scale, sometimes as a tracing, for consignment to the chosen factory. The publisher works in close touch with the manufacturer and prepares the inks through a series of tests. The real talent is to be able to co-ordinate the technical, commercial and artistic aspects. The dictates of manufacturing often seem frustratingly restrictive to the creative artist, so one may legitimately ask why the manufacturers do not do the design work themselves. In fact publishers often show a flexibility that manufacturers lack. The latter are professionals fully conversant with all the technical requirements, masters of their craft, but their concern with wallpaper does not have the freedom and spontaneous inventiveness of freelance artists. It must be added that they are often prisoners of their materials.

Publishers, on the other hand, bring out ranges that are more original, not to say more daring, and which are produced in smaller quantities; hence their obligation to sell at a higher price to cover the risks of failure. Manufacturers are well aware of all these things and have increasing recourse to design workshops or designers from outside their own design departments or else distribute work of young artists – thus fulfilling the suggestions of the judges of the fabrics and wallpaper sections of the 1925 exhibition.

In this way Leroy uses the designer Primerose Bordier, while Essef have taken up the services of Zofia Rostad. Gruin publishes the Arbutus collection, which was created by J.-M. Wilmotte and Dutilleul; the G.P.P company, comprising fifty shops, asked the Yves Taralon studio to create over a hundred wallpaper décors *in situ* for a mail order catalogue; and Cofac is the French distributor for the Linda Beard collections, which are published in Great Britain by Coloroll, and use Rebequet and John Wilman for new designs.

The first publisher in France was Adolphe Halard who, with the help of Pierre Motel, had opened his shop Nobilis in 1928 in the rue Bonaparte with imported wallpapers, which were an innovation at the time. With rigorous standards of quality, delicate designs and consistently good taste, these papers, which were quite opposite to the traditional product, were immensely successful. They brought a breath of fresh air to the French market. On the strength of this success, Adolphe Halard decided to publish his own papers, which were printed by Dumas, and use René Gabriel who had just closed his shop Au Sansonnet. Together they created very spare, essential designs with an almost childlike freshness; their partnership was to last until Gabriel's disappearance in 1950. Adolphe Halard then surrounded himself with artists with no background in wallpapers, who under his supervision became most valuable designers. They included painters, engravers, glass designers, a decorative art teacher and a furniture designer: Suzanne Fourcade, the painter Pierre Lardin with his charming narrative drawing, the glassmaker Jacques Le Chevalier and Paule Marot who together set out to rejuvenate old designs, often floral, by simplifying them. Paule Marot in particular created a style that influenced an era. In recognition of his artists, Halard printed their names on the borders of the papers, as if they were signed works of art.

For the export market, Nobilis called in the painter Portel, a tapestry designer for the Gobelins,

Three papers designed by Ferré, Dutilleul, and Wilmotte for Paul Gruin's Arbutus *series. French, 1979-80.*

who created huge stencil designs, rich and highly coloured, which became a craze in America. Portel's pupil Gourmelin, a designer and illustrator discovered by Halard, revitalized *toiles de Jouy* with his witty and sharp design. But his greatest discovery was without a doubt Suzanne Fontan, in 1942. Having worked since the age of fourteen in the Primavera studios, she became a window-dresser at the Bon Marché store and designed her first wallpapers for the Société Française de Papiers Peints.[15] Unlike many others, she filled her papers with people. She loved joy and nature and simplicity, was inspired by a flower in a gatekeeper's garden, a bird, an evocative poetic name, or a tree, and her designs are alive with a spark of natural simplicity. She was far removed from fashion – 'I think it is for us artists to engender it with the help of nature and chance events'[16] – and restrained by the dictates of the trade: 'of course there are technical restrictions. We "applied artists" are the industry's poodles on a lead ... let's change the subject.'[17] This Colette of wallpaper designed with a love of both her work and her fellow creatures, writing: 'I think work should be an activity through which one can build hours of joy and relaxation or communion, that is to say the pleasure of life, not a money-making machine with its ghastly results ... I think sometimes of the people who will live with my designs ... and I suggest they go and gaze on the wistarias, lilacs and roses that I am trying to convey faithfully to them, with their scent too if only I could ...' Her one regret is the shortness of each day: 'I feel so bitter that I cannot paint, make music, sing, dance, sleep, laugh and make my fellows laugh, love animals and little children for eighteen hours out of twenty-four.'[18]

The compositions of this great lady of wallpaper are always young and lively, full of gaiety and dreams, answering people's need for escape and contact with nature.

In 1976, with an eye to the future, the Nobilis International shop opened at 40 rue Bonaparte, offering, in addition to its own range, wallpapers and fabrics from all over the world which all shared the same high standard of quality. With two stores and four smaller shops, a staff of a hundred, and 1000 outlets world-wide, the Société Nobilis (under the management of Adolphe Halard's children, François, Jean, Denis and Anne-Marie), publishes traditional machine-printed papers, screen-prints, panel designs, panoramas and *trompe-l'oeils*. They are the exclusive importer of wallpaper from all over the world including their best-seller, grass-cloth, and work with the best manufacturers, who use the latest techniques and are always on the look-out for new talent. Although the Nobilis image is one of established distinction, they also have an eye to the future, which is the proper role of a publisher.

Letters at Play. *Frieze by René Gabriel for Nobilis. French, 1935.*

The Circus. *Frieze by Pierre Lardin for Nobilis. French, 1935.*

Positano. *Les Dominotiers. French, 1980.*

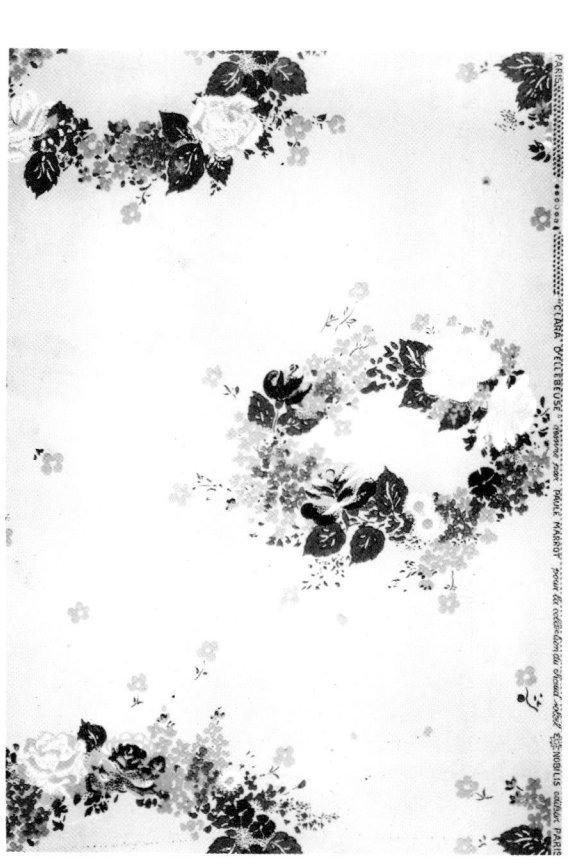

Clara d'Ellebeuse. *Designed by Paule Marot for Nobilis's* Chaud soleil *series. French, 1937.*

Châteaux of the Loire. *Designed by Suzanne Fontan for Nobilis. French, 1950.*

Beauty is Here. *Designed by Francoise Estachy for Nobilis. French, 1965.*

Whereas Nobilis turned to fabrics from wallpaper,[19] Manuel Canovas and Patrick Frey came to publishing wallpaper from a background in fabrics. Canovas set up his fabrics company in 1965. It was his silkscreen chintzes that led him towards wallpaper. A lover of screen printing, because of its matte, gouache-like quality, he designs his own patterns and supervises the printing in the workshop. He is very demanding, always striving for quality and gets his papers screen-printed in Switzerland and his vinyls in the United States. A man of refined taste and a keen archaeologist, he has drawn inspiration from extensive travels in Latin America and from nature, which he views as much as a botanist as an artist. He is a lover of colour and admires the interior designer David Hicks, whose vibrant palette he finds enchanting. Canovas' first designs were strongly coloured (acid green, strong yellow, Indian pink, sky blue), but later became more gentle with graduated tones. He has been expanding his range of wallpapers and has recently done a series of more geometrical designs. In his opinion, a good wallpaper should go just as well with old-fashioned as with modern furnishings, and hang in the main room of a house alongside harmonious, but not exactly matching, fabrics. Though it is rather stifling, the fashion for co-ordinates he finds beneficial in that it has disciplined public taste. Manuel and Sophie Canovas are the dynamic directors of an expanding business that comprises a showroom in the place de Furstenberg in Paris, a company in New York, ten showrooms in the United States and 8000 points of sale world-wide. Manuel Canovas confided to me that 'people think I am a man of fashion. I hate fashion – I have classic tastes'.

Often in the past, fabric and paper manufacture was a family business, and publishers today have kept up this tradition. Patrick Frey, for example, in 1975 succeeded his father who founded the business in 1935. For this thirty-year-old director, his father is still the master who taught him his trade. As for his mother, Geneviève Prou the designer, she taught him, he says, 'to see the world'. The Pierre Frey-Pierre Patifet group,[20] of which Antoine Frey is managing director, exports 35% of its production. They have two showrooms in Paris, one on the right bank, in the fine seventeenth-century house where Lully once lived and one on the left bank at St-Germain-des-Près, a just return to home ground.[21] Five years ago the wallpaper department was started, considered by Patrick Frey an essential complement to fabrics. He admits he does not know how to wield a pencil, but knows how to choose the designer who will best be able to realize his idea. He draws inspiration from the environment or from beautiful historic documents and usually puts the execution in the hands of the Zuber company. He aims to create fabrics and wallpapers with which

The Songs of France. *Designed by Gourmelin for Nobilis. Co-ordinated fabric and paper. French.*

Migration. *Grass-cloth, with co-ordinated fabric, from Nobilis's* Estompes *series. French, 1979.*

Java. *Soft geometric pattern inspired by handwoven cloth. Canovas. French, 1979.*

everyone from seven to seventy-seven years old can 'feel at home and be happy'. He is in favour of co-ordinates in colour but not design, and tries to stand apart from the uniformity of contemporary products. His fabric *The Elephant Gardener* has a co-ordinated wallpaper, *The Extraordinary Garden,* and another fabric, *The Alphabet,* to go with it. All these different designs are linked into one family by their colour range of soft pink, green and blue. It is rare for Pierre Frey not to exhibit his wallpapers *in situ* since he feels they are not finished articles in themselves and the buyer's imagination must be helped along.

An interior designer called Jean Vigne and a photographer called Jean-Louis Seigner set up a joint venture at St-Germain-des-Prés. They went into wallpaper publishing purely for love of the medium and distribute to two hundred outlets in Britain, Switzerland, Italy and Germany. Their papers are screen-printed. In 1974 they brought out their first 'Art Nouveau' style in blue pastel tones, and it was featured with a double-page spread in *La Maison de Marie-Claire,* an interior design magazine. They did not continue this style, though it was immensely successful with Laura Ashley. Every twenty years they bring out a new series, inspired by current events – for instance the 1970 'tachiste' design based on a moon photograph by NASA. They have modernized chintz designs and *toiles de Jouy* and use 'rétro'-style flowers. The simplest things, like a free-range white hen, a pavement, strawberries and cherries, a grating, a school notebook are turned into wallpaper designs, which they usually print on varnished or vinyl paper. They are against co-ordinates but favour complementary colour harmonies, and also produce friezes in the style of comic strips. They belong to the group of young fashion-conscious publishers.

If wallpaper is clothing for walls, then Mauny belongs to handsewn couture. In 1935 he bought up from Robert Gaillard, at the place de la Madeleine, his stock of old blocks and opened a small shop in the rue Franklin in Paris. At the back of the shop, in a workshop run by André Fénard with Raymonde Baudry as assistant, the tracings were made, the backing prepared, borders and decorative panels hand-painted from old documents, while in the little workshop at Montfermeil the paper was block-printed as in the early days. Today there is still a workshop master and three assistants to continue this fine craft tradition for a clientele that is 60% American (a nation that has always loved fine wallpapers and grand French décors). Three quarters of the production is for special orders. Their most faithful and enthusiastic customer was Nancy McClelland who came to buy wallpapers and panoramas for her New York shop. In 1936-37, Mauny introduced the first grass-cloths. In 1960 his son Patrick came into the business, intending to

Frieze and paper from the Folia *series. 1980.*

Malita. *P. Frey, 1980.*

Wall with Wistaria. *Designed by Suzanne Fontan for Nobilis. Printed by hand on vinyl-backed paper, with co-ordinated papers of trellis-work and wistaria. French, 1979-80.*

Bahia. *P. Frey. French, 1980.*

Benares. *P. Frey. French, 1980.*

Taking Flight. *Paper in 4 sheets. Zuber. French, 1974.*

Robespierre. *Paper and frieze reprinted by Mauny from a paper of the French Revolution. French, 1930.*

practise as a landscape architect, but he fell in love with block printing and became managing director of the firm. Paradoxically block printing, which is the oldest technique for producing wallpaper, is capable of creating the most contemporary designs. The changes that have revolutionized the profession – progress in the design of machinery, to cite just one example – are not in any way denied by Mauny's craft. He reminds us that tradition can live on, that the human element cannot be forgotten.

Notes (pp. 165-91).

1. This family business has been run for twenty-two years by Dr Ulrich Borges. With a factory at Lüstringen, near Osnabrück, the firm uses computer-operated flexographic machines. They print 60,000 rolls of paper a day.
2. According to the report of the 1925 Paris exhibition, 'England, which in the past produced papers by Crane and Morris, showed nothing in this field that was worthy of note.'
3. John was in charge of sales, Arthur of the shop and showrooms in Berners St, and Harold ran the factory in Chiswick.
4. In 1981 the Laura Ashley company consisted of 2 factories and 68 shops, employing a total of 1,000 people.
5. *Les arts modernes décoratifs*, Gaston Guénioux, 1925.
6. Besides the usual fabrics and printed velvets, damasks and cretonnes, the exhibition showed materials such as artificial silk and lincrusta. After the war, synthetic materials became tremendously popular because of the prohibitive cost of natural fibres.
7. Since 1921 the major stores had created studios to encourage a taste for decorative arts in the public as a whole. In 1921 La Maîtrise opened at the Galeries Lafayette, in 1922 Primavera at Au Printemps, and in 1923 Pomone at Au Bon Marché.
8. In twenty years the use of wallpaper grew spectacularly. Production leapt from 16,139 tonnes in 1957 to 30,467 tonnes in 1966. (These figures apply to the base paper and not to the finished product.) 43 million rolls of wallpaper were produced throughout France. In 1979, sixteen factories produced 70 million rolls, together with 30 million rolls imported from abroad.
9. This is one of the most popular wall-coverings today. The Nobilis, Fardis and Follot companies are the main importers of grass-cloth from Korea and Japan. Nobilis sells 800 rolls of it a day.
10. G. Fagu was secretary of the Chambre Syndicale des Fabricants de Papiers Peints de France.
11. This exhibition at the Musée des Arts Décoratifs toured the provinces and showed more than 400 papers and fragments from the eighteenth and nineteenth centuries. It was a revelation for the public, and the press was unanimous in its praise.
12. Denise René launched a series of mass-produced works of art.
13. The colours most frequently used were salmon pink, lavender blue, pearl grey, lime green and pale yellow.

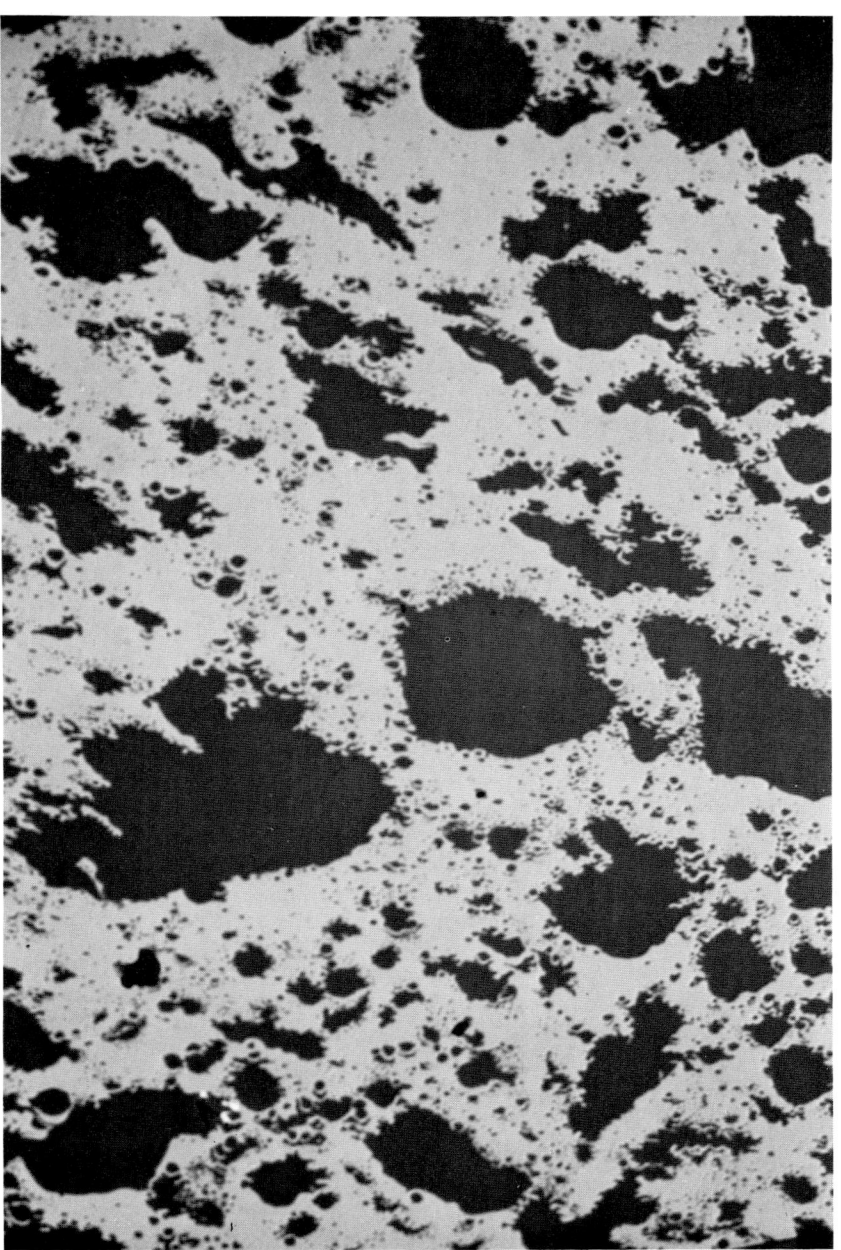

NASA. *Jean Vigne. French, 1978.*

14. Madame Borgeaud set up the Besson boutique, and her son is currently chairman of the Turquetil firm.
15. Suzanne Fontan was taught by Clavel, Paul Dumas and Jacques Camus. The last she described as the 'avant-garde creator of the mid 1920s, when I first stuck my beginner's nose into the glorious profession of French wallpaper design.' (Letter to F. Teynac, 10 July 1979.)
16, 17, 18. Letter to F. Teynac, 10 July 1979.
19. Suzanne Fontan, the sister firm, was established in 1932 and specialized in furnishing fabrics.
20. The sister firm was established in 1953.
21. His new collection *Oak-leaf*, printed from a wooden cylinder, is a monochrome design and has co-ordinating borders designed after old documents. These wallpapers are sold exclusively by Brunschwig in New York.

Lilies and partridges. From an original design by Philippe Delasalle. Mauny. French, 1920.

Vase and bouquet. From a 17th-century design. Mauny. French, 1920.

Important wallpaper exhibitions

1849 Select Specimens of British Manufacture and Decorative Art, Society of Arts, London.

1851 The Great Exhibition (class 26), London.

1862 International Exhibition (class 30, subclass B).

1867 Exposition internationale (wallpaper section), Paris.

1878 Exposition internationale (wallpaper section), Paris.

1882 Exhibition at the Palais de l'Industrie (wallpaper section), Paris.

1889 Exposition universelle (wallpaper section), Paris.

1900 Exposition internationale (wallpaper section), Paris.

1905 Exposition internationale, Liège.

1907 Exhibition of wallpaper, Kunstgewerbe Museum, Berlin.

1908 Franco-British Exhibition, White City, London.

1909 Exposition de papier peint et toiles, imprimées et pochées, Musée Galliera, Paris.

1911 Tapeten Ausstellung, Hamburg.

1914 Exhibition of wallpaper at Malmaison, organized by Charles Follot.

1925 Exposition internationale des arts décoratifs et industriels modernes, Paris.

1928 Toiles imprimées et papier peint, Musée Galliera, Paris.

1933 150ᵉ anniversaire de la conquête de l'air, 1783-1933, Musée Galliera, Paris.

1936 Première exposition des papiers peints panoramiques, Galerie Carlhian, avenue Kléber, Paris.

1937 Deuxième exposition rétrospective de panoramas en papier peint ancien, Galerie Carlhian, Paris.

1937 Exposition des arts et techniques de la vie moderne, Paris.

1937 Wallpaper, Historical and Contemporary, Albright Art Gallery, Buffalo (NY).

1938 Two Centuries of Wallpaper, Buffalo (NY).

1938 300 Jahre Tapeten, Hamburg.

1939 Wallpaper Design and Production, Cooper Union Museum, New York.

1945 Historical and British Wallpapers, Suffolk Galleries, London.

1945 Alte und neue Bildtapeten, Städtischen Museum, Osnabrück.

1946 Troisième exposition rétrospective de panoramas en papier peint ancien, Galerie Carlhian, Paris.

1946 Old French Wallpapers, Columbus (NY).

1948 -59 Salon des arts ménagers (wallpaper section), Paris.

1951 The Festival of Britain, South Bank Exhibition, London.

1951 Bauausstellung Constructa, Hanover.

1953 Internationale Tapeten Ausstellung, Mathildenhöhe, Darmstadt.

1953 Les papiers peints et les décorateurs du XVIIIᵉ siècle à nos jours, Musée Galliera, Paris.

1956	Three Centuries of Taste and Comment, exhibition of wallpaper at Foyles bookshop, London.	1968	Papiers peints du XVIIIe au XXe siècle, Musée des Beaux-Arts, Dijon.
1959	Dernière année où fut présenté le papier peint à la rotonde du Salon des Arts Ménagers, Paris.	1969	The Magic of Wallpapers, Kunstgewerbe Museum, Zurich.
1960	A Century of Sanderson 1860-1960, Sanderson, London.	1969	Une fête de papiers peints. Métamorphoses au Palais-Royal. With the participation of French wallpaper manufacturers: Brépols, Paul Dumas, Follot, Gaillard Motel, Inaltera, I. Leroy, P.P.V.L., Turquetil, Verkindere.
1960	I.T.A. 60 (Internationalen Tapeten Ausstellung), Munich.		
1961	Des fleurs dans la cave, first press showing of wallpaper in the cellars of the Eiffel Tower, executed by G. Aubry after an idea by J. and G. Fagu.	1973	Salon du bricolage, Foire de Paris (wallpaper section), Paris.
		1973	Historic Wallpapers in the Whitworth Art Gallery, Manchester.
1962	Les décorateurs et le papier peint, Musée Galliera, Paris.	1976	Papiers peints 1925, Bibliothèque Forney, Hôtel de Sens, Paris.
1963	The Wallpaper Museum and Archives. An Exhibition of Commemorative Papers (1850-1953), Sanderson, London.	1977,	Paritex, Porte de Versailles, Paris.
		1978	Paritex
		1978	La belle histoire du papier peint, Nobilis, Paris.
1963	Papiers peints anciens, Bibliothèque Forney, Hôtel de Sens, Paris.	1979	Paritex.
1966	Décors insolites chez Tristan de Salazar en l'hôtel des Archevêques de Sens, Bibliothèque Forney. Decorative schemes by H. Béchard, R. and M. Carlhian, J. Damiot, Gallet, R. Guiraud, Jansen, Mauny, C. Olivier-Merson, J. Prud'homme-Béné, Quentinharmand, Raphael, J. Royère.	1980	A London Design Studio 1880-1963. The Silver Studio Collection, Museum of London.
		1980	De 1880 à 1890, exhibition of wallpapers from Maison Germain, Lyons.
		1980	Paritex.
		1980	Papiers peints, histoire et techniques, Rixheim (collection of the Musée de l'Impression sur Etoffes, Mulhouse).
1967	Trois siècles de papiers peints, Musée des Arts Décoratifs, Paris. Touring exhibition to Lyons and Rennes.		
1968	Exhibition of the Centre de Commerce Français in Tokyo.	1982	'Papier peint 1780-1860'. An Exhibition of French 18th- and 19th-Century Wallpaper, Maclean Gallery, London.

PART THREE
Wallpaper and the arts

Balzac's room in the Château de Saché, with wallpaper reproduced by Mauny after the original.

We felt it would be appropriate to add to this book a few pages dealing with references to wallpaper in literature and painting. Even this brief and necessarily partial selection serves to show to what extent wallpaper is a part of our pleasures and joys, and even of our griefs.

Drapery with lions. Wallpaper described by Balzac in correspondence with Madame Hanska, 1802.

CHAPTER ONE
Wallpaper and literature

Writers have never overlooked wallpaper as a backcloth to the human comedy – or tragedy. As Oscar Wilde lay dying in 1900, he commented: 'My wallpaper is killing me ... One or other of us will have to go.'

For Balzac wallpaper was 'a fashionable decoration, a grotesque and shabby invention'. Nevertheless, he did use wallpaper several times to set the scene, for example in a student's digs: 'Our room, no more than seven feet high, was covered with horrid blue paper with floral designs'.

In *Le père Goriot*, he described the Vauquer family's boarding house thus: 'The saddest sight of all was the drawing room, with its horsehair chairs and armchairs covered with striped material, alternately matte and shiny.... The floor was uneven, and the walls panelled up to elbow height. Above the panelling ran a varnished paper depicting scenes from the life of Telemachus, with the principal personages in colour.... In the panel between the lattice windows the boarders could feast their eyes on the banquet offered to this son of Ulysses by Calypso.' (In fact, the banquet scene is not from *Telemachus in Calypso's Isle* but from *Antenor*, though scenes from both were often used in conjunction.) *Le père Goriot* was written at the château de Saché in 1834, and Balzac's description is based on a paper that was actually used in one of the rooms in the château (which M. Métadier, the present owner, remembers from before the Second World War.)

Balzac mentions wallpaper once more in *Le père Goriot*: 'Madame Vauquer had done up the three rooms of the apartment, on condition of an advance payment which, she said, covered the cost of decorations: yellow calico curtains, varnished chairs covered in Utrecht velvet, a lick of paint, and wallpaper that would have disgraced a provincial tavern.... Eugène [de Rastignac, the hero of the novel] could hardly conceal his amazement on visiting the Goriots for the first time, and comparing the slum the father lived in with the neat appearance of his daughter. There were no curtains on the windows, the wallpaper was coming away from the walls with the damp, exposing the plaster below, which was yellowed with smoke.'

Elsewhere, in *Les illusions perdues* (1837, this passage dating from 1819-23), Balzac talks more cheerfully of wallpaper: 'The small apartment had three rooms, on the fourth floor of a house in the rue de la Lune ... The bedroom was quite presentable,

Cheap floral paper. Machine-printed. 19th century. Halard coll.

197

with a green wallpaper with red borders, and two mirrors, one over the chimney and the other over the chest of drawers. The second-hand carpet... hid the cold bare tiles of the floor. The chest and glazed wardrobe would do to hold the lovers' things... And the rent was no more than a hundred *écus*.'

For Dostoyevsky, wallpaper was a background for misery, as in these passages from *Crime and Punishment* (1860). 'He woke up feeling sick and irritable, in a bad temper, and looked around at his room with venom. It was a tiny box, perhaps six feet across, with an air of misery with its yellowing dusty wallpaper coming away from the walls everywhere ... Down in the corner, at the bottom of the wall, was a spot where the paper had come away from the wall and was torn. He at once began enlarging the hole under the paper: "Everything will get in there," he thought, "That's gone already, and the purse as well." ... Raskolnikov turned towards the wall and picked out one of the white flowers on the dirty, yellow wallpaper, and concentrated on it. How many petals had it, how many ridges on each petal, how many of the small brown marks? He felt his arms and legs growing numb, drifting away from him, but he did not try to move, but continued to stare at the flower.'

As for new wallpaper, it was merely a façade hiding the old wretchedness: 'There were just two workmen there, putting up new wallpaper. It was a white paper with lilacs on it: the old paper had foxed and faded with wear. This depressed Raskolnikov immensely. He hated the new wallpaper, as if any change was to be regretted.'

Wallpapers were not always synonymous with poverty and stinginess. Here is Eugène Sue's description of Rigolette's room, from *Les mystères de Paris* (1844): 'The walls were covered with a wallpaper of green bouquets of flowers. The floor with its red tint glowed like a mirror... Over the grey stone fireplace, which looked like marble, two simple flower-pots as decoration, painted a bright emerald green... The curtains were in Indian cotton, grey and green, with woollen braiding, cut and trimmed by Rigolette herself, and hung by her own hand on the fine wrought-iron curtain rods across the casement windows. The bed was covered with a matching counterpane... Every item in the room contributed to its dainty effect.'

A more modest interior is described by Jules Romains in *Le 6 octobre* (1908): 'Madame Maillecotin lived in lodgings in the rue Compans: three rooms, with kitchen, on the ground floor. Only the dining room faced the street... The niche and the stylobate were painted chocolate-brown. The wallpaper was on a yellowish ground, with a double design in quincunx pattern, of a small vase of formal flowers and a cornucopia.'

In Emile Zola's *Germinal* (1885), we find wallpaper hinting at social class: 'Madame Hennebeau, his wife, explained that nothing had been done about the office, which was still papered in faded red.'

The bourgeois taste for luxury appears in Léon Gozlan's *Le faubourg mystérieux* (1861): 'Curtains in pink silk are only possible with lace curtains beneath them... And to create the necessary harmony in the scheme, I suppose that half a dozen chairs, a *causeuse* and two armchairs also finished in red silk, to go with the curtains, will be needed... With such furnishings, you must have a wallpaper with a border, in gold and white, cool as marble.'

In *Le plus beau rêve d'un millionaire* (1863) Léon Gozlan describes the new apartment buildings of Haussmann's Paris: 'She was in charge... of the choice of wallpapers, and would only buy ones with historical subjects. She went in for *The Inca's Sun Worship*, *The French Entering Madrid* and *The Refuge for the Die-Hards of the Army of the Loire*... "Good grief", said Fleuriot, seeing these papers which were more suitable for restaurants than homes, "What old-fashioned taste".'

The designs had indeed been published forty years before. (Incidentally in our opinion it is a great pity that modern restaurants do not still have such decorations.)

Katherine Mansfield describes a rather less than perfect restaurant paper in 'The Indiscreet Journey' (*Something Childish*, London, 1924):[6] '"You are two?" asked the waiting-boy, flicking the table with a red and white cloth. His long swinging steps echoed over the bare floor. He disappeared into the kitchen and came back to light the lamp that hung from the ceiling under a spreading shade, like a haymaker's hat. Warm light shone on the empty place that was really a barn, set out with dilapidated tables and chairs. Into the middle of the room a black stove jutted. At one side of it there was a table with a row of bottles on it, behind which Madame sat and took the money and made entries in a red book. Opposite her desk a door led into the kitchen. The walls were covered with a creamy paper patterned all over with green and swollen trees – hundreds and hundreds of trees reared their mushroom heads to the ceiling. I began to wonder who had chosen the paper and why. Did Madame think it was beautiful, or that it was a gay and lovely thing to eat one's dinner at all seasons in the middle of a forest...'

In Tolstoy's *Anna Karenina* (1876-77), wallpaper symbolizes change: 'Something there was new... from the French wallpaper... to the carpet with its all-over floral design.'

But in Turgenev's *First Love* (1860), wallpaper is seen no longer as merely an element of decoration, but as a product of industry, a reflection of working-class society: 'Our villa consisted of a central building, in wood, with a colonnade flanked by two low wings. The right hand wing was empty, and to let. In the left hand one there was a small wallpaper factory... I went there often. Ten or so thin lads, their hair unkempt and their faces already showing the effects of drinking, dressed in dirty tunics, leant on the wooden levers of the presses. Their weight moved the press plates, printing the brilliant arabesque designs onto the wallpaper.'

Industrialization figures in Alphonse Daudet's story 'Froment jeune et Risler aîné' in *Moeurs parisiennes* (1881): 'A rotary press, my dear Frantz, a rotary press with twelve faces, able to print in a single revolution a design in twelve to fifteen colours, red on pink, dark green on pale green, without error, without splashes, without a single line encroaching on the next, or any colour blotting or staining another... such a machine, with its almost human artistry, is a revolution in wallpaper... I myself designed, at the same time, an automatic device to hang the paper on the rods of the dryer.'

Only an artist's words can do justice to Chinese paper: 'With Madame de F... I saw at Maigret's a Chinese paper, for walls. Maigret told us that our own skill was nothing to theirs in strength of colour, as he had tried to match part of the pink ground: the result rapidly became awful. The paper is good value for money, considering. All the birds are painted by hand, as, so he told us, are all the decorations, including the pale bamboos, heightened with silver, which cover the plain pink background. The design is covered with birds and butterflies and so on... Their perfection is not the result of minute inaccuracies in imitation, as is the case with our ornamental designs. Rather it results from the whole animal being included in the presentation of the whole scene and the choice of colours, all done with an inspiration that selects and presents the object so as to make an ornament from it, as with the animals on Egyptian monuments and manuscripts.' (Eugène Delacroix, *Journal*, I: 1822-52, Paris, 9 October 1847.)

Marcel Proust found his hotel wallpaper a moral support: 'My dressing room was covered with a bright red paper decorated with black and white flowers, which I thought I would have quite a bit of trouble getting used to. But these flowers were merely new to me, and only made me enter into contact, not conflict, with them, made me change, perhaps, the gay songs I sang on rising, and gave me the will-power to turn and face the world quite differently from how I used to in Paris; it was like a gaudy screen reflecting the new house's setting, quite different from my parents' home, which was embued with a pure air.' (*Le côté de Guermantes*, 1920.)

When the couturier Paul Poiret was called up in 1914, he shared a hotel-room in Lisieux with a friend: 'We used to dine with the well-known painter Derain, who was in a cycle regiment, which afforded us the occasion to escape from a life of

The Allied Victory, 1918: Troops on the Champs Elysées.
Teynac coll.

Distemper paper. One of ten panels from Elton Lodge, Kent. Chinese, first half of the 18th century. V&A.

boredom and danger into our favourite subject, the arts. Our lodging was an old inn, the Hôtel Maure, where I had to redecorate my room to get it clean. I chose a red, white and blue wallpaper, to remind me why I was there. I have heard it said that the owner of the hotel still today shows off the paper as if Bonaparte himself had hung it . . . This was the setting for Derain's attack on my portrait.' (*En habillant l'époque*, 1930.)

Anatole France's memories were younger ones: 'It was there that my soul found its shape, to grow and create its own mythic world . . . between these four walls, scattered with blue flowers, the terrifying images of love and beauty, at first vague and distant, appeared to me.' (*Le petit Pierre*, 1918.)

Guy de Maupassant recalled 'the Jupiter room, where the local merchants used to hold meetings, and which was decorated with a blue paper carrying a vivid design of Leda leaning on the swan' (*Bel ami*, 1885), while Chateaubriand found himself 'seated beside the filthy alcove where I had to sleep, with nothing to do but look at the figures on the wallpaper.' (*Mémoires d'outre tombe*, 1821.)

Writing in a German newspaper, Octave Mirbeau admitted that wallpaper could affect his mood: 'The colour of my room is the reason for my sadness, my unhappiness and my lack of calm these days: it has a ghastly wallpaper in a sort of brown, the colour of burnt gravy, with something earthy and yellow in it, which only makes me think of abysmal ideas and unworthy comparisons.'

And one finds traces of it in Flaubert's diary, in unexpected circumstances: 'All sorts of idiots had written their names on the great pyramid of Cheops, for instance "Buffard, 79 rue St Martin, wallpaper maker"'. (Gustave Flaubert, *Notes de voyage*, 1849.)

The Belgian poet Georges Rodenbach (1855-98), in the passage on his home from the poem *Jeunesse blanche* recalled 'the flowery wallpaper, on which we would count the garlands of roses to help pass the slow, sad days of illness.'

But the most unusual reference to wallpaper is in Octave Aubry's *Le second Empire, Souvenir d'un contemporain*, published in 1935: 'The wearing of crinolines was the starting point for one very odd idea: I mean wearing wallpaper as dresses. So that you do not think I am making this up, let me quote an extract from a contemporary magazine, so that the truth will not be in doubt. "Here is an unusual fancy for your wardrobe: it only has one drawback, that it is cheap — a serious fault at a time when only the costly is chic. The idea is a dress of wallpaper. Stick onto any old crinoline covered with stout fabric a sheet of paper that will stretch and resist water and wear. For the price of a cotton dress you can have a silver dress or a moiré one, in a whole range of colours and designs. According to the calculations of M. Louis Fiquier such a dress will last six months. Even if only for a week, what matter? Other clothes, and more beautiful ones at that, are only worn three or four times! With this system, ladies of fashion could buy their dresses by the roll, and chorus girls, like dowagers, would become a real backcloth. Couturiers will be replaced by interior designers — the lucky ones will have regular appointments — to redecorate the living room and Madam's wardrobe at the same time.'".

Vases of flowers and garlands. French, c. 1780. Halard coll.

CHAPTER TWO
Wallpaper and painting

As wallpaper was a feature of interior decoration from the seventeenth century on, one would expect to see it represented in paintings, as the background to interiors. This is not, however, the case. It is no surprise that it does not occur behind the sitters in formal portraits, who generally pose in front of a huge baroque drapery or perhaps a tapestry, indicating their wealth and status. But it is more curious that the genre painters, although they paid attention to the finest details – a gilded wooden moulding, or the pattern on a carpet – hardly ever found it necessary to include wallpaper in their compositions. When they set a domestic or gaily flirtatious scene in an intimate setting that might well include one of the new paper hangings, they were conscious of the extent to which a flowery, coloured backdrop would dominate the picture. So they toned it down or, better still, made it disappear completely, keeping in only the vertical line of the woodwork or the diagonal of a curtain to give the composition a suggestion of three-dimensional space. To find wallpaper in paintings in the eighteenth and nineteeenth centuries, one must study the English house portraits beloved of amateur draughtsmen and painters. Even in the realist period in the nineteenth century, painters seldom took pains to depict wallpaper in detail. A careful examination of Victorian narrative paintings will only occasionally reveal an illustration of wallpaper of the period.

Things were to change radically from the moment painting abandoned space created by perspective. One could say that Cézanne, at the end of the nineteenth century, was the first to exploit the possibilities for description and for composition, in painting wallpaper. When one is talking about Cézanne's decision to break with Renaissance three-dimensional space, and to assert a new reality tied essentially to the surface of the canvas itself, one realizes the importance that the flat wall covered in wallpaper was to have henceforth in pictorial

Degas, The Belleli Family. *Oil on canvas.* c. *1858-59. Louvre.*

Henri Matisse, Woman on a Sofa. *Walter Guillaume coll.*

Henri Matisse, Woman in a Turban. *Walter Guillaume coll.*

composition. Proof lies in the number of Cézanne's paintings in which it plays a decisive role. At least twenty-five have been catalogued. Even without entering the debate about dating the works on the basis of the two types of wallpaper in Cézanne's homes, one geometrical and one with a branch motif, one can see in the still-life which Venturi dates to between 1879 and 1882 the major compositional elements the painter has built up from the patterns in the papers. The diamond pattern is as strong in colour and presence as the fruit on the table and therefore makes the whole composition revolve around a single vertical plane.

When Maurice Denis did a group portrait of his friends the Nabis (the new 'prophets' of painting, Vuillard, Bonnard, Roussel) he had them pose round a Cézanne canvas in homage to the visual teaching the artist had given them. Thus, in the paintings of the Nabis it is not surprising to find a strong predilection for painting wallpaper. But what was for Cézanne above all compositional, became for the Nabis decorative as well. A painting is, according to Maurice Denis's famous formula, 'a flat surface covered with colours assembled in a certain order'.

In the years after 1900 these colours acquired a new vitality, from the flowers and vines that wound their way round every piece of furniture or household object, and of course even the wallpaper on every wall. The Nabis, as specialists in intimate, overcharged atmospheres, were in the forefront of this profusion. Vuillard would sit a girl mending socks in a flower-covered armchair that appeared to be cut out flat from a heavily decorated wall, while Bonnard, with his paintings of nudes, knew how to use the shimmering of the light on a wall alive with flowers to build up, together with a sofa-cover, a unified moving surface on which to place the young woman's body.

Of all the Fauves Matisse without a doubt is the most important, the one who played most successfully on the emotive charge of the wall's original colour; he liked to contrast the flowered designs on wallpaper with the pure arabesques of his odalisques. Sometimes the wallpaper pattern became obsessive and took over everything including the floor. As with Cézanne, some of their paintings can be grouped and dated according to the wallpaper. Thus, *Le boudoir, Le nu au turban blanc* and *Femme au canapé,* with their very similar backgrounds, seem quite clearly to have been painted in 1921 when Matisse was staying at the Hôtel Méditerranée in Nice. But this is still the more anecdotal side of the rôle of wallpaper in painting. The artists' compositional use of it is a great deal more interesting.

For progressive artists such as the Fauves and the Cubists, art became a spiritual exercise which should not be affected by the artist's own feelings, whether emotional or physical; the subject itself and the individual's particular way of handling it impede the aim of objectivity in relation to the idea of the thing to be depicted. Painters therefore used an entirely new style with cut-out and glued paper and, of course, wallpaper. The most famous example is Picasso's large painting, *Femmes à la toilette*, painted in 1938. Perhaps the most remarkable feature of this large canvas, more than 40 feet (12 metres) square made of odd pieces of wallpaper stuck on like a jigsaw with very little use of oil paint, is that it started out as a sketch for a tapestry. Picasso was therefore using wallpaper to indicate colour tones and for the chance encounters it afforded. The substance of wallpaper, however, did not come into it, as the design was to be woven directly in wool at the Gobelins workshop. On occasion Picasso did use fragments of actual wallpaper in his paintings, as in *Homme à la pipe*, where it is used to depict a flowered shirt. But more often he faked it, producing clever *trompe l'oeil* imitations which, as Golding put it, 'are a technical tour de force which required a complete knowledge and mastery of the techniques of academic illusionism'. In this case one could say that Picasso is parodying himself, and cleverly laughing at the more intellectual experiments of the Cubist era when real or fake materials (such as wallpaper imitating wood for the analytical fragments of a guitar), tended to reintroduce reality. Picasso, as André Fermigier has pointed out, had a 'do-it-yourself' side to him, which would find fun everywhere, and an extraordinary ability 'to make something out of nothing, the most sophisticated work from the most ghastly wallpaper'.[1] This playful use of wallpaper can also be found in Dada collages, where little pieces of paper find a place alongside bits of bus tickets or pieces of lace. Schwitters' rebus constructions – the famous Merzbau destroyed twice over in the last war – were in the same spirit and most probably included pieces of wallpaper.[2] The various forms of abstract art, Orphism, Constructivism, Suprematism, Tachism, did not favour either the representation or use of wallpaper.

One might think that the connection between wallpaper and painting would break completely with this last disappearance. However, the following was written in 1977 by a young painter for an exhibition of his work at the Museé d'Art Moderne de la Ville de Paris as a manifesto: 'Juxtaposition: a principle by which components are placed regularly with no overlap, on a surface that they cover completely. These components can all be similar (and form a thread, with all the juxtapositions printed with identical components) or have one different element, the changing of this element following a system'. How could one better define or describe wallpaper?

As we know, once the limits of abstraction were reached, art returned once more to realism, but a

Henri Matisse, Interior with Aubergines. *Oil on canvas. 1911-12. Musée des Beaux-Arts, Grenoble.*

Pablo Picasso, Women Dressing. *Oil on canvas with wallpaper fragments. Musée Picasso, Paris.*

hyper-real realism which, at its best, achieves a degree of poetry by making the viewer look, as it were, through the wrong side of an extremely clear glass. The knot of a tie, a shoe lace, are blown up to an enormous scale, so they seem to be new things beyond reality. Recently Wolfgang Becker has taken to doing the same with pieces of wallpaper, and this, as far as we know, is the most recent use of wallpaper in the world of painting.

Notes (pp. 201-04).

1. A. Fermigier, *Picasso*, Paris, 1969.
2. Kurt Schwitters (1887-1948), painter, sculptor, poet and one-time adherent of Dada. The word Merz comes from the word *Kommerz*, or commerce.

Pablo Picasso, Man with Pipe.
Oil on canvas with wallpaper and newspaper fragments.
Paris, spring 1914. Musée Picasso, Paris.

CHAPTER THREE
The flower as a recurrent motif in wallpaper

Artists have generally felt at one with nature and so have often used flowers in their decorative creations. This theme can be traced from the beginnings of wallpaper through to modern designs: whether heraldic, stylized, naturalistic, 'rétro' or modernized, flowers retain a constant tenderness and delicacy through the ages and reflect each period's aesthetic preferences.

The Tudor rose

This first known use of the flower in wallpaper goes back to the sixteenth century. The lining paper (below) in the Victoria and Albert Museum in London from about 1550, with its Tudor rose emblem and branching foliage gives us a clear-cut, almost botanical image, but is at the same time stylized with thick hatching to give the effect of volume. These wood-cuts printed in black on a grey ground call to mind goldsmiths' work. This example prefigures the different directions wallpaper design was to take, towards faithful, even photographic, representation of flowers, and towards inventive stylization facilitated by the printing processes.

Domino flowers

By the end of the seventeenth century, the *dominotiers* had fully mastered the making of wallpaper. De Fourcroy's paper (above) was the first to use an overall floral design. The delicacy of the drawing is brought out by the yellow and blue highlights scattered among the sepia mass of foliage. The flowers in this design are extraordinarily detailed.

Climbing flowers

In the anonymous English paper (right), the flowers are essential elements of the composition, scale is ignored and the flowers are as important as the animals and people. The artist has set out, in a manner clearly influenced by calico prints and *chinoiserie* designs, to give a rhythm to the whole by means of a sinuous line accentuated by pattern repeats, which on close study reveal the details (the composition still works with the paper reversed because the background is plain).

Poppies and birds by De Fourcroy. Printed in black heightened with sepia, yellow and blue by stencilling. French, c. 1700. Musée des Arts Décoratifs. Paris.

Paper from Ord House, Berwick upon Tweed. Block-printed with stencilled colours. English, c. 1700. V&A (Note the influence of 'indiennes' and Chinese designs.)

Tudor rose. Lining paper. English, first half of the 16th century. V&A.

Velvet flowers

The velvet of flock paper gives flowers a look of tactile softness. Paradoxically, while the flower on this paper (left), which dates from 1735, is almost realistic, the aesthetic preference at the time was for imaginary flowers. The perfect symmetry, and the single colour with reversed out design in chiaroscuro, of this design are most lyrical, and put this paper on a level with the great damasks it sets out to imitate. The flower entirely fills the design.

The flower border

The simple natural grace of the Bassano frieze (opposite, above left) belies its Italian origins and calls to mind the ceramic tradition dating back to Luca della Robbia. Composed of shrub or climbing flowers, this is a printed border with no drawing or lines, volume being indicated solely by the colours which give an impression of single brush strokes.

Calico flowers

Conversely, in the French paper of the same period (below) which includes similar flowers, the black printed design underlines the stencil colour areas.

Flock paper from the Privy Council Chamber. English, 1735. V&A.

Domino paper with bands of flowers. Block-printed with stencilled colours. (Note the influence of 'indiennes'.) DTM.

The undulating vertical line is repeated in inverted symmetry. This block print, directly derived from calico ornamentation, is nevertheless a perfect example of the French aesthetic outlook of the time.

1. Domino paper with floral border. Bassano, 18th century. DTM.

2. Decorative panel used as a screen. Distemper paper designed by J.-B. Réveillon (detail). French, c. 1785. DTM.

3. Putti and roses. Distemper paper. French, 18th century. Halard coll.

4. Bouquet of flowers within a garland. Follot coll.

5. Athenian Vase with Flowers. Design no. 394, by J.-L. Malaine for the Nicolas Dolfuss company. French, 1797. MISE.

1. Bamboo. Gouache paper. Chinese, 18th century. MISE.

2. Bouquet of dahlias. Manufacture Française de Papier Peint. French, c. 1840. Bibliothèque Forney, Paris.

3. Floral paper. Sanderson. English, 1914.

4. Wallpaper decoration of roses and dahlias. Machine-printed for Zuber. French, 1852. MISE.

5. Flowers in frames. Jules Riottot. French, c. 1845. Bibliothèque Forney, Paris.

Chinoiserie flowers

The ornamental compositions of Chinese wallpaper transformed the European sense of space and reinterpreted perspective by juxtaposing a succession of planes. In this panel (opposite, above left), peach blossom and bamboo punctuate the surface, raised above a foreground of blooming peonies and opulent waterlilies, drawn with the precision one would expect in a herbal. The characteristic beauties of Chinese painting have here been adapted to appeal to European taste.

Roses and love

Eighteenth-century bucolica entailed a burgeoning of flower themes in all the arts, to which wallpaper made a large contribution. Garlands, festoons, columns, borders, seed beds, bouquets – every kind of floral ornament went into wallpaper. In this anonymous design (p. 207, centre left), from the reign of Louis XV, the elegance of the composition is matched by its theme.

The flower bouquets of Réveillon

If there is one decorative theme that typifies the talent of J.-B. Réveillon, it is without a doubt the bouquet. One need only examine the beribboned example in the Follot Collection (p. 207, below left) or the screen panel in the Kassel museum (p. 207, above right), to be convinced of this. In the first example the bouquet, which is the principal motif, is elegantly surrounded and picked out with flowers and bows. In the second, though it takes up only part of the Pompeian-style panel, the bouquet is nonetheless handled with the greatest delicacy.

Peasant flowers in a palace

During the restoration work on the Petit Trianon at Versailles in 1980, the re-hanging of the mirrors brought to light evidence of very charming flowered papers of a simplicity quite out of keeping with the palace's grandeur (above right). Gorgeous scatterings of pinks, violets and other wild flowers covered the backing of the mirrors. These had been in place under Louis XV and Louis XVI, were removed with the Revolution and then replaced under the Directoire by these wallpapers and borders. At this time the Petit Trianon was kept by a hotel- and cabaret-owner who rented rooms there. Under the Empire, the décor and the mirrors returned, but the flowers remained, so to speak, an invisible reflection of the past.

Fragments of 18th-century block-printed paper discovered during the restoration of mirrors at the Petit Trianon, Versailles.

Flowered Athenian

The large decorative composition dated 1794 on p.207, below right, is block-printed with exceptional technical skill, on a par with easel painting. It is the work of Malaine, flower painter at the Gobelins and director of the Zuber factory; he was both artist and technician. The flowers (tulips, lilac, peonies, fritillaries and holly-hocks) are sensitive and lively, in contrast to the cold lifelessness of the gilded bronze, marble and porcelain. The naturalistic treatment of the flowers is in the Flemish tradition. This decorative panel is comparable with the Van Spaendonck painting dated 1785 in the château de Fontainebleau.

Flowers as architectural ornament

When gathered into a heavy garland, fresh flowers can be turned into architecture. The sublimation of the real flower, accentuated by its shadow, goes beyond *trompe l'oeil* to an expressive form specific to wallpaper and is not found in either painting or fabrics. This frieze (below) recalls the woven garlands worn at classical feasts.

Frieze with garland. Dufour, French, 1825. Follot coll.

Spangled bouquet of coloured flowers in a grisaille medallion. Designed by Carl Herting. German, 1860. DTM.

The reign of Flora

Through all the technical developments of machine printing, flowers have never lost their pre-eminence, whether they are found on wallpapers freely drawn, burst from architectural scrolls as in Riottot's paper from 1845 (p. 208, below right), are deliciously beribboned in blue satin or just arranged to make a decorative panel.

Like an illustration from a herbal, Delicourt's iris (far left) is portrayed in all its detail, from the bulb to the flower, and is surrounded by an unusual frame of trained branches.

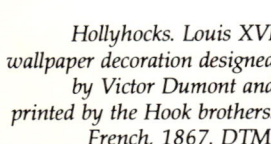

Iris in a rustic frame. Delicourt, French, 1855. Bibliothèque Forney, Paris.

Shimmering flowers

In a dull-coloured scroll done as an architectural *trompe l'oeil* (left), a bouquet sparkles with gold; such flowers were the speciality of a skilled firm which transformed floral reality through the brightness of metal foil. Carl Herting's design, of botanical precision, is covered with fine leaves of metal that reconstruct the whole flower and entrap the light.

Garden flowers

In this large architectural *trompe l'oeil* décor (left), with gold highlights, the eye is led to a rustic garden where hollyhocks are burgeoning in glory. The light concentrated on the flowers brings them to life. In this cameo of grey and green, the hollyhock petals are the only hint of the warm colours that are so very important in nature.

Hollyhocks. Louis XVI wallpaper decoration designed by Victor Dumont and printed by the Hook brothers. French, 1867. DTM.

A revival rose

William Morris's woodblock-printed roses recall the earliest English papers. With great economy of means, he devoted his attention to flat surface without relief or shading. Flowers like climbing roses cover the wall. Morris is here returning to the traditional simplicity of the Elizabethan garden, as did Walter Crane (below right). In this frieze (right), Morris presents a profusion of flowers with particular emphasis on the ornamental curves of the flower stems, in an almost Art Nouveau manner.

Oriental-style flowers

With the same intentions as Mackmurdo, Voysey used curves and counter-curves but to an overall

The Rose. Designed by William Morris. English, 1877. V&A.

Tokyo. Designed by C.F.A. Voysey and machine-printed by Essex and Co. English, 1894-5. V&A.

Frieze of roses, by Walter Crane. English, c. 1880. V&A.

effect; poppies, underlined by the movements of the lines in the drawing of the petals, take up the whole of the design (above). The flowers are stylized and two-dimensional.

Flowers in profusion

Floral profusion and exuberance are expressed in the Sanderson paper on p. 208 with a juxtaposition of flowers – roses, peonies, chrysanthemums, asters – richly blooming in mauve and pink tones that sing against the greens of the foliage. All is imbued with the inimitable charm of English papers, to create a soft and agreeable atmosphere.

Le Mardelé. *Primavera.*
French, 1918-26.
Bibliothèque Forney, Paris.

Roses. Designed by Paul Dumas for Follot. French, 1930. Bibliothèque Forney, Paris.

Vase of tulips. Woodson Wallpapers. English, 1978.

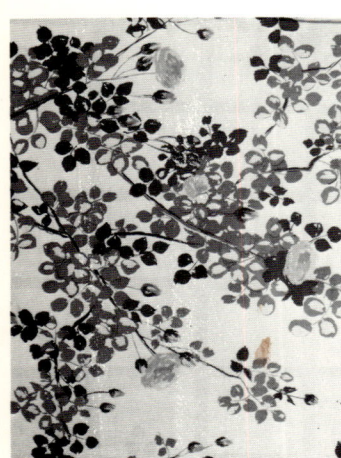

Allons voir si la rose...
Designed by Suzanne Fontan for Nobilis. French.

Tango flowers

A pale rose winds across a broad black ground, against a vigorous rhythm of invented foliage. Here is an explosion of colour like that of Bakst's décors for the Ballets Russes and Dunan's precious lacquers – the fire of the orange ennobles Le Mardelé's pastel blue rose. Flowers have become the aesthetic embodiment of the period.

'Fauve' flowers

The heavy, full-petalled roses (left), painted in broad, free strokes of red, recall the Fauvist experiment. The flowers, arranged in tight balls, stand out from the surface. This paper with its determinedly pictorial treatment moves away from the imitation of real flowers.

A childhood garden

It is as if nature has been brought back into our drawing-rooms by Suzanne Fontan's flowers, with the title *Allons voir si la rose...* (below left). There is poetry to be found in the delicate treatment and sweet colours. Their old-fashioned charm harks back to the gardens of our grandmothers, which we in our technological age regard with nostalgia.

'Tachiste' flowers

Painted in blobs of colour, these tulips (left), gathered into silhouetted bouquets, are no more than patches of colour without line or relief. The space has been destroyed, and the repetitive rhythm of the flower motif is now only a tonal variation. Once again flowers are subject to the influence of pictures.

The perennial flower

Influenced perhaps by current ecological trends, this paper (below left) teems with clearly drawn, tastefully coloured flowers. It derives as much from the seductive nineteenth-century English garden as from oriental exoticism and the exactitude of herbals, and carries on the living tradition of floral designs for wallpaper.

Savina. Canovas. French, 1979.

/ PART FOUR
Manufacturing techniques

*Interior of a wallpaper manufactory. Oil on canvas. Artist unknown.
Inscribed 'Wm. Hardy, Junction Dock St, Hull' on stretcher. English, c. 1842-57.
Ferens Art Gallery, Kingston-upon-Hull.*

CHAPTER ONE
Early techniques

This covers the various wallpaper manufacturing processes from the sixteenth century up to the appearance of the machine in the nineteenth century. Most of the sources for defining the early procedures and technical terms are contemporary ones, such as Diderot and d'Alembert's *Encyclopédie*, Louis-Sébastien Lenormand's *Manuel du fabricant d'étoffes imprimées et du fabricant de papier peint* (Roret, 1830), and *the Album de l'Industrie* (Combet and Co 1903) and *A travers l'industrie française* by Paul Poiré (Hachette, 1897).

The raw material

Paper can be made from three different materials: rags, straw and wood. Originally it was always made from a base of cotton or linen rags, sorted by hand and divided into white, partly white, coloured, etc., which then determined the various qualities of paper. Nowadays rags are only used for the most expensive kinds of paper.

Hems were unpicked, buttons removed and heavy thicknesses reduced with a jagged blade (shredding). Then the rags were beaten out, washed, dried and heaped into a tank or steeping-vat where they fermented for more than a month, so as to soften before they were shredded. After shredding they were mixed with more or less water according to the thickness of paper desired in stamping-troughs, where they were then kneaded for one or two days to produce a pulp the consistency of whey. The pulp was then placed in a kind of sieve or mould, in the form of a wooden frame filled with a web of shafts and perpendicular brass wires, which left their impression in the paper. The sieve was the size of the sheet of paper to be made. The pulp was then shaken to dry it and spread evenly in a thin layer on which a piece of felt was laid and turned over. This operation was repeated to make a pile of 150 to 200 sheets of paper with felt between each layer: they were then squeezed hard with a hand-press to draw off all the water. Once squeezed out, the sheets of paper were put out to dry on racks.

This manufacturing process hardly changed from its beginning up to the end of the eighteenth century.

Steeping was a chemical operation achieved with chalk and soda. The use of machines to replace the slow manual procedures began with experiments by Louis-Nicolas Robert, a worker with François Didot at Essonnes, was delayed by the Revolution and perfected in England by Bryan Donkin at the beginning of the nineteenth century; it was thereafter widely adopted. From the middle of the century onwards, the process of making continuous lengths of paper, which were dried and wound directly onto large rolls speeded up production considerably and made it possible to deal with an ever-increasing demand.

But it was the use of wood in place of rags in the making of pulp that brought about the most important revolution in the paper industry. Wood is used nowadays in 95% of production, the remaining 5% being made of straw, esparto grass, bagasse or reeds.

There are two distinct stages in making paper from wood: the making of paper pulp and that of the paper itself. Pulp is manufactured either mechanically (by grinding, crushing or breaking up) or chemically (by bisulphite, sulphate or monosulphate processes, or else by the Celdecor-Pomilio process for straw). Pulp in liquid form is converted by pulp presses into slabs like heavy cardboard which may contain up to 30% water. These are then taken to paper factories and put back into suspension in water in large vats. But this phase is dying out, as paper factories are increasingly integrated with pulp mills.

Paper making itself includes a range of mechanical processes (refining, purification, coating, pressing, smoothing, drying, rolling), the last of which can change the appearance of the sheet by surface treatment or calendering. The paper is produced as a continuous sheet, which involves obtaining a thin but strong material from a liquid solution, in enormous machines which churn out paper at a rate of between 3 and 35 miles an hour. The main rolls are cut into narrower rolls which can be used as they are, or turned into separate sheets. Of the many different kinds of paper, papers with a high bulk are used to make wallpapers.

Marbled paper (sixteenth century)

'Paper marbler. This is a worker who knows how to paint paper, or rather to stain it in different colours, sometimes in an irregular arrangement, sometimes imitating marble and producing an effect that gives pleasure to the eye, when the worker is skilled, has some taste and uses good paper and good colours. Marbled paper is used for a fairly large number of purposes, but its principal use is for the covering of sewn books.' (Diderot and d'Alembert, *Encyclopédie*.)

The method of manufacture followed a process of Turkish origin, of which there is an early description in Francis Bacon's *Natural History* (1623). Unlike wood engraving, it permitted an immense range of designs, due as much to the mix of the colours as to the hand of the craftsman who 'combed' the surface of the water in the vat.

To obtain the marbled effect, the paints were scattered one after another with a paint brush over the surface of the water, starting with blue which covered the vat, forming veins and branches, then the red which repelled the blue, the yellow which settled between the two other colours, and so forth. The worker's skill consisted in knowing how much of each colour to use. The surface of the water was then gently raked with the comb, so that each tooth formed a wave of colour. This could be repeated as required. The sheet of paper was then laid gently on the paint, which covered the water and which would stick to the paper in the pattern left by the comb. The paper was lifted off onto a wire frame which was placed over a basin so that the excess gum and water could drip off. It was then hung on the rack to dry, and when dry gently rubbed with white or yellow pure wax on a perfectly polished marble surface. Once polished, the sheets were folded into sections of twenty-five. The whole skill of the marbler lay in the way he combed them, using differently shaped tools and a varying number of marks.

Marbled paper has continued to be made up to the present day with very little change in this technique.

To put gold threads on a marbled paper a stencil of the design to be gilded was made, and laid on the already marbled paper. Acid was applied through the stencil, then gold leaf. The surplus was removed with cotton-wool (cotton). The stencil was then removed, revealing the figure of the final design on the marbling. At the end of the seventeenth century, the *dominotier* Lebreton made marbled paper mixed with gold and silver of such a high standard that he was made a member of the Académie Royale des Beaux-Arts. Jean-Michel Papillon, the great innovator in wallpaper design, still admired and talked of Lebreton's work in the eighteenth century.

This very curious technique seems to have originated for two economic reasons. Printers needed decorated paper to hide the binding threads on the inside covers of books (which would show through plain paper); and, as several hundred or even several thousand copies were made of each book, a vast quantity of such paper was needed. In the seventeenth century the *dominotiers*, who had the exclusive right to make decorative paper, could not use wood engraving, because under contemporary regulations this was the prerogative of the printers, and, besides, a polychrome paper would have required more than one block. Marbling was the perfect solution: it was a decorative paper which could be produced by the *dominotiers* in a polychrome design and in large quantities. (The fact that the designs differed from copy to copy did not matter as no one was likely to possess multiple copies of the same book.)

The tools of the trade

The paper marbler's materials included a wooden vat several inches larger than the piece of paper to be marbled, a churn and plunger, a leather sieve, a large paint brush, combs of various designs, pots and brushes for the paints, a drying-rack, a stone and pestle for grinding the paints, a scoop or a piece of leather with a cutting edge, a knife, a scoop to clean the water, several square frames made of four slats, bound together with upright crossed wires, in groups of five, trestles to hold the tubs, a smoothing-iron, pots, combs and other tools.

The preparation of water for marbling

To make a ream of paper, or five hundred sheets, half a pound of gum tragacanth was mixed with fresh water, and stirred once a day. This was then decanted to fill half a large stoneware pot. After churning the mixture for a quarter of an hour, the

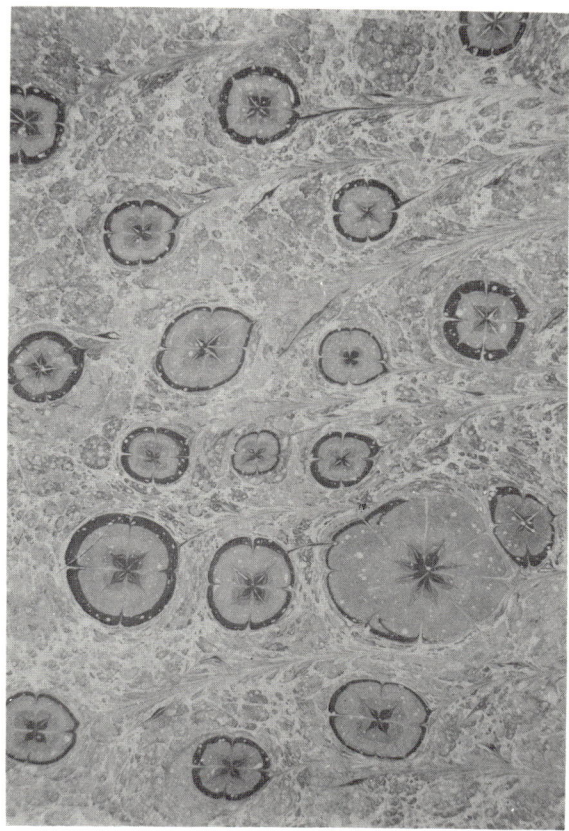

Making marbled paper. Alberto Valese, Venice, 1980.

Sheet of marbled paper. Alberto Valese, Venice, 1980.

rest of the pot was filled with water. The solution was passed through a sieve, the remaining gum being kept for re-use. When all the water had been put into the vats the density was tested, either by stirring with a stick which would cause froth to appear, or by passing the comb over the surface, which would leave neat flaky waves. One could correct the mixture by adding gum or water according to the required density.

Paints used by the paper marbler

The paints used were clear and even. The *dominotiers* tried continuously to improve the quality by taking special care over their preparation. The recipes for some colours were as follows. For blue, indigo crushed in water on a stone; for red, lake crushed with water in which Brazil-wood has been boiled, with lime added; for yellow, three spoonfuls of ox-gall mixed in a pan of water in which ochre has been soaking for three days; for green, two spoonfuls of crushed indigo and ochre soaked in a pint of water, mixed with three spoonfuls of ox-gall; for violet, red, to which are added four or five drops of soot crushed with indigo; for white, four spoonfuls of ox-gall beaten into a pint of water; for black, a spoonful of ox-gall with a pinch of soot and a piece of gum.

Maker of marbled paper. BN.

Mosaic paper (seventeenth century)

To imitate mosaics of flowers or landscapes, the *dominotiers* used a process which was a combination of marbling and printing methods. They used wooden blocks, engraved with wide, well-hollowed lines a centimetre deep. The block was then placed on the tub of water, on the surface of which floated the paint; the raised parts of the wood absorbed the paint, leaving a network of blank areas in the water. The wood block was then removed and the paper laid down so that it took the colour except where the wood had soaked it up. Depending on the design to be reproduced, the operation was repeated until all the paint was used up.

Papier de tapisserie (seventeenth century)

The French word *papier de tapisserie* refers both to paper that imitates high warp tapestry, and to wallpaper in general. Hanging a paper on the wall came to be called in French *tapisser*. Even today wallpaper is often called *tapisserie* in French.

In imitating tapestries the draughtsman would draw out the chosen subject on sheets of paper pasted together in the same format as the tapestry. When the drawing was ready, it was cut into sheets of suitable size for printing. The *dominotier* would then engrave each section onto wood blocks, with small strokes, using the veining in the wood to imitate the weave of the tapestry. The blocks were then inked, and the sections printed. Once the ink was dry, the sections were painted or highlighted in different colours, then put together, their edges overlapping, to recreate the original design.

Architectural landscape wallpapers were produced by the same means. Only the black outline was printed in ink, the other colours being applied with a stencil made of thin card. This had to be waterproof if it was to last. It was therefore coated with a mixture of burnt walnut oil, litharge mixed with the ash of old stencils and of horses' bones. The coated card had to be absolutely dry before use.

A yellow ink, extracted from boiled buckthorn berries, was later added to the colours used for *papiers de tapisserie*, as was Burnt Siena; flesh colours did not appear till the end of the eighteenth century. For fixing, gum arabic was used. In spite of this, the colours did not always adhere properly to the paper and sometimes came away on the fingers or the brush. There was also the further difficulty of the fragility of the paper support. To counteract this a texture imitating tapestry was added to the paper, and a canvas lining was tacked to the wall before hanging the paper.

Block printing (eighteenth century onwards)

Preparing the paper

Until the invention of the continuous paper roll and of offset printing, wallpaper was printed on sheets of paper stuck end to end, then sized and sometimes smoothed and finished. Generally, twenty-four sheets, joined at their broadest edges, made up a roll, or what British manufacturers called a 'piece'.

In order to make the piece, the paper was laid flat at one end of a table much longer than the finished piece. With a small flat piece of boxwood rounded on one side, twelve sheets were laid out, each one overlapping the next by an inch or two. The paper gluer would then place a heavy stone on these twelve sheets, laid out to his left, to secure them in position, and lay out twelve more sheets to his right in the same way. He then spread flour paste over the twelve sheets on his right, then over the ones on his left, taking care not to overlap one side more than the other, so that the edges of the section would be constantly in a straight line (which he checked against the edge of the table). Once the first twelve sheets had been pasted, a thick plank would be laid on them, with a heavy stone on top, and left to set. The other twelve sheets would be stuck together in the same way, and the whole would thus make up the piece, which was then printed

Preparing the ground

The ground is merely paint applied to a sized surface. First, round, long-bristled brushes are used to apply the still-warm size. The worker takes a brush in each hand and rapidly goes over the entire surface of the paper section. At the same time, one or two assistants follow him with long, wide brushes, like those used in France for sweeping floors. With them they go lightly over the places where the first worker has spread the size, so as to even it out thoroughly. This procedure is carried out on very long tables so that the sections can be stretched at full length.

Once the section is sized, it is laid out on poles so that it can dry easily, and when it is completely dry, an even tint of paint is applied and dried in the same way before going on to the next stage.

Smoothing the paper

The instrument used is a piece of wood, just over 3 inches long, which is attached by a forked handle to a strong wooden pole, itself fixed to the floor by an iron bolt long enough to have a certain pliancy. This vertical pole also has a fork projecting from it further down, which holds a copper cylinder that revolves on two pivots. The cylinder is about 1½ inches long and 1 in diameter (3.5 x 2.7 centimetres). It is not perfectly round: the ends are of a slightly smaller radius than the middle, and the edges are rounded. This is to prevent the corners cutting the paper.

The smoother is long enough to reach the edge of a sturdy table of very flat hard-wood, on which the work is done. The tension in the overhead beam means that the smoother runs on the table with a more or less even pressure. Greater evenness can be achieved by attaching a weight to the end of the beam, which gives a leverage effect. The worker lays the section on the table upside-down, with the coloured side to the table. Holding the smoother in the cup of his hand and moving it in all directions, he smooths the paper perfectly, but does not polish the colour, which remains matte.

Glazing the paper

The tool used for giving a glazed or satin finish is the same as the one used for smoothing, the only difference being the fitting at the end of the pole. This time it is not a metal cylinder, but a rough short-bristled brush, mounted on a swivel which allows it to lie flat on the table in any position. The worker lays the section on the table the right way up, the colour face up. He dusts it with a very fine Briançon chalk called talc or mica, and brushes it hard. This operation polishes the coloured side.

Manufacturing the blocks

For printing wallpaper, wooden blocks like those used for printed canvas are used. They carry in relief the design to be reproduced in colour on the paper. To avoid warping, they are made of three small pieces of wood, each just under ½ inch (about 9 millimetres) thick, of which two are white woods and the third is apple or pear wood, these being more compact and having a fine grain. The three pieces are glued tightly together across the grain. The design is engraved on the perfectly smooth, flat surface of the third.

The draughtsman draws only the outline of the shapes that are to appear in relief, with very thin clear lines, before he hands the block over to the engraver. As many blocks must be prepared and engraved as there are shades to be reproduced.

The blocks cannot be very large if they are to be handled easily and give a good finish. The drawings on each block must co-ordinate perfectly and show no gaps or spaces. The draughtsman therefore marks the block on every corner with a register mark which the engraver respects. The trick is to put these marks into flowers, stems and suchlike, so that they will disappear when the printing is finished. All the blocks intended to be part of a single design must bear the same register marks so that all the sections of the design tally. The engraver, with gouges, chisels, scoops and so on, digs out the wood surrounding all the lines which are to remain in relief and are used to apply paint to the paper. He scores all the shaded areas deeply with a thin sharp chisel before removing the surrounding wood and at this point drives tiny wooden wedges into the block for delicate lines or dots, if the design requires them.

As many blocks are required as there are shades in a design so, to print a rose, three reds each darker than the last must be applied, plus a white for the pale parts, making four different blocks for one single flower. Just as many are needed for the leaves and for the stem. And if yellow and violet flowers are added, assuming that each of these colours includes four other shades, the one bouquet of three flowers will require twenty separate blocks.

Since the blocks have register marks, the design can be repeated to cover the whole piece, with no risk of confusion. The engraver places the mark so that when the second block is applied, the trace of the previous one is hidden by the new colour; when the section is finished, there should be traces only of the first and last register marks.

Printing from wood blocks

The tray for the paint is about 10 inches (24 to 27 centimetres) deep. It is filled with paper scraps covered with water to a depth of about 6½ inches (16.2 centimetres). A wooden frame, on which a piece of calf skin has been tightly stretched, is placed so that it rests on the water. The frame fits tightly into the box, and any gaps are sealed with waterproofed battens so that the water will not seep up. On the skin is laid a second frame made of a piece of broadcloth which, like a sieve, will take the paint to be used for printing. One frame is needed for each colour. The water serves as a mattress so that the block will touch the cloth evenly and an equal quantity of paint will be picked up at every point.

The sturdy bench on which the printer works measures about 4 inches (10.8 centimetres) thick by about 6½ feet (2 metres) long, 2½ inches (6.5 centimetres) wide, supported by strong square legs with good cross-bars. At the back of the bench is mounted, solidly and permanently, a very strong wooden cross-beam which serves as a support for the lever which is used continually in the printing. This lever is about 8 feet (2.5 metres) long and is used to press the block down to the required extent. This method is preferable to the older system of tapping the blocks with hammers, which had the drawback of noise and the risk of shifting the blocks, as well as wearing them out faster. The table is

Engraved woodblock.

Wooden cylinder for copperplate engraving.

Engraved wooden cylinder for printing.

covered with several thicknesses of cloth nailed to the edges to form a kind of mattress, to facilitate the printing and to save wear of the block.

With everything laid out in this way, the printer stands in front of his bench, with the tub of paint to his right and pulls out the sized paper from its roll, which revolves freely on a thin iron rod resting on two wooden brackets that are firmly attached to the underside of the bench. The cloth in the paint tray is coloured with a brush, as lightly as possible. The printer takes the block in his right hand, presses it gently onto the cloth and then places it carefully on the paper at the point shown by the register marks. Then he places on the block a trestle-shaped wooden clamp and brings down onto this the lever fixed to the cross-beam, presses firmly, then releases it, removes the clamp and delicately lifts off the block without letting it slip. He puts more paint on the cloth if necessary and then repeats the same manoeuvre until the section is finished. It is then taken to the rack to dry completely before the next colour is applied.

All the colours are printed in the same way, with various blocks to give the different shades, and it is in this part of the process that the quality and evenness of the work are determined. The borders are printed in the same way and with equal care. Depending on the size of the design, there will be one, two, three, or four across the width of the roll.

Once a section is completely printed with one colour, the printer checks it and if he notices any mistakes, corrects them by applying the missing colour with a paint-brush. Care must be taken to correct each colour as it is printed before going on to the next stage. When all the various phases are complete, the wallpaper can be delivered to the customer.

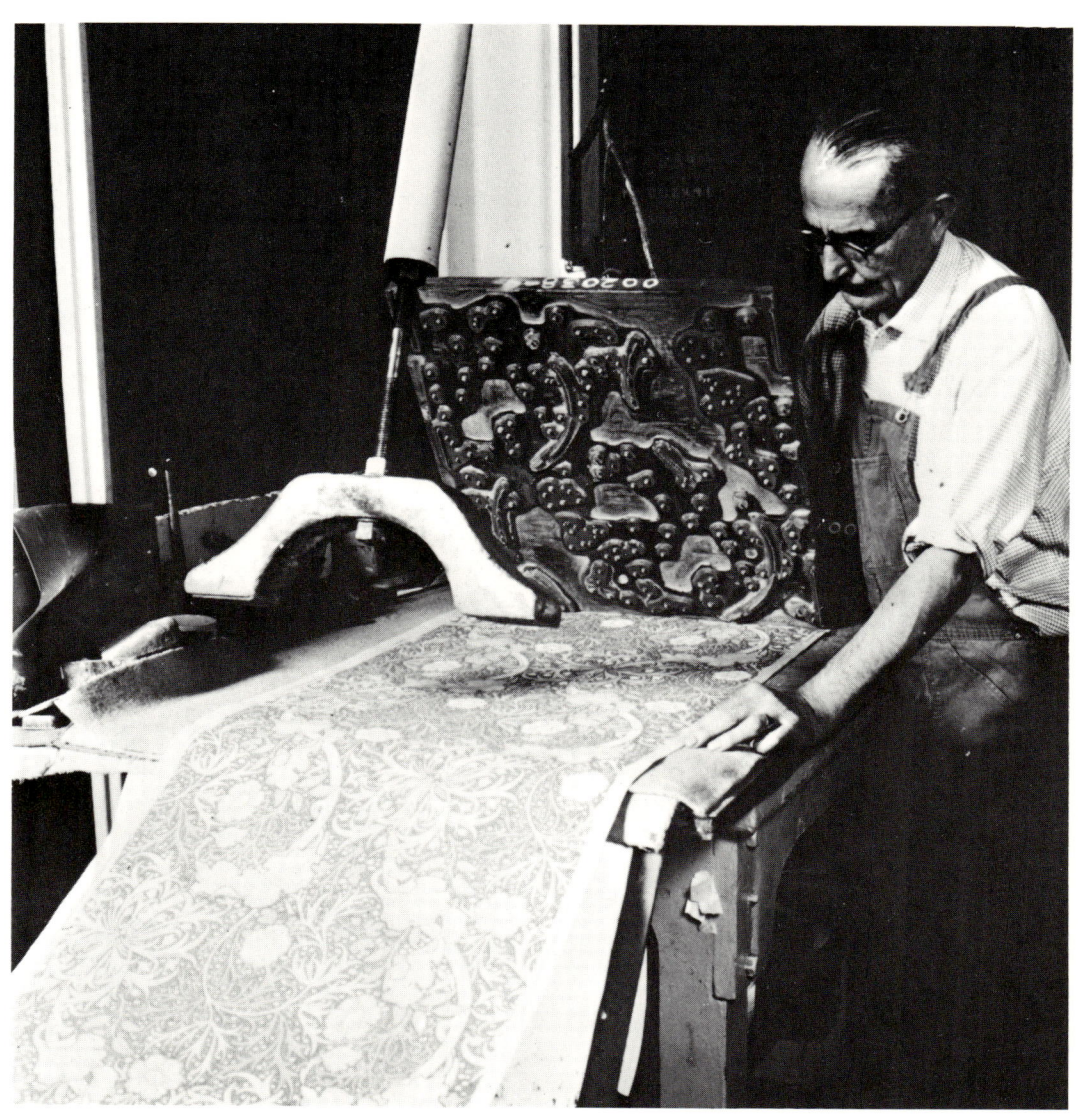

Block printing the final (eighth) colour on Seaweed, *a design by William Morris.*

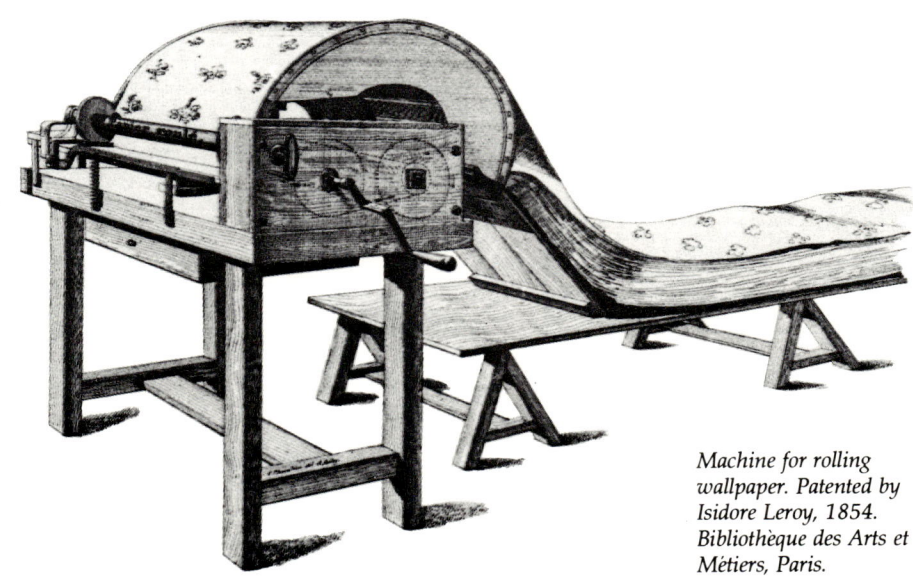

Machine for rolling wallpaper. Patented by Isidore Leroy, 1854. Bibliothèque des Arts et Métiers, Paris.

THE MANUFACTURE OF WALL PAPERS.

The white paper comes into the factory from the paper-mill in large rolls. It varies in weight according to the particular use to be made of it; much heavier stock is required, for example, for "leather" paper than for the ordinary wall hangings. The first step in the process of printing is what is called "grounding." This is applying a tint over the whole surface of the paper by a machine made especially for the purpose, in which color is applied evenly over the surface by a series of brushes. Then the paper is caught up in loops and carried by an endless chain over steam pipes, thus becoming dry as it slowly makes its journey of about four hundred feet. It is then reeled up, and is ready for the printing. These grounding machines can carry two widths of paper simultaneously, so that the process is a rapid one. "Mica papers" are grounded in the same way as those in plain colors.

The next step is the printing. This is done on machines such as that represented in the engraving. This machine can print twelve colors at a time. Machines capable of printing in eight colors are quite common and largely used.

The pattern having been designed and the colors chosen, there must be a roller for each separate color, with the corresponding part of the pattern cut on it, and the rest left blank. The rollers consist of a body of wood, with the pattern worked on them in brass and felt. The work on the rollers must be done with great accuracy, for the different parts of the pattern must be adjusted to a nicety.

THE TWELVE-COLOR PRINTING MACHINE.

READY FOR REELING UP.

Everything being ready, the rollers and their troughs of color are adjusted, the reel of grounded paper begins to pass over the great cylinder. Here it gets a spot of crimson, the blushing center of a rose perhaps, while the next roller imprints the dark green of a leaf. And so it touches roller after roller until the whole pattern is produced in completeness and beauty. As it emerges from the machine it is caught on sticks that rest in notches on an endless chain, and so in graceful festoons is slowly carried over steam pipes, which rapidly dry it. If there is any gold in the pattern, at one point in its progress over the drying coils the paper passes through an auxiliary machine, which deposits gold dust on the proper parts, which have been printed in varnish instead of color; the gold adheres to the varnish, while the colors have become sufficiently dry not to hold it. In some of the papers the gold, or bronze, or other metal is applied by hand. The portion to be bronzed is printed in varnish, then it is liberally dusted over with the metal powder. When the superfluous powder is brushed off, the masses of gold, or silver, or bronze shine out, with the result of enhancing the beauty and effectiveness of the whole.

Following the paper along, we reach the end of the moving railway which carries it. Here the sticks which have supported it in its long festoons are thrown out, and the paper placed upon a movable rack, ready to be reeled into rolls for the market.

Some papers are hand-printed. This is done in working off specimens, that effects may be determined and patterns fixed upon. It is done also in the production of special patterns made to order, or in cases where the quantity to be printed would not warrant the expense of preparing the rollers for the machine. It is done also in those cases where the pattern is, as it were, built up by layer after layer of "flock," resulting in very rich effects. Some of the "leather" papers have raised figures upon them. These papers, which are very thick and heavy, are stamped in a machine similar to other machines for the same general purpose. Some of the most gracefully elegant papers are embossed. After the printing and gilding, they are run through a sim-

[Continued on page 339.]

"FLOCKING."

THE MANUFACTURE OF FINE WALL PAPERS.

*A magazine article on late 19th century wallpaper making, including descriptions of applying the ground,
drying the paper, printing in twelve colours, flocking and gilding.
From the* Illustrated London News, *1881.*

Flock wallpaper (early nineteenth century)

From the seventeenth century, attempts were made to give wallpaper some resemblance to velvet or to Savonnerie tapestry by covering it either partially or entirely with different coloured cloth clippings. Colour tones were initially achieved by applying clippings of various colours with a brush to the appropriate points in the design.

The worker first applied a glue to the paper and then, along the lines prepared in this way, he sprinkled cloth clippings or powdered cloth of the colour chosen for that part of the design. This excessively time-consuming work made such papers very expensive. They were also susceptible to humidity and moths. Nowadays, the making of flock papers has reached a high standard and a faster rate of production.

The procedure for printing ordinary wallpapers is also employed in the manufacture of flock paper, except for the size which is thicker than that used for wallpaper.

Washing the clippings: the cloth clippings are usually white so that they can be dyed to the colour and shade required. They are thoroughly cleaned and bleached in soapy water heated to 75° centigrade, then rinsed in warm water and dried. They are then plunged in a solution of sulphuric acid, washed and dried.

Dyeing the clippings: after bleaching the cloth is not allowed to dry completely. It is thrown into a bath of dye of the shade required. It is then taken out of the dye-bath, laid out on tiles nailed to racks and dried.

Milling the clippings: when the dyed clippings are completely dry, they are transferred to a conical-shaped grinder with spiral lines incised all over its surface which turns inside a hollow cone called a bushel, covered inside with cutting blades also arranged in spirals. Once the wool is in the mill, the head of the bushel is adjusted by turning a screw, depending on how fine a grinding is required.

Sifting the powder: beside the grinder are sieves similar to those used for sifting flour, through which the milled clippings are passed. The powder is graded according to the fineness required, and the residue is sent back for milling and re-sifting.

Printing: the tools used by the printer are the same as for ordinary wallpaper (see above). The bench, paint tray, lever and blocks are identical. In

Manufacturing flock paper.

Detail of flocking machine: the electric grille sorts the synthetic fibres by static electricity.

*Trompe l'oeil ceiling with coffering.
Zuber. French, early 19th century. MISE.*

the workshop the only additional feature is a large drum with a hinged lid, placed to the worker's left, on the end of the bench, with the bottom made of tightly stretched calf skin. The cloth powder is poured into this drum.

The block used for applying the glue to the paper carries a relief of only those parts of the design that are to be flocked. The glue is made of linseed oil made sticky with litharge ground with white lead. It is spread on the cloth in the colour tray. The worker presses the block onto the cloth, which transfers the glue in the same way as the paint, spreads the glue evenly over the block with a rag or brush and places the block on the paper, following the register marks. When a sufficient area has been covered, the paper is placed at the bottom of the drum and powdered by hand with the wool dust. The lid is then closed, and with two long sticks the worker rhythmically beats the skin covering the base. The wool dust rises inside, falls back onto the paper and penetrates deeply into the glue. The paper is then taken out and tapped from behind with one of the sticks so as to detach any powder that is not fixed. The procedure is repeated till the piece is finished and it is then laid on a rack to dry thoroughly.

Retouching: the velvet effect thus produced is of a uniform shade. To make it more pleasing to the eye, shading must be added to bring out the design. In a drapery design, for instance, the folds must be brought out. This is done once the piece is thoroughly dry. The workman lays it on his bench as before and with a suitable block applies a dye to the parts that are to be shaded. Highlights can be added in the same way.

The manufacture of flock or velvet paper was developed throughout the nineteenth and twentieth centuries, and different methods of printing and fixing the powder succeeded each other. Nowadays the flock particles (a synthetic material) are applied electrostatically.

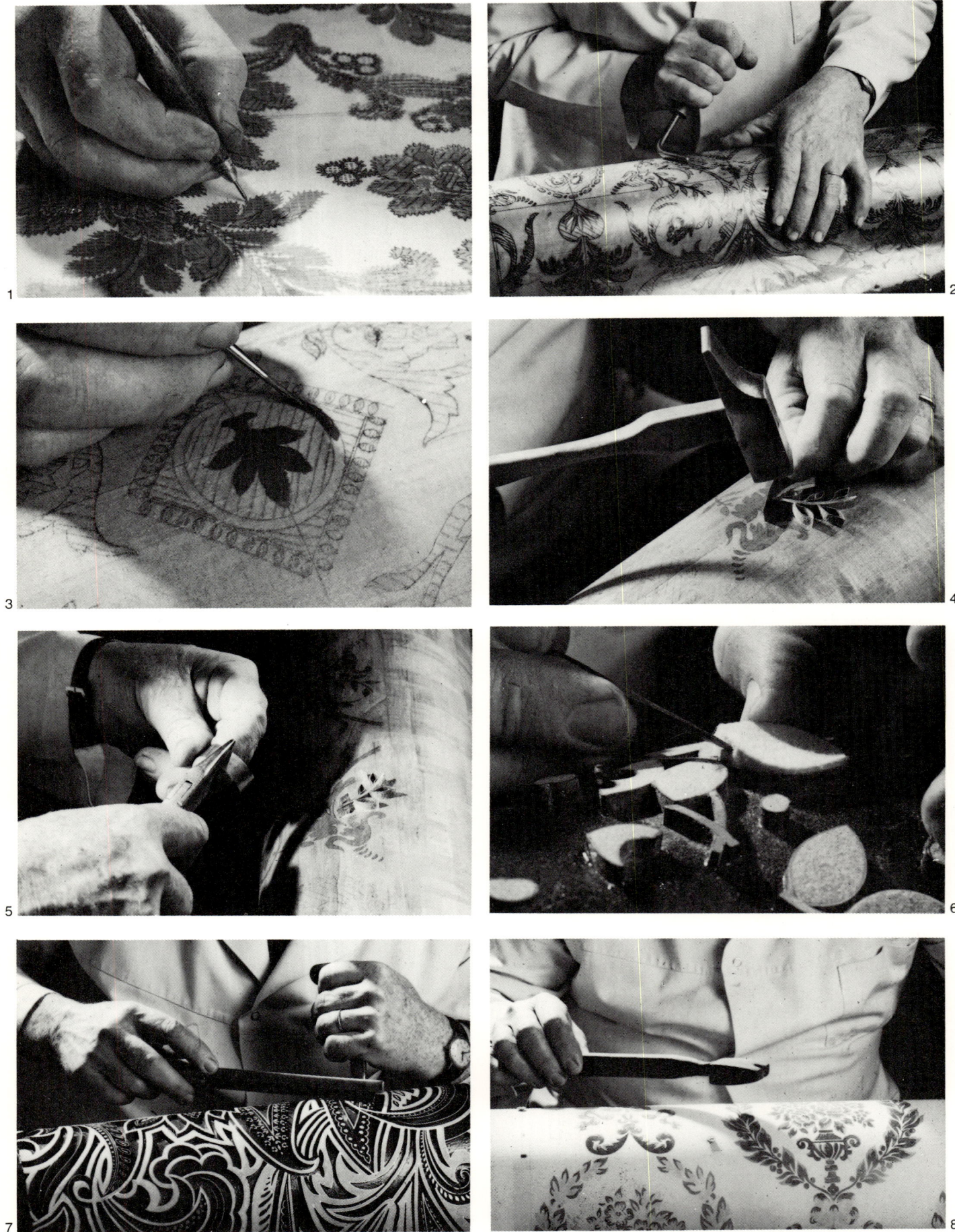

CHAPTER TWO
Industrial techniques

Cylinder or drum printing

The aim of this process is to print on a single machine run as many colours as are required. The design is engraved on cylinders of pear-wood, lead or copper.

In the case of wood engraving the design is first etched onto plastic film with a dry-point. This film is then coated with lithographic black ink, which is absorbed only by the etched lines. It is wrapped round a wooden cylinder, the inked side next to the cylinder, and rubbed, so that the ink is transferred to the wood and reproduces the outline of the design. Following the usual wood-engraving practice, the parts of the cylinder which will print the design are painted red and varnished for protection. The printer then cuts out the design by carving a line about ¼ inch (5 millimetres) deep, and digs out the unwanted part with a cutter working at right angles to the axis. The drawing therefore comes out in relief ready for surface printing. Printing rollers thus produced are relatively fragile, but do not wear out easily.

Cylinders made of lead are employed when the design is composed of a large number of identical patterns or for some standard base patterns. Dies are made by pouring lead into moulds in the shape of the pattern. They are then made to fit round the roller, which will have been poker-worked to accommodate them. Though it is cheaper, this process has several drawbacks: the engraved surface is fragile and hard to repair, and the rollers are difficult to manipulate because of the weight and wear out quickly.

In copper engraving, the design is transferred to a wooden cylinder in the same way as for wood engraving. The chaser marks each cylinder and colours the surfaces to be etched. One cylinder is necessary for each colour in the design. The engraver gouges out the wood to a depth of about ¼ inch (5 millimetres) following the outline of the coloured patterns. He then fits into the inlays a copper thread, which is bent with pliers to follow the pattern. It is these copper lines that pick up the oil-based colours and apply them to the paper. (For large areas a copper outline must be packed with felt). The engraver then checks that the copper thread projects evenly, filing it down where necessary. As a final check a sheet of tracing paper is laid against the engraved roller. The engraver takes a little flat hammer which he coats with paint and gently taps the cylinder. The marks of the relief show up on the paper, and can thereby be used as a simple check against the original design.

Mechanical sizing, surfacing and gilding

Size is a mixture of flour-based glue and oil-based colour, and is applied to give it a porous surface for the distemper or paint.

The paint used to make the size is thinned with a fairly clear hide glue, made from old leather, scraps of harness and suchlike. The sizing is done on a machine consisting of a table, at the back of which a large roll containing about 930 yards (850 metres) of paper hangs horizontally. There are two methods for applying the paint: in the first a belt of cloth is passed by continuously rotating rollers through a trough full of oil-based paint, and then is rolled against the paper. In the second, the sheet of paper as it arrives on the table slides beneath a box full of paint with a narrow slit in the bottom through which it flows continuously.

Once the sheet of paper has been coloured, it is fed onto the table and worked over with horizontal brushes moving back and forth across the paper to even out the paint. Leaving the table, the sheet of paper slides onto a roller, and is then picked up by flat rods which lift it onto a horizontal network of

Copperplate engraving.
1 Outlining the design with a dry-point
2 The design applied to the roller.
3 Painting the design.
4 Recreating the outline in copper.
5 Shaping the copper.
6 Filling the outlines with felt.
7 Finishing off the copper outlines.
8 Checking against the original design.
ESSEF.

ropes hung near the ceiling the whole length of the workshop where steam-heated pipes are laid all over the floor. The paper hangs in festoons. The movement of the ropes pulls the rods along and the paper moves slowly forward as it dries. When they reach the far end of the workshop, the rods are turned by an ingenious device so they describe a semi-circle and transfer the paper to a second set of ropes working in the opposite direction. By the end of this run, the paper is dry and is rolled up on another machine. The sizing of high-quality papers goes through this process several times, according to the number of different colours. Papers which require a surfaced background go on to surfacing after the sizing stage.

Tinting machine. Patented by Isidore Leroy, 1861. Bibliothèque des Arts et Métiers, Paris.

Mechanical surfacing is accomplished by a much quicker method than sizing. The roll, as it comes out of the preceding stage, is placed at the back of a surfacing machine. The sheet of paper is first passed over a belt of wet cloth which dampens it lightly, then under a polygonal strainer with holes in its sides. This strainer is fitted with talc and rotates continuously on a horizontal axis. As each of its faces comes into position over the paper, it releases a charge of talc which is held by the dampness of the paper. The paper is then exposed to a series of rapidly rotating horizontal cylindrical brushes, which spread the talc evenly and produce the finish. When it leaves the machine, the paper is wound mechanically to form another roll.

A glossy or polished finish is sometimes imparted to wallpaper by rubbing the suface with a hard stone, flint or agate; this is what is used for marbled papers at the final stage of manufacture. Some may also be varnished.

The gilding or silvering to be seen on some deluxe wallpapers is achieved by printing an oil or turpentine-based mordant, or adhesive, into the parts that are to take the metal, which is applied in one of two ways.

The first of these, consists in covering the whole surface of the paper with very thin leaves of brass which are pressed on with a roller. They are then wiped with cotton wool and the mordant left to dry. The surface of the paper is dusted down, so that the metal is left sticking only to the parts covered with mordant. The remaining dust is carefully collected to be used in the second gilding process.

This is identical to the method used for flock papers. It consists of replacing cloth dust with metallic dust.

To give the metallic parts of the design a shiny surface, one simply passes the paper between two rollers, one of perfectly polished cast iron, and the other, immediately underneath, of paper. The sheet of paper is fed between them, with the gilded side next to the metal cylinder; the pressure of this cylinder is sufficient to polish the gilded areas. Silvering is done by a similar process.

Machine printing (nineteenth century)

Machine printing was originally steam driven. The paper is fed between horizontal cylinders whose continuous rotation moves the paper along. One of the cylinders has the design in relief on its surface: this is the printing roller, which is continually re-charged with paint from a cloth belt, moved by rollers and passing through a tank where it is impregnated with paint. If the design to be reproduced on the paper comprises, for example, six colours, the machine will have six pairs of rollers, each of which will print one colour. In this process, the most difficult problem is the adjustment or 'register' of the machine, which means setting all the rollers in such a way that each will print the design precisely in the intended place. Once the machine has been set up, a test is run and examined by the operator. He then rectifies the rollers' lateral movement to correct any mistakes and produce a print as clean as desired. This objective is reached by trial and error, as the result of a series of small adjustments that is always fairly lengthy. Once the

*Three colour printing machine.
Patented by Isidore Leroy, 1861.
Bibliothèque des Arts et Métiers, Paris.*

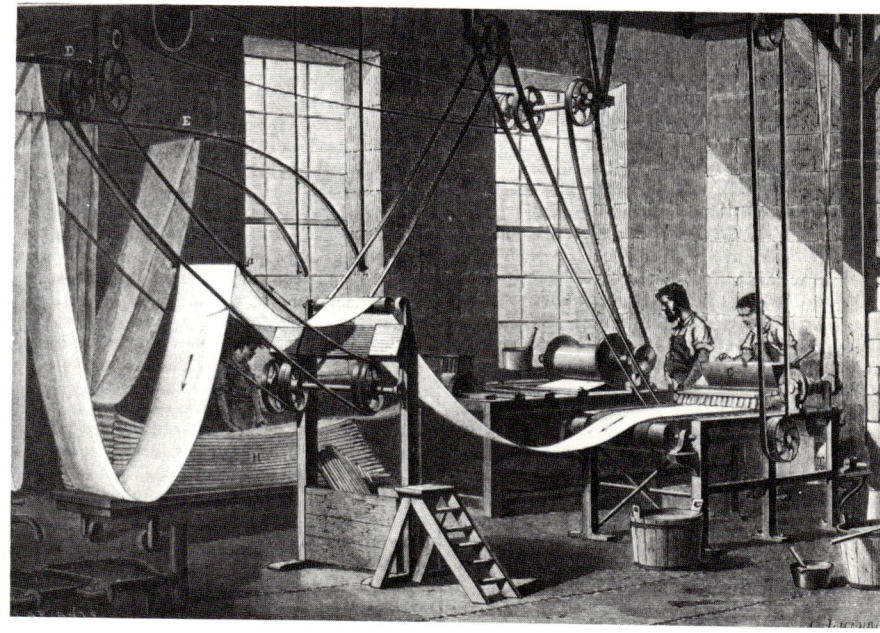

Machine for applying a base colour, with drying system. From P. Poiré, A travers l'industrie française Paris, 1897.

machine is set, it remains only to feed in the paper, which the rollers pass on from one to the next. Finally it emerges from the machine with the design printed in full colour.

Machines exist that can print up to eighteen colours, and there is a method that makes it possible to go beyond this number without increasing the number of rollers. This ingenious process consists of creating the design in such a way that across the same width, or 'track', three colours (for example, red, blue and green) are always printed in the same order – red on the right, blue in the middle and green on the left. These three colours can be printed off the same roller if the paint tray is divided into three compartments, the right one holding red, the middle one blue, and the left one green. Using this system on an eighteen-roller machine, one can print up to fifty-four colours at a time.

When it leaves the machine, the paper is dried by the same process as for sizing.

Printing stripes

For all the ingenuity and variety of different striped patterns – tartan, check, criss-cross and so on – they are printed by a very simple apparatus.

The different colours of which the stripes are made up are put into the compartments of a

Eight-colour cylinder printing machine.

triangular brass receptacle. Its lower edge has very narrow slits which let the paint through evenly. This scriber is placed at the end of a table about 25 feet (9 metres) long. The paper is placed beneath the slit and fixed between two straight wooden rods. It is then attached to a cord going round a pulley. When this cord is pulled the paper passes at an even speed beneath the scriber's lower edge which deposits trails of ink to make the stripes. The different sizes of the slits in the trough allow an infinite number of arrangements for the stripes. Some of them, for instance, can be blocked with a wax resist and the paper will then retain merely the colour of the sizing in this place. When the wet paper reaches the end of the table, it is lifted and hung on the rack to dry.

Stripes can sometimes be used as a background. In this case the paper is then printed with an engraved cylinder in the usual way, with flower designs and suchlike. A design of transverse stripes can be used to produce a tartan-style paper.

Sanitary printing (late nineteenth century)

In the early 1870s several British firms adopted a method of machine printing with copper rollers etched with an intaglio design, which was reminiscent of eighteenth-century calico printing. Papers printed in this way used oily paints and had a smoother surface, making them to a certain extent washable. They took designs easily and were therefore especially suitable for detailed pictorial patterns, as well as being cheap to produce. Thus, by the 1880s sanitary-printed nursery paper, papers illustrating historical and topical events, and novelty papers, were all extremely popular.

Photogravure

In contrast to most types of printing, which are in relief, photogravure uses copper or steel cylinders hollow-engraved by a photochemical process The design is prepared by a process of photographic separation in which coloured filters break down the original into separate negatives, each on a single colour base that together reconstitute the design when printed on top of each other. This technique makes possible an infinite range of colour combinations and graduations. The cylinder is etched with microscopic little pits that fill up with paint. When applied to the paper, they appear as tiny dots almost imperceptible to the eye, and recreate the original design. The colours are usually on a nitrocellulose or vinyl resin base, with a high-quality pigment.

Although three printing stages (yellow, red and blue) are enough, some machines have eight printing heads, which produce greater delicacy and therefore better quality. They are completely automatic and are equipped with instantaneous drying tunnels.

Flexography

Flexography was invented in England in the nineteenth century and used to be called aniline printing (as it traditionally used dyes derived from distilled coal). The difference between this process and photogravure is that the printing surface is made of rubber, cut in relief. Originally the design was etched or moulded onto rubber plates, which were fixed around a metal cylinder, but nowadays the rollers themselves are made of rubber, and the design is cut into them by laser. The ink is transferred from a duct to the printing cylinder via a rubber-covered roller and a metal cylinder called an Anilox, that is etched with a regular cell pattern. The amount of ink used depends on the number and size of these cells, which act as reservoirs. Flexography is especially suitable for wallpaper making because of its capacity for high-speed work (made possible by quick-drying ink) and because the softness of the printing roller allows it to print evenly on coarse paper or vinyl. In addition, the printing surface, being cylindrical, creates a continuous pattern, an obvious advantage in wallpaper. Because the rubber rollers are relatively cheap to produce, flexography is a much less expensive process than photogravure. For these reasons, most wallpaper is printed by flexography.

Screen printing

Screen printing produces a first-class reproduction with no irregularities. The technique has various names: silkscreening, serigraphy, frame printing or, in the United States, hand printing. It first appeared around 1930 and was developed initially in the United States during the 1960s.

Tracings are made of each part of the design according to colour, and copied photochemically onto silk screens stretched on wood or metal frames. The part of the mesh which is not to let through the printing ink is sealed with a photosensitive covering impervious to light. This screen forms a stencil. A long table 75 by 4 feet (23 x 1.3 metres) wide makes it possible to work on two rolls of paper at a time. The corresponding frames for each colour are laid on one after the other, and an assistant applies the oil-based colour in paste form through the screen with a scraper. This operation is repeated for all the frames. The process can be used to apply the glue for flock papers.

New materials

Lincrusta

This is a wall-covering derived from linoleum, invented by the English engineer Frederick Walton in 1860. The process was widely used for imitating Spanish leather, ceramic tiles, or panelling.

The pulp is made of oxidized linseed oil, mixed while hot with plant resin, sawdust, chalk, zinc oxide and a coloured dye. The pulp is applied while hot to the paper base and passed between two cylinders, one of which is engraved and prints a design in relief on the surface of the material, which is then put to dry. Stencilled, polychrome, or silvered decoration can then be added. The solid, waterproof, washable wallpaper with a design in relief produced by this means lost its market to plastic and vinyl in the mid twentieth century.

Vinyl

Vinyl wallpaper is a substance derived from PVC (polyvinyl chloride). This plastic film is used to waterproof the backing it is applied to, rendering it impervious to steam and damp and protecting it against bulging or cracking. In the 1950s successful trials showed that PVC could be used for coating fabrics. Wallpaper manufacturers immediately took up this technique and it developed very fast.

There are two methods of manufacture for vinyl paper. In one of these, soft PVC is pressed between two cylinders, making a film which is applied to the paper. The whole is then heat-pressed to make a homogeneous material. The English method is to cover paper with soft PVC by means of a scraper and then transfer it to a high temperature kiln: this is called scraper coating. The first vinyl wallpaper was made by ICI.

Tinted vinyl film is equivalent to the ground in block printing: it can then be printed by photogravure or flexography.

This new product increased the market for wallpaper by making it serviceable for kitchens and bathrooms. Vinyl is not only washable and impermeable, but non-fading and heat-resistant: it is strippable – the vinyl layer can be stripped from the backing paper which then stays on the wall as an underpaper to take a new décor. Germany, which was initially unfavourable to vinyl, has produced since 1979 what the La Marburg company calls 'Second-generation Wallpapers' (Suprofils). These papers are printed with expandable vinyl inks that reproduce patterns in relief adding a light and shadow effect. In addition to the qualities listed above, vinyl Suprofils are wear-resistant, virtually flameproof and can be painted over.

Flexographic printing machine. CSPP.

Bibliography
Acknowledgments
Sources of illustrations
Index of names

Bibliography

Ackerman, Phyllis, *Wallpaper: Its History, Design and Use,* Heinemann, London, Frederick A. Stokes, New York, 1923.

Album de l'industrie, Combet, Paris, 1903.

Amic, Y., and Brunhammer, Y. 'Histoire des papiers peints', *L'Oeil,* no. 149, Paris, May 1967.

Anscombe, I., and Gere, C., *Arts and Crafts in Britain and America,* Academy Editions, London, 1978, Rizzoli, New York, 1979.

Armstrong, Sir Walter, *Art in Great Britain and Ireland,* Heinemann, London, 1909, R. West, Philadelphia, 1980.

'L'art en France sous le second Empire', exh. cat., Grand Palais, Paris, 1979.

'Art Nouveau and Alphonse Mucha', exh. cat., HMSO, London, 1963.

Baltrusaïtis, J., 'Jardins et pays d'illusions', *Traverse,* nos. 5-6, Paris, 1976.

Barioli, G., *Mostra di Remondini,* Calcographie stampatori bassanesi, Bassano, 1958.

Berra, R., *British Wallpaper Base,* preface to an album of Sanderson papers, London, 1962.

Blanc-Subes, J.-F., 'Les papiers peints du XVIIIe', *L'Estampille,* no. 108, April, 1979.

Blum, A., *Origines du papier,* Tournelles, Paris, 1935.

Bourgeois, A., *Manuel du commis papetier,* J.-B. Baillière, Paris, 1927.

Boutin, L.-C., *Manuel de technologie de tenture murale,* Paris, 1957.

Brisson, B., 'L'aventure du papier peint', *L'Estampille,* no. 78, June 1976.

Brooke, I., *Four Walls Adorned,* Methuen, London, 1952.

Broquelet, A., *L'art appliqué à l'industrie,* Paris, 1909.

Brunhammer, Y., 'Le papier peint en France de 1750 à 1850', *Jardin des arts,* no. 41, Paris, March 1958.

____, *Les années 25,* Musée des Arts Décoratifs, Paris, 1966.

____, 'Le papier peint peut être un art contemporain: le passé en témoigne', *La maison française,* no. 209, Paris, July 1967.

Buffet-Chalier, L., 'Le papier peint', *L'Oeil,* no. 74, Paris, February 1966.

Carlhian, R., 'Papiers peints dits panoramiques', *Arts et métiers graphiques,* no. 55, Paris, 1936.

____, 'Le papier peint ancien', *Connaissance des arts,* Paris, 1952.

'Carlhian Collection of Scenic and Panoramic wallpapers, The', exh. cat., London, January 1937.

'150e anniversaire de la conquête de l'air', exh. cat. on the history of ballooning, together with a wallpaper retrospective, Musée Galliera, Paris, November 1933.

Chavance, R., *Le papier peint et le décor de la maison,* Société Isidore Leroy, Paris, 1929.

Christ, Y., 'Le papier peint connaît une nouvelle époque, mais les grands peintres le dédaignent toujours', *Arts,* no. 883, Paris, 26 September 1962.

Clark, F., *William Morris: Wallpapers and Chintzes,* Academy Editions, London, 1973.

Clouzot, H., 'La tradition du papier peint en France aux XVIIe et au XVIIIe siècle', *Gazette des beaux-arts,* Paris, February 1912.

____, 'Papiers peints de l'école napoléonienne', *Gazette des beaux-arts,* Paris, July 1914.

____, 'Au temps où les murs parlaient', *Renaissance de l'art français,* Paris, September 1920.

____, 'Le papier peint à travers les âges', *Architecture,* Paris, 25 April 1922.

____, *Le papier peint en France du XVIIIe siècle au XIXe siècle,* G. Van Oest, Paris, 1931.

____, *Tableaux et tentures de Dufour et Leroy,* A. Calavas, Paris.

Clouzot, H., and Follot, C., *Histoire du papier peint en France,* Moreau, Paris, 1935.

Cordonnier-Detrie, P., *Jacques Gaugain, cartier-dominotier en la ville du Mans au XVIIIe siècle,* Le Mans, 1928.

____, *Quelques découvertes sur l'imagerie populaire mancelle dans l'art populaire en France,* 1930.

———, 'Trois papiers domino de Jacques Gaugain et de sa veuve, *Bulletin de la société d'agriculture, des sciences et arts de la Sarthe*, Le Mans, 1930.

Cornforth, J., *English Interiors 1790-1848: The Quest for Comfort*, Barrie and Jenkins, London, 1978.

Crace, J.G., *The Crace Papers*, 2 lectures on the history of paper hangings delivered to the RIBA in 1839, annotated by A.V. Sugden and E.A. Entwisle, J.G. Hammond, Birmingham, 1839, London 1939.

La Décoration, 'Connaissance des arts' series, Hachette, Paris, 1963.

Degaast, G. and G., 'La technique de fabrication du papier peint, la gravure en plombine', *Arts et métiers graphiques*, no. 61, Paris, January 1938.

'Deutsches Tapetenmuseum', cat., Kassel, 1955.

'2e exposition rétrospective de panoramas en papier peint ancien', exh. cat., Galerie Carlhian, Paris, May 1937.

Dictionnaire historique des arts, métiers, professions exercés à Paris depuis le XIIIe siècle, Paris, 1906.

Diderot, D., and d'Alembert, *Encyclopédie*, Paris, 1784-90.

Le dix-neuvième siècle français, 'Connaissance des arts' series, Hachette, Paris, 1957.

Dossie, R., *The Handmaid to the Arts*, London, 1758.

Dubosc, G., 'Le papier peint à Rouen, à propos du congrès des fabricants du papier peint', *Journal de Rouen*, 8 September 1903.

Dubosq, F., 'Métamorphoses au Palais-Royal', *Jardin des arts*, no. 175, June 1969, nos. 176-77, July-August 1969.

Duchartre, P.L., *L'imagerie populaire*, Paris, 1925.

Duhamel du Monceau, H.L., *L'art du cartier*, Paris, 1762.

Duvaux, L., *Journal, liste de factures, 1748-1758*, preface by Louis Courajod, Paris, April 1872.

Entwisle, E.A., *The Book of Wallpaper*, introduction by Sacheverell Sitwell, A. Barker, London, 1954.

———, *A Literary History of Wallpaper*, Batsford, London, 1960.

———, *Wallpapers of the Victorian Era*, F. Lewis, Leigh-on-Sea, 1964.

———, *French Scenic Wallpapers, 1800-1860*, F. Lewis, Leigh-on-Sea, 1972, Textile Book Service, Broadway (NJ), 1964.

'Exhibition of Wallpaper, Historical and Contemporary', exh. cat., The Buffalo Fine Arts Academy, Albright Art Gallery, Buffalo (NY), December 1937.

'Exposition bibliothèque Forney, 1800-1835', exh. cat., Mireille Guibert, Paris, 1978.

'Exposition de Bagatelle à Monceau, 1778-1978', Musée Carnavalet, Paris, 1978.

'Exposition de papier peint et toiles imprimées et pochées', exh. cat., Musée Galliera, Paris, 1909.

'Exposition internationale des arts décoratifs et industriels modernes', Paris, 1925.

Fagu, G., *Le papier peint*, Paris, 1957.

———, *Le papier peint dans la décoration*, Paris, 1963.

Fichtenberg, M., *Nouveau manuel complet du fabricant de papier fantaisie, papiers marbrés, jaspés, maroquinés, gaufrés, dorés,...*, Roret, Paris, 1852.

Figuier, L., *Les merveilles de la science et de l'industrie*, Jouet et Cie, Paris.

Floud, P., 'The Wallpaper Designs of C.F.A. Voysey', *Penrose Annual*, vol. 52, 1958, pp. 10-14.

———, 'The Wallpaper Designs of William Morris', *Penrose Annual*, vol. 54, 1960, pp. 41-45.

Follot, F., *Causerie sur le papier peint à la bibliothèque Forney*, Delagrave, Paris, 1887.

———, *Musée rétrospectif de la classe 68 à l'exposition universelle de 1900 à Paris, papiers peints*, Belin frères, Saint-Cloud, 1901.

Fowler, J., and Cornforth, J., *English Decoration in the Eighteenth Century*, Barrie and Jenkins, London, 1974.

Frangiamore, C.L., *Wallpaper in America: From the Seventeenth Century to World War I*, Norton, New York, 1980.

———, 'Wallpapers Used in Nineteenth-Century America', *Antiques*, CII, New York, December 1972.

Gabrielle, N., *Catalogo del Museo dell'Arredamento Stupinigi*, Turin, 1966.

Garnier-Audiger, *Manuel du tapissier décorateur et marchand de meubles*, Paris, 1830.

Germann, S., 'Regional Schools of Harpsichord Decoration', *Journal of the American Musicological Society*, Richmond (VA), 1979.

Grand-Carteret, J., *Papeterie et papetiers de l'ancien temps*, Paris, 1913.

Greysmith, B., *Wallpaper*, Studio Vista, London, Macmillan, New York, 1976.

Gruin, le Mardelé and Auberge, *Manuel de l'industrie et du commerce du papier peint*, Paris, 1935.

Gusman, P., 'J.-M. Papillon', *Biblys*, Paris, 1925.

———, *Panneaux décoratifs et tenture murale du XVIIIe et du commencement du XIXe*, Massin, Paris.

Haemmerle, A., *Die Buntpapiere*, Callwey, Munich, 1961.

Hamilton, J., 'Early English Wallpapers', *The Connoisseur*, July 1977.

Harvard, H., 'Papiers peints', *Dictionnaire de l'ameublement*, vol. 4.

'Historic Wallpapers in the Whitworth Art Gallery', cat., Univ. of Manchester, Manchester, 1972.

Hourticq, L., *Histoire générale de l'art*, Hachette, Paris, 1920.

Huisman, D., and Patriks, G., *L'esthétique industrielle*, 'Que sais-je?' series, P.U.F., Paris, 1961.

Jackson, J.B., 'An essay on the Invention of Engraving and Printing in Chiaroscuro', London, 1754.

Jacqué, B., 'Les débuts de l'industrie du papier peint à Mulhouse, 1790-1794', *Revue d'Alsace*, no. 105, Colmar, 1979.

Jacqué, B. and J., *Chefs-d'oeuvre du Musée de l'Impression sur Etoffes de Mulhouse*, vol. III, Gakken, Tokyo, 1978.

Jacquet, P., 'Musée de l'Impression sur Etoffes',

Bulletin trimestriel de la Société Industrielle de Mulhouse, Mulhouse, no. 761, 4/1975.

'Jardins 1760-1820, pays d'illusion, terre d'expériences', exh. cat., Hôtel de Sully, Paris, May 1977.

Jenkinson, H., 'English Wallpapers of the Sixteenth and Seventeenth Centuries', *Journal of the Society of Antiquaries*, London, July 1925.

Jugaku, Bunsho, *Paper Making by Hand in Japan*, Meiji-Shobo, Tokyo, 1959.

Katzenbach, L. and W., *The Practical Book of American Wallpapers*, Philadelphia and New York, 1951.

Labarte, J., *Histoire des arts industriels*, Morel, Paris, 1872-75.

Laboulaye, C., *Notice technologique sur l'invention des gaufrages du papier peint et observation sur le procès en contrefaçon intenté à Messieurs Desfossé... et autres par M. Balin*, Paris, 1879.

Lalande, J., *L'art de faire le papier*, Paris, 1761.

Lardet, A., 'Les papiers peints panoramiques', *L'Estampille*, no. 5, December 1969.

Leblanc-Hardel, F., *Imageries populaires ayant trait aux papiers cartes du XVI*^{e} *et XVII*^{e} *siècles*, Liesville, Caen, 1867.

Leiss, J., *Bildtapeten aus alter und neuer Zeit*, Broschek, Hamburg, 1961.

Lenormand, S., *Nouveau manuel complet du fabricant d'étoffes imprimées et du papier peint*, Roret, Paris, 1832.

Levêque, J.-J., *L'univers d'Hubert Robert*, 'Les carnets de dessins' series, Scrépel, Paris, 1979.

Longfield, A.K., 'History of the Dublin Wallpaper Industry in the Eighteenth Century', *Journal of the Royal Society of Antiquaries in Ireland*, Dublin, Vol. 77, iv, 1947.

Martin, A., *L'imagerie orléanaise*, prefaced with a study by P. Duchartre, biographical note by Dr Garsonnin, Orléans, 1929.

Martin, G., *Le papier*, 'Que sais-je?' series, P.U.F., Paris, 1975.

Mathey, F., 'Les panoramiques ou le panorama d'une société', *Art et décoration*, no. 30, Paris, 1953.

McClelland, N., *Historic Wallpapers*, J.B. Lippincott, Philadelphia and London, 1924.

———, 'Papiers peints français dans les demeures américaines', *Renaisssance de l'art français*, no. 5, Paris, May 1928.

Métadier, P., 'Balzac à Saché', *Bulletin de la Société d'Honoré de Balzac de Touraine*.

Metken, S., *Geschnittenes Papier*, Callwey, Munich, 1978.

Meyer-Riefstahl, R., 'La décoration du livre oriental', *Art et décoration*, no. 32, Paris, August 1912.

Mick, E.W., *Altes Buntpapier*, Die Bibliophilen Taschenbücher, Harenberg Kommunikation, Dortmund, 1979.

Moussinac, L., *Étoffes imprimées et papiers peints*, Levy, Paris, 1924.

'Mucha 1860-1939', exh. cat., Grand Palais, Paris, 1980.

Muhammad Agha-Oghli, *Persian Bookbindings of the Fifteenth Century*, Univ. of Michigan Press, Michigan, 1935.

Nouvel, O., *French Wallpaper Designs*, Zwemmer, London, 1981.

Oligs, H., *Tapeten: Ihre Geschichte bis zur Gegenwart*, Braunschweig, 1970.

Oman, C., and Hamilton, J., *Wallpapers. A History and Illustrated Catalogue of the Collection of the Victoria and Albert Museum*, Sotheby Publications, London, 1982.

'L'Ornementation des papiers imprimés des clavecins anversois', *Revue belge d'archéologie et d'histoire de l'art*, fasc. 2, Brussels, 1932.

'Les papiers peints et les décorateurs du XVIIIe siècle à nos jours', Musée Galliera, Paris, June 1953.

Papillon, J.-M., *Traité historique et pratique de la gravure sur bois*, Simon, Paris, 1776, and an unpublished m.s. in the Bibliothèque Nationale, Paris, 1776.

'Le Parisien chez lui au XIXe siècle, 1814-1914', exh. cat., Hôtel de Rohan, Paris, 1976.

Pasquier, J. du, and Blanc-Subes, J.-F., 'Papiers peints du XVIIIe siècle à Bordeaux', *L'Estampille*, no. 115, November 1979.

Passamani, B., *Guido al Museo Civico di Bassano*, Bassano, 1975.

Poiré, P., *A travers l'industrie française*, Hachette, Paris, 1897.

Poiret, P., *En habillant l'époque*, Grasset, Paris, 1930.

Poisson, P., *Nouveau manuel du marchand papetier*, Paris, 1854.

Réveillon, J.-B., *Exposé justificatif pour le Sieur Réveillon, entrepreneur de la Manufacture Royale de Papiers Peints Fauxbourg Saint-Antoine*, Paris, 1789.

Rioux, J.-P., *La révolution industrielle 1780-1880*, Le Seuil, Paris, 1971.

Saint-Sauveur, D. de, 'A Barbentane, le XVIIIe siècle est bien vivant', *Le Figaro-Magazine*, Paris, December 1979.

Saulnier, R., *Un gentilhomme dominotier à Besançon au XVIII*^{e} *siècle*, S 73, 1933.

———, *Une lignée de cartiers dominotiers bisontins*, S 64, 1934-35.

Savage, G., *Histoire de la décoration intérieure*, Somogy, Paris, 1967.

Savary des Bruslons, J., *Dictionnaire universel de commerce contenant tout ce qui concerne le commerce qui se fait dans les quatre parties du monde*, J. Estienne, Paris, 1723-30.

———, *Le parfait négociant ou industrie générale pour ce qui regarde le commerce des marchandises de France par les frères Etienne*, Paris, 1770.

Save, C., 'Panorama du papier peint', *L'Estampille*, no. 17, January 1971.

Seguin, J.-P., preface to the Zuber album of panoramic papers, 1971.

Sembach, K-J., *Style 1930*, Office du Livre, Paris, 1971.

Spencer, I., *Walter Crane*, Studio Vista, London, and Macmillan, New York, 1975.

Spoerlin, *Fabrication du papier peint dit iris ou irisé*, Risler, Mulhouse, 1823.

Sugden, A.V., and Edmondson, J.L., *A History of English Wallpapers 1509-1914*, Batsford, London, 1925, Scribner's, New York, 1926.

Sugden, A.V., and Entwisle, E.A., *Potters of Darwen: A Century of Wallpaper Printing by Machinery, 1839-1939*, Manchester, 1939.

Thiéry, L.-V., *Guide des amateurs et des étrangers voyageurs à Paris*, 3 vols, Paris, 1786-88 (repr. 1928).

'Toiles de Nantes des XVIIIe et XIXe siècles', exh. cat., Musée de l'Impression sur Etoffes, Mulhouse, 1977.

'Toiles imprimées et papiers peints', cat., Musée Galliera, Paris, 1928.

'Trois siècles de papier peint', exh. cat., Musée des Arts Décoratifs, Paris, 1967.

'3e exposition rétrospective de panoramas en papier peint ancien', exh. cat., Galerie Carlhian, Paris, 1946.

Tschoudi Madsen, S., *Art nouveau*, Hachette, Paris, 1967.

Vachon, M., *Les arts et les industries du papier en France*, Paris, 1871-94.

Veronesi, G., *Into the Twenties. Style and Design 1909-29*, Thames and Hudson, London, 1968; US edn as *Style and Design 1909-29*, Braziller, New York, 1968.

'Wallpaper. A picture book of examples in the collections of the Cooper Union Museum', cat., New York, 1961.

Waring, J., *Early American Stencils on Walls and Furniture*, Dover, New York, 1968.

Waterer, J.W., *Spanish Leather*, Faber and Faber, London, 1971.

Watkinson, R., *William Morris as Designer*, Trefoil Books, London, 1979.

Zuber, I., *Papiers peints*, vol. II: *Histoire documentaire de l'industrie de Mulhouse et de ses environs au XIXe siècle*, Veuve Bader, Mulhouse, 1902.

Acknowledgments

The authors and publishers gratefully acknowledge the assistance of: Christian Baulez, Claire Constans and Daniel Mayer, Musée National du Château de Versailles; Alain Erlande-Brandenburg, Musée de Cluny, Paris; Jacqueline Jacqué, Musée de l'Impression sur Etoffes, Mulhouse; Paul Métadier, Château de Saché; Bernard de Montgolfier, Musée Carnavalet, Paris; Ernst Wolfgang Mick, Deutsches Tapetenmuseum, Kassel; Jeffery Daniel, Geffrye Museum, London; Jean Hamilton, Victoria and Albert Museum, London; Clelia Alberici, the Bertarelli Collection, Museo di Castello Sforzesco, Milan; Gian Domenico Romanelli, Ca' Rezzonico, Venice; Peter Irmgard, Historisches Museum, Basel.

and of the following institutions: Cabinet des Estampes de la Bibliothèque Nationale and Musée des Arts Décoratifs, Paris; Print Room of the British Museum and British Library, London; Museo Civico di Bassano del Grappa; Museo Correr, Venice; Museo dell'Arredamento, la Palazzino della Caccia, Stupinigi, Turin.

Thanks are also due to: Didier Bonnet, Martine Bouton and Martine Hérold, as well as Henri Béchard, Daniel Bohême, Jacques Boucher, Robert Carlhian, Bernard Chasset, Marianne Clouzot, Margaret Coventry, Françoise Dorget, Janine Fagu, Marilyn Gaucher, Arnaud Griton, Jean, François and Denis Halard, Armelle Häury, Bernard Jacqué, Philippe Laxton, Patrick Mauny, Claude Mercier-Ythier, Charlotte Poggioli, Madame Jean Raindre.

Finally, the authors would like to express their most sincere gratitude to Mireille Guibert of the Bibliothèque Forney, Paris.

Sources of illustrations

The following abbreviations have been used: a – above; b – below; btm – bottom; c – centre; l – left; r – right; t – top. *Figures are page numbers.*

Archives Photographiques Paris/SPADEM: 220 bl.
Ashmolean Museum, Oxford, reproduced by courtesy of the President and Fellows of Corpus Christi College, Oxford: 21a.
Bibliothèque Forney, Paris: 69al, 71, 95br, 97cl, br, 102 cl, 128bl, 130(5), 131b, 132c, 134(3,4), 138 bl, br, 140al, 160bl, 162br, 175 (3-7), 176, 177, 178, 179, 180a, c, 208ar, br, 210cl, 212ar, al.
Bibliothèque Nationale, Paris: 22, 25a, 26, 35, 36, 39, 40, 95a, 217b.
Bonnefoy: 59c.
Bozzetto, Venice: 53b.
British Museum, London: 76b.
Bulloz: 37, 212br.
Carlhian: 106, 108b.
City of Kingston-upon-Hull Museums and Art Galleries: 214.
Cooper-Hewitt Collection, New York: 125a, b.
J.-C. Dewolf: 41, 43bl, 46cr, 162ar.
Pierre Dumoulin: 25c, b.
John Freeman Group, London: 56al, 77, 153a, r, 168al, ar.
Geffrye Museum, London: 162al.
Historisches Museum, Basel: 81b.
Iphot, Grenoble: 203a.
Joël Lelièvre: 11, 23, 24, 25tac, 28-34, 42, 43al, ar, br, 47, 48, 49, 50, 51, 52a, 54, 56ar, 58cl, bl, r, 59a, b, 60l, 65ar, br, 68, 72, 73b, 74r, 80ar, 81a, 84, 85, 87, 89, 90, 92, 93, 95c, 96, 97l, 98b, 99bl, cr, br, 100a, 101, 102ar, br, 103, 104, 105, 106a, 108a, 109, 110, 111, 113cr, br, 114a, cl, 115, 116bl, br, 117, 118, 119, 121, 123, 128a, c, 134(l,1,2,5), 135br, 137, 139ar, bl, 140l, bl, tr, cr, br, 141, 154, 156, 157, 158a, 160al, ar, br, 162cl, bl, 163a, 164, 169c, 170, 171, 172, 175al, ar, 182b, 183r, 185r, 186, 187b, 189bl, 190b, 191, 192, 196, 197, 199a, 200, 206br, 207al, ar, cl, br, 208bl, 209, 210a, br, 212cr, bl, 221b, 228, 229al, ar.
Mansell Collection, London: 222.
J.-P. Merlhou: 220.
Edith Michaelis: 187a.
Musée de l'Impression sur Etoffes, Mulhouse (MISE): 60r, 70, 75, 88, 99a, 100b, 116a, cr, 132b, 133, 135a, 136, 139al, 142r, 207br, 208al, bl, 224.
Musée des Arts Décoratifs, Paris: 98a, 120, 205ac.
Museo Correr, Vennice: 52b.
Papiers Peints de France, Paris: 223b, 231.
Daniel Quat: 169a.
Réunion des Musées Nationaux, Paris: 14, 58a, 201, 202, 203b, 204.
Arthur Sanderson and Sons Ltd, London: 144, 147al, cl, 173bc, btm, 221a, 223ar, 229b.
Laurent Sully-Jaulmes: 138a, 139al.
José Tavera: 182.
Victoria and Albert Museum, London: 16-20, 21b, 38, 46al, br, 56, 61, 62, 63, 64, 65l, 66, 67r, 69r, 73a, 74l, 76, 78, 79, 80al, bl, 82, 83, 114br, 129, 130(1-4), 131a, c, 135bl, 142l, 145, 146l, r, 147bl, ar, br, 148, 149, 150, 151, 152, 153bl, 158b, 159, 161, 166, 168b, 173tr, ar, 183al, bl, 199b, 205al, br, 206al, 211.
Whitworth Art Gallery, University of Manchester: 44, 56b, 67l, 80br.
Photo X: 69bl, 112, 113a, bl, 115b, 116cl, 163b, 174, 181, 184, 185a, cl, b, 188, 189a, cr, 190al, ar, c, 217al, ar, 226.

Index of names

Figures in *italics* refer to the illustrations.

A.B. Durotapet *183*
Académie Française, L' 27, 141
Académie Royale des Beaux-Arts 216
Adam, Robert 72
Akali, Baron J.K. 124
Albermarle, Lord 71, 75
Albright Art Gallery, Buffalo 193
Aldermanbury 70, 121
Aldford House, London 20, 21, *44*
Aldridge, John 173
Alembert, d' *28*, 215, 216
Alix 177
Allen, Rev. Thomas 120
Alps 16, 108
Alsace 42, 94, 100, 107, 117, 125
Alte Kapelle, Regensburg 66
Amalfi 122
American Museum in Britain, Bath 126
Amic, Y. 182
Amy 42
Andrada, Lina de *177*
Angevilliers, Comte d' 105
Angiolini, Giovanni 50
Angoumois 70
Anisson-Dupéron, Etienne 101, 102
Anne, Queen of England 45
Anne of Britanny 15
Annison, Abbé 73
Annonay 90
Antin, chaussée d', Paris 101
Antwerp *25*
Appenines 105
Arabia 7, 9, 57, 141
Arbre Sec, rue de l', Paris 88, 90
Arc de Triomphe, Paris 119
Arcadia 106, 125
Archevêques de Sens, Hôtel des, Paris 194
Ariosto 123
Arnold, Johann Christian *85*, 85, 86
Art Union 129

Art Workers' Guild 148, 152
Arthur, Jean-Jacques 101
Arthur and Grenard 107
Arthur and Robert 79, *102*, 101-02, 107, *108*, *111*, 122
Artois, Comte d' 91
Arts and Crafts Exhibition Society 148
Ashley, Bernard 174
Ashley, Laura *174*, 174, 188, 191
Ashmolean Museum, Oxford 19
Atelier Hook 123, 210
Atelier Martine 155, *162*, 177, 178
Atelier Pomone *175*, 191
Atlantic Ocean 121
Atwell, Mabel Lucy 147, *173*
Au Bon Marché 191
Au Printemps 191
Au Sansonnet 177, 184
Aubert, Didier 37, 38, 73
Aubry, Georges 193
Aubry, Octave 200
Auffay *68*
Augsburg *25*, *48*, 48, 49
Austria 70, 119, 152, 155, *157*, 157, 158, *163*, 178, *179*
Aushwahl Verlag Cadi 165
Auteuil 155
Avignon 54, *84*

Bacon, Francis 216
Baeschin 177
Bagatelle gardens 105, 107
Bagneux 27
Bagneux, rue de, Paris 74
Bakst, Leon (Lev Samoïlevitch Rosenberg) 164
Baldo 85
Baleni, Guaniesi 50
Balin, Paul *58*, 141, *162*
Balk 48

Ballets Russes 155, 212
Baltimore 125
Baltrusaïtis, Jurgis 106
Balzac, Honoré de 141, *196*, 197
Bammenthal 167
Banks, Sir Joseph 62
Baratti, Antonio 50
Barberot 26
Barcelona 164
Barker, Robert 102
Basel *48*, *81*
Bassano 37, 48, 50, *51*, *52*, 52, *53*, 54, 54, 55, 206, *207*
Basset 40
Bastille, Paris 91
Batavia 57
Battersea 77, 78
Baudelaire, Charles 155
Baudry, Raymonde 188
Bauhaus 144, 154, 156, 158, 163, 165
Baumann bank, Frankfurt 85
Bawden, Edward 173
Bayley, William 45
Bayonne 125
Bayreuth 156
Beard, Linda 184
Beaton, Sir Cecil 173
Beauvau, rue, Paris 117
Béchard, Henri 182, 194
Beck, B.G. 85
Becker, Wolfgang 204
Bedford, Duke of 62
Bedford Park 146
Behagel, Jakob 86
Behagel brothers 86
Behrens, Peter 157, 158
Belgium 154, 164, 200
Bell, Thomas 83
Bellanger 105
Belleville 175
Bellevue 73

241

Bellicard, see Cochin and Bellicard
Bénard de Moussinières, Eugène Balthasar Crescent 98; see also Jacquemart and Bénard
Benedictus 175, 178
Bengal, Bay of 57
Benoit, Guillaume 42
Bently, Richard 80
Benucci, Antonio 50
Bérain, Jean 67
Bercy, Château de 22, 36
Berlin 84, 85, 155, 156, 163, 193
Bernardin de Saint Pierre, Henri 103, 117, 122
Berners St, London 173, 191
Bertarelli Collection 52
Bertinazzi, Carlo 50
Berwick-upon-Tweed *64, 205*
Besançon 42
Besford Court, Worcester *20*, 20, 173
Besson boutique 191
Bettuzzi, del 50
Beverley 18
Bewick, Thomas 79
Bexley Heath 145
Bianchi, Giulio Cesare 50
Bianchini 155
Bibiena family 104
Bibliothèque Forney, Paris 194
Bibliothèque Nationale, Paris 94, 95, 102
Bing, Samuel 152, 153, 154, 164
Binyon, Brightwen 146
Birchin Lane, London 61
Birge company, M.H. 153, 167
Blanc, Charles 141
Blanche de Castille 15
Blondel, Merry-Joseph 117, *118*, 124
Blue Paper Warehouse 70
Blumenrain *81*
Board of Trade for Schools of Arts and Crafts, Prussia 164
Boileau, Etienne 15
Boilly *106*, 122
Bokhara 48
Bolney 35
Bologna 50
Bonaparte, rue, Paris 178, 182, 184, 185
Bonnard, Pierre 202
Bons-Enfants, rue des, Paris 91
Bordeaux 42, 125
Borden Hall, Kent 20
Bordier, Primerose 184
Borgeaud, Mme 184, 191
Borges, Ulrich 167, 188
Bosmelet, Château de, Normandy *68*
Boston, MA 120, 121, 122, 124, 125, 126
Bougainville, de 117
Bouillon, Duc de 71
Boulard 40

Boulogne, de 71
Bourdichon, Jehan 15
Bourier, Jean-Pierre 42
Bourmaux, Elisabeth 42
Bourton-on-the-Water 79
Boussac company 168
Boutet de Monvel, Louis Maurice 155, 164
Boutique Américaine 168, 182
Bramsche 165
Brauchitsch, Margaret von 156
Brentford *46*
Brépols 194
Breslau 84
Brighton 62, 64, 81, 173
Bril, Paul *175*
Briscoe, John 44, 70
Brissot de Warville, Jacques-Pierre 121, 126, 153
Britannia 125
British Museum, London 52
Broc, Jean 117, *119*, 122, 128
Broke Hall, Suffolk 20
Bromwich, Thomas 79, 80
Brück, Paul 156
Brunhammer, Yvonne 182
Bruno, Paul 158
Brunschwig et Fils, Inc. 192
Brussels 155, 157, 164
Brutus 95
Buffalo 164, 193
Buffard 200
Bumstead, Josiah 126
Burchardt, Adolf 156
Burchfield, Charles 167
Burges, William, 145, 146
Burgos *106*
Burne-Jones, Edward 146
Butling, Edward 44
Butterfield, Lindsay 20
Byzantium 57

Ca' Rezzonico, Venice *52*, 54
Cabinet d'Estampes, Bibliothèque Nationale, Paris 36, 141
Cabinet du Roi 117
Cadogan, Lord 78
Café Procope, Paris *97*
Cailleux Collection 107
Calcutta 57
Caldecott, Randolph 146
Calderwood, Mrs 85
Calicut 57
Callot, Jacques 27
Calypso 197
Cambridge *18*, 18, 21
Campagna 105
Camus, Jacques 178, 192

Canaletto, Giovanni Antonio 77
Canei 167
Canova, A. 117
Canovas, Manuel 185, 186, *188, 212*
Canovas, Sophie 186, *188, 212*
Canton 57, 121
Cape of Good Hope 57
Cardon, Emile 131
Carlhian, R. and M. 181, 194
Carlhian Collection 107, 122
Carlton Hill 102
Carlton House, London 81
Carminati Palace, Venice *52*, 54
Carmontelle (Louis Carrogis) 102, 103, 105
Carré St Martin, rue, Paris 40
Carrières 74
Carrousel, place du, Paris 102
Carrousel, rue du, Paris 90
Carson, Pirie and Scott 164
Casa Vicens, Barcelona 164
Castel Béranger, Paris 155, *160*, 160, 164
Castel Sant Angelo, Rome 107
Castello Sforzesco, Milan 52
Castiglione, Giovanni Benedetto 50
Castletown House, Co. Kildare 35
Cathay 57
Cattaneo, Geronimo 50
Caze, de 73
Centre de Commerce Français, Tokyo 194
Century Guild *148*, 151, 157
Cerio, Letizia 165
Cézanne, Paul 155, 201, 202
Châlons-sur-Marne 177
Chambers, Sir William 75
Chambre Syndicale de Fabricants de Papiers Peints de France 182, 191
Champagne 70
Champs, Château des 71
Champs Elysées, Paris 154
Chanteloup 64
Chardon, Jacques 27, 40
Charenton, rue de 74
Charles I 68
Charles X 100, 128
Charleston 120
Charmettes, Château des *59*
Charonne, rue de 88
Charterhouse Designs *169*
Charvet, Jean-Gabriel 112, 122
Chateaubriand, Vicomte de 200
Chatou 105
Chauveau, Charlotte-Madeleine-Thérèse 27, 40
Chauveau, François 40
Chauveau, Jacques 40, 79
Chauveau, Pierre-Joseph 40
Chauveau, René 27, 40

Chauveau, René-Bonaventure 27
Chavant, Fleury 141
Chelsea 81
Chenevard 40, 100
Chenevard and Pernon 98
Cheops 200
Chéreau, Jacques 74
Cheronnet, Louis 179
Chestnut St, Philadelphia 121
Chevallier 42
Chevillon 40
Chevillon, Marie-Madeleine 26
Chicago 152, 153, 164
Chicago Auditorium 164
China 7, 9, 35, 36, 42, 44, 45, 54, 57, *60*, *61*, 61, 62, *63*, 64, *64*, *65*, 68, 71, 73, 74, 79, 80, 81, 85, 86, 98, 107, 121, 141, 154, 167, 169, 199, *205*, *208*, 209
Chippendale, Thomas 45, 64
Chiswick 173, 191
Christ Church Mansion, Ipswich 71
Christiansen, Hans 156
Christ's College, Cambridge *18*, 18
Church of Rome 15
Cietti 86, 101
Clandon Park, Surrey 71, *74*
Clarkson, Thomas 163
Claudius-Petit, Eugène 182
Clavel 192
Claverton Manor, Bath 126
Clerc and Margeridon 123
Clésinger, J.-B. 120
Clichy, rue de, Paris 155
Clisson 105
Cloître St Germain, rue du, 73
Clough, Ebenezer 124, 125
Clouzot, Henri 7, 24, 27, 36, 119, 177
Coates, Victoria 174
Cochin, Charles-Nicolas 86
Cochin, Noël 26
Cochin and Bellicard 86
Cocteau, Jean 175
Cofac 184
Cogniet 128
Colbert, Jean-Baptiste 59
Cole, Henry 131, 145
Cole and Sons *58*, 170, *171*, *173*, 173
Colefax, Sybil 174
Colette 154, 185
Colignon 88
Colin, Paul 178
Cologne 157, 158
Colonial Williamsburg Foundation, VA 21
Coloroll 184
Columbus, NY 193
Compagnie des Indes 61
Compans, rue 198
Company of Mercers 20

Comtesse d'Artois, rue, Paris 74
Connaissance Fabrics 171
Constantinople (Istanbul) 57
Conti, quai 101
Cook, Captain 113, 122, 125
Cooper, J.S. 131
Cooper Hewitt Museum, New York 125, 126, 167
Cooper Union Museum, New York 193
Copenhagen 183
Cordoba 16, 18
Cordonnier-Detrie, P. 142
Coromandel 57
Corpus Christi College, Oxford 19
Couronne, Palais de la 117
Cournon 107
Courtalin 90, 91, 94
Coutts bank, Strand, London 62
Couture, Thomas 120, *139*
Cowtan, Mawer 81, 128, 131
Crace, Edward 81
Crace, Frederick 81, 173
Crace, John 81
Crace, John Gregory 81
Crace company 81, 129
Cradock, Mrs 101
Crane, Walter *148*, 148, *150*, 152, 156, *159*, *161*, 173, 191, *211*, 211
Crépy the elder 40, 74, 75
Crown Decorative Products Ltd 183
Crystal Palace, New York 126
Cuthbertson and Co. 131

Dahls Tapetfabrik 183
Dalí, Salvador 165
Damiot, J. 194
Dampierre-sur-Salon 126
Daniell, Thomas and William 108, 122
Danzig 84
Daphne 126
Darius 183
Darly, Mathias 45
Darmstadt 193
Darwen 129, *132*
Daudet, Alphonse 199
Dauphine, place, Bordeaux 42
Dauptain 128
David, Louis 86, 119
Day, Lewis F. *150*, *151*, 152, *159*, 173
Day, Lucienne *173*, 173
Decorative Art Society 128
Defoe, Daniel 103
Degas, Edgar *201*
Deglane 154
Deighton, Edward 80
Delacroix, Eugène 199
Delafosse, Charles 88
Delagarde, Etienne 90

Delasalle, Philippe *192*
Delaunay, Robert and Sonia 175
Delft 66
Delicourt, E. 117, 123, 131, *210*, 210
Delille, Abbé 103
Deltil 10, 110, 113, 116, 122, 123, 124
Denis, Maurice 155, 164, 202
Denmark *183*
Denst, Jack 168
Derain, André 199, 200
Desfossé *65*, 103, 112, *116*, 117, 120, 123, *137*, *139*, 142, 181
Desfossé and Karth *115*, *138*, *141*
Designers Guild 174, *175*
Deskey, Donald 167
Desportes, François 123
Dessau 156
Desventes 40
Deutscher Werkbund 158
Deutsches Tapetenmuseum, Kassel 209
Dickenson, Joseph 121
Diderot, boulevard, Paris 178
Diderot, Denis 27, *28*, 215, 216
Didot St Léger, François 90, 127, 215
Dijon 194
Ditzel, Roland 167
Dodd, George 131
Doddington Hall, Lincs *78*
Dolfuss, Nicolas 88, 107, *207*
Dominotiers, Les *183*, 185
Domus Aurea, Rome 16
Donkin, Bryan 215
Donnell, Edna K. 78
Dossie, Robert 45, 80
Dostoyevsky, Fyodor Mikhaylovich 198
Douglas Ford House 46
Dresden 84
Dresser, Christopher *146*, 146
Drottingholm 64
Drouard, see Lapeyre and Drouard
Drummond, John 173
Dublin 121
Ducal Palace, Venice *51*, 52
Ducuing, F. 132
Dufet, Michel 181
Dufour, Joseph 64, 107, 112, 113, 117, 119, 126
Dufour and Leroy 101, 117, *119*, 119, *120*, 122, 123, 127, *128*
Dufour company *71*, *77*, *97*, 100, *109*, *117*, *118*, 122, 124, *134*, *209*
Dufy, Raoul 155, 164, 177
Dugourc, Jean-Démosthène 101, 102
Dumas, Paul 155, *177*, 177, 178, 181, 184, 186, 192, 194, *212*
Dumont, Victor 123, *210*
Dunan 212
Dunand 123
Dunbar 121

243

Dunoyer de Segonzac, A. 155, 164
Dupin, Hampshire, French and Co. 44
Duras 42
Dutilleul *184*, 184
Duvaux, Lazare 71

East End, London 21, 79
East India Company 45
East Indies Company 57
Eastlake, Charles Lock 131
Eccard, Anthony 81
Eckhardt, Francis, Frederick and Anthony George *80*, 81, *83*, 83
Eckmann, Otto *156*, 156
Ecole des Beaux-Arts, Paris 141
Eden 108, 112
Eder, Johann Georg 48
Edinburgh 102
Edmondson, J.L. 7
Egypt 7, 100, 124, 167, 169, 170, 199
Ehrmann, Eugène 122, 123, 142
Ehrmann and Fuchs 112, 113
Ehrmann and Schuler *116*, 123
Eiffel Tower, Paris 193
Eitel, W. 165
Ekwits 77
Elizabeth I 20
Elizabeth II 173
Elton Lodge, Kent *199*
Engelbrecht, Martin *24*, *37*
Engelhardt company 86, 156
England 15, *17*, 18, *19*, 19, *20*, 20, 21, 22, *44*, 44, 45, *46*, 50, 54, *56*, 57, *58*, 59, 61, *62*, 64, *65*, 66, *67*, 67, *69*, 70, 71, *73*, 73, 74, 75, *76*, 77, 78, *79*, 79, *80*, 80, *81*, 83, 83, 85, 86, 87, 105, 120, 124, 126, 127, 128, *129*, 130, 131, *132*, 132, *135*, 141, *142*, 145, 145, 146, *147*, 148, *149*, *150*, 151, 151, *152*, 152, *153*, 153, 154, 156, 158, *159*, *161*, 162, 167, 170, 170-74, *171*, *173*, *174*, 175, 191, *199*, 201, *205*, 205, *206*, *208*, 211, 211, 212, *212*, *214*, 215, 231
English Channel 125
Enkhausen brothers 156
Enrichemont, Princesse d' 71
Erfurt 103
Ermenonville 105
ESSEF *182*, 184, *227*
Essex *83*
Essex and Co. *151*, *161*, 211
Essonnes 127, 215
Estachy, Françoise *186*
Etats Généraux 91
Etruria 85, 86
Euderlin, Anna Maria 48
Euderlin, Jacob 48
Eugénie, Empress 142

Eure-et-Loir *60*
Europe 7, 9, 16, 18, 22, 45, 48, 50, 52, 57, 59, 61, 64, 66, 70, 71, 75, 77, 81, 84, 85, 86, 90, 105, 108, 118, 121, 126, 144, 145, 151, 154, 156, 157, 164, 168, 169, 170, 209
Evelyn, John 57
Ewart, William 141
Exposition Internationale des Arts Décoratifs et Industriels Modernes 167, 175, 177, 178, 191, 192

Fagu, G. 183, 191, 193
Fagu, Mme G. 182, 193
Falguerolles 9
Far East 57
Fardis 191
Fawley Court, Bucks 18, 80
Fénard, André 188
Fénelon (François de Salignac de la Mothe) 118, 122
Fermes, Hôtel des 98
Fermigier, André 203, 204
Ferouillat 107
Ferré, Charles *184*
Figuier, Louis 200
Flammersheim and Steinmann 158
Flanders 7, 18, 62, 67, 70, 84, 209
Flaubert, Gustave 200
Fleuriot 198
Florence 50
Foley, Edwin 20
Folie Méricourt 88
Folie Regnault 88
Folie Titon 88, *90*, 90, 91, 98
Follot, Charles 7, 178, 193
Follot, Félix 36
Follot Collection 209
Follot company *72*, *172*, *176*, 177, *178*, 178, 181, 183, 191, 194, *212*
Fontainebleau, Château de 100, 209
Fontan, Suzanne 178, *182*, 185, *186*, *189*, 191, *212*, 212
Fontenay 88
Foucray *171*
Fourcade, Suzanne 184
Fourcroy, de *205*, 205
Fourdrinier brothers 128
Fournier, J.-P. 40
Fowler, John 174
Fox Linton, Mary 174
Foyle Ltd, W. and G. 193
Fragonard, Evariste *95*, 128
Fragonard, Jean-Honoré 126
France 42
France 7, 9, *11*, *14*, 15, 16, 18, 20, 21, 22, 22, *35*, *36*, *39*, 40, 42, 42, 44, 45, 46, 48, 50, 57, *58*, *59*, 59, 64, 66, 67, 68, *69*, 70, 71, 72, 73, 74, 74, *75*, 75, 77, 79, 80, *81*, 83, *84*, 85, 86, *89*, 91, *92*, *93*, 94, *95*, 95, *97*, *98*, 98,99, *100*, 101, *102*, 103, 105, 107, *108*, 108, *109*, 110, 111, 112, 113, 114, 115, 116, 117, *118*, 119, 119, 120, 120, 121, 124, 125, 126, 127-28, *128*, 129, *131*, 131, *132*, 132, *134*, 135, 136, *137*, *138*, *139*, *140*, 141, *141*, 142, 144, 145, 151, 153, *154*, 154-55, *158*, 160, *162*, 163, 164, 167, 168, 170, 171, 172, 175, 175, 175-92, *176*, 177, *177*, 178, *179*, *180*, 181, 182, 184, 185, 186, 187, 188, *190*, 191, 192, 196, 200, 201, 202, 203, 205, 206, 207, 208, 209, 210, 212, 218, 221, 224
France, Anatole 200
Frankfurt 84, 85, 165
Franklin, rue, Paris 188
Fressinet, Jean 177
Freudenberger family 155
Frey, Antoine 186
Frey, Patrick 186, 188, *189*, 190
Frey-Patifet group 186
Fröhlich, Mathias 48
Fryer, Greenough and Newbury 83
Fuchs 112, 115, 123, 142; *see also* Ehrmann and Fuchs
Fulton, Robert 103
Fumeron 181
Furstenberg, place de 186
Fürth 48

Gabriel, René 177, *180*, 184, *185*
Gabrielli, Noemi 75
Gaillard, Robert 188
Gaillard-Motel 182, 194
Gailerie Carlhian, Paris 193
Galeries Lafayette, Paris 191
Gallé, Emile 151
Gallet 194
Gallet, Michel 86
Gama, Vasco da 57
Gamble, John 128
Garnier 74
Gaudí, Antoni 154, 164
Gaugain, Jacques, *see* Sillé
Gaugain, Mme, *see* Elisabeth Bourmaux
Geffrye Museum, London 151
Gelée, Claude, *see* Claude Lorraine
Genlis, Mme de 71
Genoa 16, 18, 71, 84, 141
George I 71
George III 81
George IV 62, 81
George Hill House, Sussex *80*
Gérard, Baron 117, 119
Germany *24*, *37*, 44, 45, 46, 48, 48, 49, 50, 50, *59*, 59, 61, 62, *66*, 66, 67, 70, 71, 77,

84-86, *85*, 85, 86, 107, 154, 155, 156-64, 165-67, 178, 188, 231
Gessner, V. 108, 122
Gesvres, quai des 40
Giampicoli, Giulio 50
Girardin, Marquis de 105
Girault 154
Gloucestershire *62*, 79
Gobelins factory 71, 86, 87, 101, 107, 184, 203, 209
Godwin, E.W. 146, *153*
Goes, Hugo *18*, 18, 20
Goethe, Johann Wolfgang von 85, 153
Golden Lion, Ludgate Hill, London 80
Golding 203
Goriot family 197
Gough, Lord *145*
Gourmelin 184, *187*
Gozlan, Leon 198
G.P.P. company 184
Graf Wallpapers Inc., Philip, *169*
Grand Palais, Paris 124, 154
Grant company, Moses 125
Grantil 177, *187*
Gråsten, Viola *183*
Great Britain 20, 21, 35, 45, 79, 83, 102, 119, 125, 126, 128, *132*, 141, 146, 152, 154, 156, 157, 170-74, 178, 184, 188, 218, 230
Great Marlborough St, London 81
Great Exhibition (1851) 119, 126 129, 131, *135*, 141, 193
Greder, Captain de 27
Greece 86, 98, *102*, 117, 124, 125, *128*, 157
Greenaway, Kate 146, *147*
Grellou 181
Grenard 101; *see also* Arthur and Grenard
Gropius, Walter 154, 158, 163
Gros 119
Groult, André 177
Gruin, Marcel 177
Gruin, Paul 177, *184*
Gruin company 184
Guaranty Building, Buffalo 164
Gué, J.-M. 108, 122
Guéden, Colette 178
Guénioux, Gaston 191
Guérard, Charles-François 27
Guérin 101, 119, 128
Guérite *139*, 142
Guichard 141
Guilbert, Yvette 154
Guild, Tricia 174
Guillou-Dumont *138*
Guimard, Hector 154, 155, *160*, 164
Guiraud, R. 194
Gusman, Pierre 27, 75
Guyatt, Richard 173
Guyenne 70

Haddam, C.T. 125
Haemmerle 75
Hague, The 81
Haichele, Simone 48
Halard, Adolphe 179, 184, 185
Halard, Anne-Marie 185
Halard, Denis 185
Halard, François 185
Halard, Jean 185
Hall and Proetz 167
Hamburg 154, 156, 193
Hancock, Thomas 121
Hanover 85, 193
Hans company 177, *179*, 181, 182
Hanseatic League 84
Hanska, Mme *196*
Hardy, William *214*
Harpe, rue de la, Paris 87
Harrington House, Gloucs 79
Hartford 126
Hartford, Lady 79
Hartmann Riesler *99*, 100
Hauntsch, Johann 67, 84
Haussmann, Baron 132
Haute-Saône 126
Haymarket, London 102
Henbus, Julius 165
Henchman, David 120
Henery, Mlle d' 74
Hennebeau, Mme 198
Henri IV 38
Henriot 91
Henry VII 18, 20
Henry VIII 18, 20
Henry Frederick, Prince of Wales *21*
Herculaneum 86
Hermes 107
Herrnhut 50
Hertfordshire *65*
Herting, Carl *210*, 210
Heywood, Higginbottom and Smith 129, *135*
Hicks, David 186
Hickstead Place, Sussex 35
High St, Brentford *46*
High St, Salem 126
Hildyard, Charles 70
Hindustan 90, 125
Hirsch Collection, Olga 18, *48*, *49*, 52
Hobbes, Thomas 21
Hoffmann, Josef 155, 157
Holland 24, 59, 61, 62, 64, *66*, 66, 67, 70, 90, 107, 174
Hollywood 168
Hook brothers, *see* Atelier Hook
Horne company 129
Horta, Victor 154, 155, 164
Houdin 178
Houdon 86

Houghton, John 45
Houses of Parliament, London 81, 131, 173
Howell, John 126, 152
Huebner, Ernst 167
Huet, Jean-Baptiste 86
Hugo, Victor 132
Huguenots 45, 67
Hull *214*
Hull, Isaac 125
Hungary 148
Hunt, Richard Morris 152, 163
Huntington, James 131
Huquier, Daniel 40, 42
Huquier, Jean-Gabriel 40, 74

ICI 183
Ile de la Cité, Paris 57
Imprimerie Royale 102
Inaltera 183, 194
Incas 118
India 20, 22, 45, 57, *58*, *59*, 61, 62, 71, 73, 80, 85, 86, 88, 94, 142
Innocent III, Pope 15
Institut d'Archéologie, Paris 42
Iphigenia 126
International Exhibitions (1862) 119, *130*, 193; (1867) 193; (1878) 146, 193; (1900) 154, 156, 193; (1905) 193
Ipswich 71
Ireland 44, 102
Irwin, Guy 173
Islam 9
Italy 16, 19, 20, *38*, *50*, 50-55, *51*, *52*, *53*, *54*, *55*, 57, 59, 66, 71, 78, 86, 104, 105, 107, 118, *120*, 125, 156, 188, 206
Iven company 156
Ivy House, Worcester *67*

Jabach, Everhard 98, 126
Jackson, G.F. 162
Jackson, John Baptist 45, 54, *76*, *77*, 77-79, *78*, 80, 173
Jacqué, Bernard 107, 126
Jacquemart, Pierre 98, 100, 101
Jacquemart and Bénard *10*, *92*, *99*, 98-101, *101*, *104*, *109*, *110*, 120, 122, 124, 127
Jacquet 71
Janes and Bolles 126
Jansen 181, 194
Japan 19, 36, 57, *58*, *59*, 61, 64, 71, 75, 146, 151, 154, 169, 182, 191
Jardin des Plantes, Paris 142
Jedo 64
Jeffrey and Co. 129, 131, 145, *146*, 148, 148, *150*, 152, 152, *153*, 158, 159, 173

Jerome, King of Westphalia 85
Joel, Isaac 85
Jones, Owen *129*, 131
Jones, Robert 81
Jourdan and Villard *114*, *119*, 124
Julien *136*
Junction Dock St, Hull *214*
Juvara, Filippo 75

Kaempfer, Engelbert 64
Kandinsky, Wassily 163
Karasz, Ilonka 169
Karlby, Bent 183
Kassel 67, 84, 85, 209
Katzenbach and Warren 167
Kelmscott Press 146
Kennedy, Jacqueline 112
Kensington Palace, London 45, 71, *130*
Kent 20, 145, *199*
Kent, William 45
Kew gardens 64
Kiesewetter 84
Kildare, Co. 35
Kingston House 154
Kingston-upon-Thames *56*, 80
Kirkall, Edward 77
Kléber, avenue, Paris 193
Klee, Paul 163
Klimt, Gustav 7, 155, 157
Koechlin Ziegler *136*
Kolbe, C.W. 85
Köchel, Johann 48
Korea 57, 181, 182, 191
Kradow, Gerhard 163
Kunstgewerbe Museum, Basel *48*
Kunstgewerbe Museum, Berlin 193
Kunstgewerbe Museum, Zürich 194
Kupferoth, Elsbeth 165, 167

L'Aigle 88
La Fontaine, Jean de 117
La Garenne Lemot, Clisson 105
La Maîtrise 191
La Marburg company 165, 167, 231
La Pérouse, J.-F. de 122
La Vallée-Poussin 86
Labo, Mario 50
Laborde, Joseph de 113
Laboureur 177
Labourey 42
Ladeuil, Marcelle 177
Lafayette, Marquis de 124
Lafitte, Louis 117, *118*, 124
Lainier family 70
Lancake (or Lancoke) 74
Lancashire 129, *132*
Landes 42

Langlois 44
Langlois, Mme 27, 38
Langlois the younger 38
Langres 27, 35
Languedoc 59
Lantier, Etienne de 118
Lanyer, Jerome 70
Lapeyre and Drouard 123
Lardin, Pierre 184
Latin America 186
Lavoisières 40
Le Chevalier, Jacques 184
Le Clerc, Sébastien 27
Le Corbusier (Edouard Jeanneret-Gris) 154, 158, 170, 179
Le Foll, Alain *181*
Le Mans 42, 44
Le Mardelé company 177, 212
Le Masson, Louis 105
Le Nôtre, André 105
Le Peletier, Claude 59
Le Raincy 103, 105
Leblond, Jean 42
Lebreton, father and son 40, 216
Lechner, Johann 48
Lecomte, Hippolyte 74, 122
Leffler de Berne 127
Leipzig 85
Leistikov, Walter 156
Leleu, Jean-François 177
Leloup, Pierre 42
Lenger, Max 156
Lenoir 88
Lenormand, Sébastien 127, 215
Lentzner, J.N. 84
Leopold, Joseph Friedrich 48
Leroy 100
Leroy, Isidore 132, 141, 177, *179*, 184, 194, *221*, *228*, *229*
Leroy company *132*
Leroy and Dumas 182
Les Invalides, Paris 119
Lesueur, Vincent 40, 79
Letourny, Jean-Baptiste 42
Lévèque, Jean-Jacques 104
Leyland, F.R. 151
Liège 193
Lindsay, Lina 173
Line and Sons, John 170, *173*
Lisbon 57, 84
Lisieux 199
Liverpool Exhibition (1886) 151, 157
London 20, 21, 44, 45, 54, 61, 62, 64, 68, 70, 71, 77, 79, *80*, 81, *83*, 83, 102, 119, 121, 126, 128, 129, 131, 146, 151, *162*, 173, 174, 193, 194, 205
London, City of 79, 83
London, Port of 79
Longueville, Hôtel, Paris 101

Loo, van 126
Loos, Adolf 152, 153, 158, 164, 170
Lorraine, Claude 104
Los Angeles 163
Lough Cutra castle *145*
Louis IX 15
Louis XI 15
Louis XIII 108, 183
Louis XIV 59, 70, 71, 126, 132, 141
Louis XV 71, 209
Louis XVI 86, 101, 132, 183, 209, *210*
Louis XVIII 100
Louis-le-Grand, rue, Paris 101
Louis-Philippe 100, 117, 128, 142
Low Countries 44, 45, 66, 70, 71
Lübeck 84
Luca della Robbia 206
Luckhardt, Wassily and Hans 163
Ludgate Hill, London 80
Lully, J.-B. 186
Lune, rue de la 197
Lüneburg 156
Lurçat, Jean 177
Lüstringen 191
Lybbe Powys, Mrs Phillip 80
Lyon, Hôtel de 40
Lyons 42, 71, 74, 75, 84, 86, 94, 100, 107, 120, 124, 194

M.L.A. *176*
Macartney, Lord 62
Mackintosh, Charles Rennie 157
Mackmurdo, Arthur Heygate *148*, 148, 151, 152, 157, *159*, 211
Macky, John 62
Maclean Gallery, London 194
Mâcon 107, 126
Madeleine, place de la, Paris 188
Mader, Alexis 117
Mader, Jules 117
Mader, Xavier *71*, *117*, 117, 119
Madras 57
Maigret *65*, *109*, *116*, *141*, 199
Maillecotin, Mme 198
Maintenon, Château de, Eure-et-Loir *60*
Mainz 45
Maison du Peuple, Brussels 164
Maison Germain, Lyons 194
Malaine, Joseph-Laurent 86, *99*, *100*, 101, 107, 142, *207*, 209
Malmaison 193
Malmerand 9
Manchester 129, 131, *135*, 141, 194
Mann, Horace 78
Mannheim 86, 156, 187
Mansfield, Katherine 198
Manufacture Française de Papiers Peints *175*, *208*

Manzon, Billy 168
Marais 88
Mare, André *175*, 178
Margeridon, *see* Clerc and Margeridon
Margueritte, Victor 175
Marie-Antoinette 141
Marie-Louise, Empress 100
Marigny, François de 86
Marine Coffee House, London 61
Marlborough, Duke of 45
Marly gardens 107
Marmontel, Jean-François 118, 122
Marot, Daniel 67
Marot, Paule 184, *185*
Maroy 87
Marseilles 26, 59, 61, 84
Martin, Guillaume 73, 75
Martin, Simon Etienne 73, 75
Martin brothers 36, 64
Marx, Karl 95
Mary II 62
Massachusetts 126
Masson 40
Mathildenhöhe, Darmstadt 193
Mathis, Juliette 168
Mathurins, rue des, Paris 40, 74
Matisse, Henri *202*, 202, *203*
Maubert 181
Mauny, Patrick 188
Mauny company 167, 181, 188, *190*, 191, *192*, 194, *196*
Maupassant, Guy de 200
Maure, Hôtel, Lisieux 199
Maurepas, Comtesse de 71
McClelland, Nancy 7, 8, 79, 117, 119, 125, 126, 167, 168, 188, 192
Mediterranean 57, 117
Mediterrannée, Hôtel, Nice 202
Meisch, Georg 48
Meisch, Johann 48
Menegazzi company 50, 52
Mercers, Company of *20*
Méréville 105, 117
Mérimée, Prosper 141
Merrii *134*
Mery *70*
Merzbau 203
Métadier, Paul 197
Métro, Paris 164
Miaco 64
Mick, Ernst Wolfgang 52
Middle East 9
Middlesex *46*
Midi 84
Milan 50, 52, 54
Mills, Zechariah *125*
Milton, John 103
Mincing Lane, London 61
Minnikin, George 44

Mirbeau, Octave 154, 200
Mirepoix, Duc de 71
Miyer 40
MLA *176*
Mogul empire 57
Molière *71*, *117*
Monceau 103
Monceau, parc, Paris 103, 105
Mongin, Pierre-Antoine 107, *108*, 108, *112*, 112, 113, 119
Montfermeil 188
Montgolfier, Bernard de 9
Montgolfier, Etienne de 90
Montgolfier, Joseph de 90
Montgolfier family 9, 90
Montmartre, boulevard, Paris 102, 103, 105, 122, 124
Montmartre, parc, Paris 103, 105
Montreuil, rue de 117
Mont-Rouge 27
Monville, de 105
Moore, Albert 146
Moors 9
Morand 42
Morgenstern, Christian 85
Morris, Rober 121
Morris, William 58, *144*, 144, 145, *146*, 146, 148, *149*, *150*, 151, 152, 156, 157, 163, 173, 191, *211*, 211, *221*
Morris and Co. 145, *147*, 173
Morris, Marshall, Faulkner and Co. 145, 146, *150*
Mortimer, Thomas 45
Mortimer Street, London 173
Morton and Co., Alexander *151*
Mosser, Monique 107
Motel, Pierre 182, 184
Mount Vernon 124
Mucha, Alfons 154
Mulhouse 107, *132*, *136*
Muller, Charles 123, *138*, 142
Munch, Johann Carl 48
Munch, Johann Michael 48
Munich 155, 157, 158, 193
Municipal Library, Mâcon 126
Münster 165
Musée Carnavalet, Paris 9
Musé d'Art Moderne de la Ville de Paris 203
Musée de l'Impression sur Etoffes, Mulhouse 194
Musée des Arts Décoratifs, Paris, 24, 191, 194
Musée des Beaux-Arts, Dijon 194
Musée Galliera, Paris 27, 177, 181, 193
Museo Civico di Bassano del Grappa 50, 52
Museo dell'Arredamento Stupinigi 75
Museum of Fine Arts, Boston 122

Museum of London 64, 194
Muthesius, Hermann 155, 156, 158, 164

Nacton Hall, Suffolk *19*
Nagasaki 64
Nanbar Byobu *58*
Nancy 178
Nantes 94, 117
Naples, Bay of 122
Napoleon I 100, 200
Napoleon III 128
NASA 168, 188
National Institute of Science and Art, France 103
Neatby, W.J. 152
Nero 16
Netherlands 57
Neufville 75
Neumeister 85
Neutra, Richard 163
New Jersey 124
New York 121, 125, 126, 152, 153, 167, *168*, 186, 188, 192, 193
Nice 202
Nile, R. 9
Nobilis *59*, *97*, *179*, 179, *180*, 181, *182*, 184, 185, *185*, *186*, *187*, *189*, 191, 194, *212*
Nobilis International, Paris 185
Normandy 21
North Africa 9
North Ockendon, Essex *83*
Northumberland *64*
Nothnagel, Johann Andreas Benjamin 84, 85
Notre-Dame, Paris 119
Nuremberg 48, *49*, 66, 67, 84

Oberkampf *103*, 122
Oberland 108
Obermann, Dominique 42
Odéon, Paris 86
Oise 178
Olbrich, Joseph Maria *157*, 157, 158
Old Brewery, Watford, Herts *65*
Old Sturbridge Village 126
Olivier-Merson, C. 194
Oman, C.C. 121
Ord House, Berwick upon Tweed, Northumb. *205*
Order of the Garter *20*
Orient 57, 64
Orléans 42, *43*
Orléans, Duc d' 91, 107
Orne 88
Orpheus 107, 126
Osborne and Little *174*, 174

Osnabrück 165, 191, 193
Oxford 19

Paestum 86
Paillard, see Pignet and Paillard
Palacio Guell, Barcelona 164
Palais de la Couronne 117
Palais de l'Industrie, Paris 193
Palais Royale 119, 182
Palais Stoclet, Brussels 155
Palazzo Carminati, Venice *52*, 54
Palermo 50
Palladianism 79
Pally, Johann 85
Pan 126
Panini 86, 104
Pankok 156
Panseron 40
Panthéon, Paris 86, 154
Pantheon, Rome 154
Paolozzi, Eduardo 173
Papiers de France 182
Papiers Peints de France *175*
Papillon, Jean I 26
Papillon, Jean II 25, 26, 38, 40, 59
Papillon, Jean-Michel 21-27, *22*, *24*, *26*, *28-34*, *35*, 35, *36*, 36, 37, 38, *40*, 40, 61, 64, 73, 75, 77, 85, 87, 94, 216
Papillon, Jean-Nicolas 26, 27
Paris 9, 15, 16, 22, 24, 26, 27, 36, 38, 40, 42, 57, 64, 66, 67, 68, 71, 75, 77, 79, 86, 87, 88, 90, 95, 100, 101, 102, 103, 107, 117, 120, 125, 126, 128, 132, *137*, 146, 153, 154, 155, 156, 158, 168, 174, 175, 178, 184, 186, 191, 193, 194, 198, 199, *204*, 204
Paritex 194
Park Lane, London 21
Pascal, Blaise 78
Passy 71, 75
Patent Office, London 45
Patifet, Pierre, see Frey-Patifet group
Paulik, Bernard 156
Paulot and Carré *134*
Peacock Room, Freer Gallery of Art, Washington DC 151
Peche, Dagobert *157*, 157, 158, *163*, 164
Peking 62
Pelle 42
Pennsylvania 121, 153
Pepys, Samuel 44
Perdoux, Pierre-Fiacre 42, *43*, 43
Pérelle 27
Pergamum 9
Perivale 173
Pernon, see Chenevard and Pernon
Perry, Michael 120
Persia 46, 48, *49*, 59, 127, 182, 183

Persian Gulf 57
Petit *39*
Petit, Egidio 50, 54
Petit Palais, Paris 154
Petit Pont, rue du, Paris 40
Petit Trianon, Versailles *209*
Petit-Jean 42
Peynet 165
Philadelphia 121, 124, 126, 152
Philip II of Spain 57
Phillip, John 120
Piazzetta, Venice *52*, *53*
Picasso, Pablo *203*, 203, *205*
Pickaërt and Sieburg 165, 167
Pignet 124
Pignet Jeune and Paillard 107, 123, 124
Pillement, Jean *65*, 86, *99*
Piranesi, Giovanni Battista 77, 79, 86, *104*, 104
Pirelli 108, 122
Plunkett Fleeson 121
Poilly, N.B. de 75
Poiré, Paul 215, *229*
Poiret, Paul 155, 199
Pompadour, Mme de 59, 71, 73, 86
Pompeii 86
Pompidou Centre, Paris 126
Ponce 86
Pontet 85
Portel, C. *179*, *180*, 184, 185
Portier, Joseph-Jean 42
Portugal 57
Posillipo *104*
Poterlet *69*, 123
Potsdam 64, 85
Potter, Charles, Harold and Edwin 129, *132*, 170
Poussin, Nicolas 104
Poyntell, William 124
P.P.V.L. 194
Pradier 117
Pragnell, H.J. 126
Pre-Raphaelites 146
Preston, Walmsley 129
Prévost, Charles 122, 124
Price, Abraham 70
Prieur, L. 86
Primaticcio 78
Primavera *178*, 178, 185, 191, *212*
Privy Council Chamber *206*
Prix de Rome 117
Prou, Geneviève 186
Proust, Marcel 199
Prouvaires, rue des, Paris 40
Prud'homme-Béné, J. 194
Prud'hon, Pierre Paul 117
Prussia 64, 164
Psyche 117
Public Record Office, London 20

Pugin, Augustus Welby Northmore 129, *145*, 145, 173
Putnam and Roff *125*
Pygmalion 126
Pyne, William 71
Pyramus and Thisbe 126

Quadrat Hoffmann 157
Quentin-Harmand 194
Quincampoix, rue, Paris 74

Rabier-Boulard 42
Radio City Music Hall, New York 167
Rambouillet 100, 105
Ramponneau *36*
Raphael (Raffaello Sanzio) 77, 194
Rappenviller 127
Rasch company 165, 167
Raskolnikov 198
Rastignac, Eugène de 197
Rebequet 184
Redgrave, Richard 131
Redouté, Joseph 141
Regensburg 66
Regent St, London 79
Reims *176*
Remondini, Giambattista 50
Remondini, Giovanni 50
Remondini, Giovanni Antoni 50
Remondini, Count Giovanni Battista 50
Remondini, Giuseppe 50
Remondini family 37, 48, 50, *51*, *52*, 52, *53*, 54
Renan, A. 151
René, Denise 191
Renner, Georg Nikolaus 48
Rennes 194
Resources Council, New York 169
Retz 64, 105
Réveillon, Jean-Baptiste 24, 59, 71, 74, 74, 75, 77, *81*, 85, 86-94, *87*, *89*, *92*, *93*, 95, 98, *99*, 101, 102, *207*, 209
Reymund, Andreas 48
Reymund, Georg Daniel 48
Reymund, Johann Michael 48
Reymund, Paul 48
Rheinburg 85
Ribeyre, Château de la, Cournon 107
Ricci, Sebastiano *52*, 54, *76*
Richelet 22
Riemerschmid, Richard 158
Riesewitz 85
Riesler, Amedée 127
Rigault 127
Rigolette 198
Riguet, Louis 177
Riottot, Jules *138*, *208*, 210

Riva del Schiavone, Venice 52
Rixheim 107, 122, 194
Rizzi, Giuseppe *50*, 50
Robert, François 101, 102
Robert, Hubert 86, 104, 105, 119
Robert, Louis 127, 128, 215
Robertson, Mary 167
Robespierre, Maximilien de 101
Rodenbach, Georges 200
Rohan, Princesse de 73
Romains, Jules 198
Rome 50, *54*, 77, 86, 98, 105, 122
Ronco, Alberto 50
Roquis 73
'Rose Moderne, La' 177
Rossetti, Dante Gabriel 146
Rostad, Zofia *182*, 185
Rouen 26, 35, 42, 67, 68, 70
Roumier *35*, 36
Rousseau, Jean-Jacques 103
Roussel 202
Rowe, Thomas 121
Royal Albert Hall, London 148
Royal Institute of British Architects 128
Royal Opera House, London 81
Royal Patent Manufactory, Chelsea 81
Royal Pavilion, Brighton 64, 81, 173
Royère, J. 194
Rückers 25
Rugar, John 121
Rugendas 122
Ruhlmann, Emile-Jacques *176*, 177, 178
Ruskin, John 131, 145, 148, 156
Russia 119, 164
Ryres and Fletcher 121

Saché, Château de *196*, 197
Saegers, A. 141
Sagrada Familia, cathedral, Barcelona 164
St Agathe 42
St Antoine, faubourg, Paris 40, 67, 74, 88, 177
St Antoine, rue, Paris 36, 74, 91
St Bernard, rue, Paris 128
St Catherine, monastery, Nuremberg 66, 84
St Chamond, Lyons 75
St Cloud 100
St Denis, faubourg, Paris 178
St Denis, parc, Paris 119
St Etienne, Lyons 75
St George 75
St Germain-des-Prés 186, 188
St Jacques, rue, Paris 26, *30*, 36, 37, 38, 40, 73, 74, 75, 88
St James's Palace, London *149*

St Martin, rue, Paris 200
St Martin's le Grand, London 44
St Merri, rue, Paris, 126
St Pandelon 42
St Paul's cathedral, London 21
St Quentin 26
St Séverin, fountain, 38, 40, 75
St Sulpice, Paris 119
Ste Geneviève (Panthéon), Paris 86
Saintonge 59
Salazar, Tristan de 194
Salem, MA 126
Salisbury, Wilts *56*
Saloomey *169*
Salubra 183
Saltfleet Manor, Lincs 71
Samarkand 48
San Mardula, via, Varese *50*
San Pietro ai Monte 105
San Staë, Venice *52*
Sanderson and Sons Ltd, Arthur *58*, *147*, 170, *173*, 173, 193, 194, *208*
Sanderson, Arthur 173
Sanderson, Arthur (the younger) 191
Sanderson, Harold 191
Sanderson, John 191
Sans Souci 64
Santa Coloma de Cervelló, Barcelona 164
Saumur, Hôtel de, Paris 38
Saussure, rue de, Paris 177
Sauvignet, Félix 119, 177
Sauvigny, Mme de 71
Savary des Bruslons 22, 67, 68
Saxony 50
Schinkel, Hermann *66*, 66
Schmidt company, Max 157
School of Arts and Crafts, Weimar 158, 164
School of Design, South Kensington 131
Schuler, *see* Ehrmann and Schuler
Schumacher and Co., F. *167*, 168
Schütz, C.G. 85
Schütz, Ernst 156
Schwibecher, Johann Michael 48, *49*
Schwitters, Kurt 203, 204
Scotland 112
Scott, Gilbert 145
Scott, Sir Walter 112, 122
Scott, Cuthbertson and Co. 131
Sedding, John D. *153*
Segerhof, Blumenrain *81*
Seguin, Jean-Pierre 102
Seigner, Jean-Louis 188
Seine, R. 119, 154, 177
Semper, Gottfried 156
Sens, Hôtel de, Paris *182*, 194
Sevestre, Jean-Baptiste 42
Sevestre-Leblond 42
Shakespeare, William 173

Shand Kydd Ltd *147*
Shaw, Richard Norman 146
Sheffield, Lord 121
Shelburne Museum, VT 126
Sheraton, Thomas 81
Sherringham, John 81, 83
Shiraz 57
Sicily 156
Sieburg, *see* Pickaërt and Sieburg
Sillé (Jacques Gaugain) 42
Silver Studio 152, *173*, 194
Simon, Master 73
Sloane St, Chelsea 81
Smith, Asa 125
Smith, Robert 131
Société des Arts, Paris 27
Société des Arts Graphiques Modernes, Nancy 178
Société du Progrès de l'Art Industriel 141
Société Française des Papiers Peints *175*, 178, 185
Society for Promoting Art, Boston 121
Society of Arts, London 129
Soho Sq., London 173
Solférino, rue, Paris 177
Solvay, Hôtel, Brussels 164
Sonnin 85
Sorbonne, Paris 38
Soufflot, Jacques-Germain 86, 90, 105
Soury 42
South Kensington *130*, 131
South Kensington Museum 141
South Seas 113
Southwark 44
Spaendonck, van 209
Spoerlin, Michel 127
Städtischen Museum, Osnabrück 193
Staël, Mme de 108
Stationers' Company 21
Steinmann, *see* Flammersheim and Steinmann
Stéphany, Henri 177, *178*, 178
Stewart, John 131
Stockholm 64
Stoclet 157
Stonegate, York 18
Stoy, Georg Christoph *25*, 48
Strand, London 45, 62
Strasbourg 84
Strawberry Hill 78, 81
Stuart, Gilbert 125
Stupinigi 54, 61, 62, 75
Stuttgart 18, 103, 179, 193
Süe 178
Sue, Eugène 198
Suffolk Galleries, London 193
Sugden, A.V. 7
Sullivan, Louis 152, 163

Sully, Hôtel de, Paris 86
Summerly's Art Manufactures 131
Sumner, Heywood 152, *153*
Surat 61
Sutherland, Graham 173
Sweden 167, *183*
Switzerland 59, 70, *81*, 91, 107, 121, 122, 125, 126, *137*, 153, 163, 186, 188, 191

Tahiti 117
Talbert, Bruce 146
Taralon, Yves 184
Tartary 48
Tassel, Hôtel, Brussels 155, 164
Tasso (Tassi Torquato) 118, 122
Telemachus 197
Temple Newsam House, Leeds 62, 71
Temple prison, Paris *97*, 101
Teynac, Françoise 192
Theatre Royal, Drury Lane, London 81
Thénard 127
Thiéry, Luc-Vincent 90
Third Avenue, New York 169
Thoyer, Nicolas 27, 40
Tiepolo, Giovanni Battista 77
Tierce 42, 68
Tiffany, Charles Louis 163
Tiffany, Louis Comfort 152, 163
Tiffany and Co. 163
Tintoretto, Jacopo 77, 78
Tissot, Lin 167
Tissot, Mme 42
Titian (Tiziano Vecelli) 77, 78
Titon du Tillet 88
Tivoli 122
Tizzi family 50
Tokyo 194
Tolstoy, Leo 198
Topaï, Angelo 50, 54
Torrance, Mrs 167
Toulet, Paul-Jean 154
Toulon 103
Tour du Pin, Marquise de la 91
Townsend and Simpson 129
Trautmann, J.G. 84
Trenzanesio Palace 54
Trocadéro, Paris *137*
Tsai-Lun 7
Tübingen 103
Tuileries 90, 107
Turgenev, Ivan 198
Turin 61, 64, 148
Turkey 44, 45, 48, 57, 66, 85, 216
Turquetil company 141, 192, 194
Tutenkhamun 167
Tweedside 79

Ulysses 197
Union Centrale des Arts Décoratifs, Paris 52, 182
Union Centrale des Beaux-Arts Appliqués à l'Industrie 141
United States of America 52, *53*, *56*, 77, 83, 103, 112, 113, *116*, 119, 120-26, *125*, 148, 152-53, 154, 167-69, *167*, *168*, *169*, *171*, 182, 183, 184, 186, 188, 193, 230
Utrecht 66, 71
Uxbridge 173

Valadier, Luigi 50, 54
Valence, Mme de 91
Valéry, Paul 182
Valese, Alberto *217*
Varese *50*, 50, 52
Vauquer, Mme 197
Vauquer family 197
Velde, Henri van de 151, 154, 158, 164
Vendôme, place, Paris 102, 119
Venice 16, *51*, *52*, 52, *53*, 54, 57, 66, 67, 77, 78, 79, 84, 85, 124, *217*
Vennet 119
Venturi, Lionello 202
Véra, André 155, 179
VERKA 163
Verkindere 182, 194
Vernet, Carle 120, *121*, 122, 124
Vernet, Joseph *97*
Vernon, Mount 124
Versailles, Château de 24, *25*, 71, 90, 125, *209*, 209
Versailles, porte de, Paris 194
Vesuvius 122
Victoria, Queen of England 62, *161*
Victoria and Albert Museum, London *18*, 18, 20, 21, *50*, 52, 64, 71, *146*, 205
Vidalou-lès-Annonay 90
Vienna 67, 84, 148, 155, 157, 158, 163
Vigers, Alan Francis *150*, 152
Vigne, Jean 168, 188, *191*
Villard, *see* Jourdan and Villard
Villayer, de 61
Villon brothers 175
Vincennes 91
Violle 27
Viollet-le-Duc, Eugène Emmanuel 145
Virgil 103
Virieux, Lyons 75
Vivarais 59
Voysey, Charles Francis Annesley *150*, *151*, 151, *152*, 152, *161*, *162*, 173, *211*, 211
Vuillard 202

Wagner, Guillou *140*
Wagner, Otto 164
Wagner, Richard 156
Wailly, Charles de 86
Waldon, Sam 121
Wales 174
Walker, David *147*, 147
Wallpaper Manufacturers Ltd 173
Walpole, Horace 78, 80
Walton, Frederick 231
Walton, George *158*
Wanstead, Palace of 62
Warde, Thomas 163
Warner, Metford 131, 146, *150*
Warrens, Mme de *59*
Warsaw 86
Washington, General George 124, *125*
Washington, Martha 124
Waterhouse, Alfred 145
Watford *65*
Webb, Philip 145, *146*, 146
Weigel Collection 75
Weimar 158, 164
Werkstätte für Kunst in Handwerk 157
Wessely and Neumeister 85
Westphalia 85
Wheeley, James *76*
Whistler, James McNeill 151
White City, London 193
White House, Washington DC 112
White Paper Makers' Company 44
Whitelands, Chelsea 81
Whitworth Art Gallery, Manchester 21, 194
Wiener Werkstätte 155, *157*, 157, *163*
Wilde, Oscar 152, 197
Wilhelm, Gottfried Philipp 85
Wilhelm II, Kaiser 154
Willament, Thomas *131*
William of Orange (William III) 67, 70
Wilkes, Francis 121
Wilman, John 184
Wilmotte, J.-M. *184*, 184
Wilson, H. *152*
Windsor castle 81
Windsor company 74
Woburn Abbey 62
Woollams, William 129, *151*, 173
Woodson Wallpapers *171*, *212*
Worcester 20, *67*, 154
Worley 167
Worshipful Company of Painter-Stainers 80
Wotton-under-Edge *62*, 64
Wren, Sir Christopher 45, 151
Wright, Frank Lloyd 164, *167*, 167, *168*, 168
Wyatt, Digby 131

Xima 177

Yanasch 167
York 18
York Wale Paper Company P.A. 153
Yorkshire 18

Young, Stephen 173
Yourcenar, Marguerite 104

Zahn, Johannis 103
Zippelius 112, *114*, 123, 142
Zola, Emile 132, 198

Zuber company, Jean *69, 70, 74, 75*, 77, *100*, 100, 102, 106, 107, *108, 112*, 112, *114, 115, 116*, 119, 122, 123, 124, 125, 126, 127, *132, 134, 135, 136, 139*, 141, *142*, 142, 167, *181*, 181, 183, 184, 186, *190, 208*, 209, *224*
Zürich 156, 158, 194

Achevé d'imprimer sur les presses
de l'imprimerie Berger-Levrault, Nancy
Dépôt légal : octobre 1982
N° d'imprimeur : 118772-10-82